W9-AQJ-621

THE ELOQUENCE OF PROTEST

Voices of the 70's

Voices of the 70's

THE ELOQUENCE
OF PROTEST

Edited by Harrison E. Salisbury

1972

HOUGHTON MIFFLIN COMPANY BOSTON

First Printing w

Copyright © 1972 by Harrison E. Salisbury
All rights reserved. No part of this work may be reproduced
or transmitted in any form by any means, electronic or mechanical,
including photocopying and recording, or by any information storage or
retrieval system, without permission in writing from the publisher.
ISBN: 0-395-13653-9
Library of Congress Catalog Card Number: 79-184116
Printed in the United States of America

Contents

Women and Men

Youth and the New Life-Styles

II. THE WORLD

For Peace

Personal Freedom

Political Oppression

Youth

Race

War

Introduction

THE WORLD IS a prison. Has humanity in its struggle to free itself from slavery to storm, cold, hunger, toil, sickness woven a net of steel, high explosives and hatred within which to indenture us all? Are we all — are all beings, jailers and jailed — confined within an amniotic sac of our own creation?

Is this what the struggle is all about? A question but not an answer. A question which claws into the brain as we look on the agony of the world while the decade of the 1960's gives birth to the unknown 1970's.

This anthology is dedicated to the agony of the world, to the trauma which is echoed in the voices of poets and philosophers alike. The agony sears these pages. In a lifetime spent on the frontiers of human conflict — in the turbulence of our own ghettos, in the Asian cesspools where men struggle to win some small grip on existence, in the bureaucratic morasses of the ideological states where clerks painstakingly seek to match blueprint to unruly life and unruly life to blueprint, in the ceaseless wars of our generation — nothing, for me, has matched the relentless agony of this moment.

Each of us sees and experiences some small part of the whole. But here in these pages we see that all divisions are artificial, including the sections and subsections in this anthology. The lines which separate nation from nation are artificial. Those which divide war from peace are artificial. The divisions we call race, or alienation, or generation or nation are artificial — they dissolve before our eyes when we lift them from the pages of our own dilemma and see that we are each part of the same experience and that the poets and the prisoners, the patriots and the philosophers, the old and the young, the black, the white, the brown, the Asians and the Caucasians, the hard-hats and the longhairs speak, as it were, in a single voice.

If this anthology possesses any positive quality I hope that it lies in the revelation of universality. This is, I believe, a moment among moments in human history. Perhaps, to be sure, it is an illusion that springs from the magic of technological communication so that when it becomes the style to wear blue jeans on campus in Berkeley it becomes the style to wear blue jeans on campus in Warsaw a few months later; when the Stones sweep the field in America they capture the juke boxes of Calcutta and Irkutsk before the echo is dead in Liverpool and Capetown. Perhaps it is because we have become one satellite-linked world so that the breath of revolution in Santerre flutters the trees of the Harvard Yard. Perhaps we have all become freaks of a single culture. But I do not think it is so simple. If we listen to these voices we find they speak in many accents. They are not all revolutionary. Some are counterrevolutionary. (Can it be that these are two aspects of the same phenomenon?)

What has happened, I believe, is that the combination of technology and theory, of communication and experience, of trial and error, of oppression and liberation has brought to the world a common voice which can be heard at one and the same time in many places and in many languages. This anthology is largely limited to those who write and speak in English (although there are some translations). The similarities far outweigh the differences. When England's poet Ted Hughes speaks in the voice of Crow he speaks for all: "There was no escape into death. And still it went on . . ."

There are no national differences in the voices of the poets. You must look on the jacket of the book to be certain that Hughes is English, Bly is American and Yevtushenko Russian. Language is almost a matter of accident and it does not seem surprising that Yevtushenko actually wrote his poem in Spanish, not Russian, or that Bly anthologizes poets of half a dozen nations in translations that have the authentic ring of original voices.

I do not mean to suggest that all voices in this book speak in the same mood. Far from it. But if, like John Lennon, they speak in despair ("The dream is over. It's just the same, only I'm thirty and a lot of people have got long hair"), they speak not for an individual but for a generation of individuals. The dream ended not just for Lennon. It ended for the Lennons and their followers in a dozen lands. And at the same time Dan Berrigan speaks of hope. He writes to the Weathermen: "The gift we can offer others is so simple a thing as hope." The line could have been written by Ho Chi Minh. Or Che Guevara. Or, as Berrigan notes, by Christ. There is in Berrigan, as there is in others, both young and old, the high note of perfect faith. Their dream has not ended, can not end and, in fact, so long as they live (and their spirit seems to be eternal) Lennon's dream has not ended even though he may think that it has.

But in a time which records depths of despair and peaks of faith there must be — and is — hatred and anger, the wild rage of passion and frustration. We hear it in the words of Dr. Paul Williamson to his son, just entering college: ". . . If you choose to try to change it [the government] by revolution, expect to get shot. Mother and I will grieve but we will gladly buy a dinner for the National Guardsman who shot you."

And there is the incandescent rage of George Jackson, writing to Angela Davis: "They've created in me one irate, resentful nigger — and it's building to what climax?" And the contempt, the utter disillusion of Robert Bly: ". . . The ministers lie, the professors lie, the television lies, the priests lie . . . These lies mean that the country wants to die."

But are the country and the world possessed by a death wish? I think not. Death comes not in a rage, not in a shrill cry of anger, not in a call to arms, not in indictment of a status quo which in every way falls short of the dream. Death comes of despondency, of lassitude and despair so profound that it drowns the spark of life. These are not the days of despondency. No sloughs here. There is a grandeur in the words of the poets (like Bly and Hughes) which is matched by the concepts of Peter Marin, who fashions out of his own personal and direct experience as the head of a California day school a vision in which "the world and time reside within, not outside, men; there is no distance, no 'alienation,' only a perpetual wedding to the world."

Here is another denominator of these voices. They are in and of the world. They know prison, they know arrest, they know beatings, they know death, they know injustice. they know poverty, they know cruelty. The world is no Garden of Eden. Life is not the dream but only its foretaste. If the 1950's were the decade of silence and the 1960's the decade of struggle, surely this threshold of the 1970's is the edge of promise.

These are strong voices. There is fire and passion and blood in their decibels. The mood is authentic and it circles the world. You could change the signatures and transpose the messages of the monks in the Saigon jail, the Panthers in the jails of the country they call Amerika, the exiles from Russia, the fighters for freedom in Greece, the Weathermen. Bernadette Devlin, the Irish flame, speaks for all: "Dare to struggle, dare to win!"

A decade ago it would not have been possible to gather an anthology that reflected a single theme in a troubled world. The world of the 1960's was disparate and the voices spoke to every wind. Indeed, many were silent. The young in America were hardly awake, and in Russia there was the quiet of resignation. Vietnam was but a cloud on the horizon and the sit-in movement was just beginning in the South.

What happened as the decade went by — and what this volume memorializes — is that eyes were opened and consciences aroused on every hand. To what? To the human condition, the social contract, man's inhumanity to man, the banality of official clichés, the injustice of rules of law and rules without law, the cruelty of "the system," whether it be a university system in California or a governmental dictatorship in Greece. With this awakening came the realization that we live not in an imperfect world but in one which is destroying itself — devouring itself and its mountains, as Robert Hatch proclaims. A dozen anthologies would not contain the catalogue of this self-destruction — the poisoning of the water, the air, the food; the torture of human souls, the orgy of waste and squander.

Were this the only theme, the voices would be more than we could stand, the agony too great for words, the pain unbearable. But human spirit intervenes. It will not believe the worst — even when it is true. George Jackson believes that he will die, but believes he will bring down the system with him (probably he does not *really* believe he will die). Fred Hampton believes he will die (of this he seems *really* certain), but believes his cause will triumph. George Mangakis does not know when or whether he will get out of Greek prison. But he gives a drop of blood to save a mosquito's life. Yevtushenko sees the spirit of Che Guevara riding in the sky. Woodstock is *felt* as a quest for the Grail ("We are stardust, we are golden. And we got to get ourselves back to the garden"). So, too, in Rainbow Farm. The commune. Another quest in which Winter sat as a seventh member and freedom became a prison out of which new life grew. And the Weather Underground. The apocalypse of the Town House giving birth to New Morning, a New Nation, built of new people, new consciousness, new land.

I don't know whether these statements, poems, affirmations, affidavits, briefs, protests, essays, philosophies, analyses, letters, declarations, vignettes, interviews, tapings add up to the mood of the 70's. I think they do. They speak for the 70's I know. I think there is a consistency here. The voices speak from the right. They speak rather more from the left and from the broad middle, from the squares, the new life-styles, the academics, the common prisoners, the Greeks, the Puerto Ricans, the Russians and the Indians, from the gentle mouth of Mary Mebane and the angry mouth of Professor K. Ross Toole, from Tom Winship rapping on the press to Judge Murray Gurfein putting down John Mitchell, from Archibald Cox pleading for the right of YAF to be heard over the din at Harvard to Russell Baker chanting "Sleep," in a surrealistic lullaby to carry us past the world where horror haunts.

If there is a leitmotif surely it rises from the unwillingness of men to abide any longer the condition of the society which they have created. Intolerance? Yes, to be sure. From those put down. From those challenged. Those who want. Those who intend to keep. Unwillingness to go on longer with what cannot be endured. Should not be endured.

From this springs eloquence. When men and women speak up and speak out — Merle Miller speaking for his homosexuality, Gloria Steinem for her womanhood, Rostropovich for his friend, Solzhenitsyn, Sergei Khrushchev speaking for his father — passion lends eloquence to words. We hear them as we have not heard them before. Robert Hatch speaks for beloved Canaan Mountain and it is as if we had not seen nor felt that mountain before. Nor is this new. So Milton spoke. So the unruly colonists spoke in 1776. So France spoke in the "Marseillaise." Words welling from emotion, and emotion itself welling from injustice and hatred — these are the most powerful weapons in the world. Man long has known this. "Arise, ye prisoners of starvation." "Workers of the world, unite — you have nothing to lose but your chains." "We hold these truths to be self-evident." "All men are created equal."

Dangerous weapons. More dangerous than missiles. More powerful than laws ("Stone walls do not a prison make"). These are the words which echo down the corridors of the centuries. They make our skin prickle. They make tyrants and men of power shift uneasily in their seats. Bullets kill. Words live — and kill. They can be said over and over and over. They cost nothing.

They need no technology, no launching pads. They spring from the lips of condemned men. They slip silently through the bars of cells. They penetrate the thickest dungeon walls. They are carried on the wind. They fly over oceans. They are heard by men of many tongues. No barriers can be set against them. No ruler is safe in their presence. Only the truth, in the end, endures. In their presence the tyrant reaches for the censor's scissors and the gag.

But words are stronger than despots. They flow on the lightest breeze. Here we find voices around the world speaking in the same tongue. It can be no accident that so many speak from prison or from the underground. We think of the patriots confined in prison in foreign lands. Let us think again. See how many of these voices speak from and of our own prisoners, our own underground. Their faces may differ from those in the labor camps of Kolyma. They do not write in Cyrillic or Greek. But they speak in the same voice — against injustice, against intolerance, for freedom, for a better world. They speak for hope.

Author's Note

I want to acknowledge a special indebtedness to the Op-Ed page of the *New York Times,* where much of this material first appeared, and to my colleagues there. I also owe a special debt to Stephan P. Salisbury for his guidance and assistance, particularly in the selection of the poetry which is included in this anthology.

I
AMERICA

W HEN WE TURN to the past for parallels to the present we quickly perceive how deep was the crisis on which the 1960's turned into the 1970's. Only twice in American history has our society been so stirred — in the midcentury days leading up to and including the Civil War and in 1929–30 when the Great Depression roused fears that the economic system would not survive and that its disaster would bring crashing down our political system as well.

No single event (if we exclude the Vietnam war) brought us to the brink in 1970. Instead, we found the foundations of government and custom challenged at every turn and the banner of challenge raging forward into almost every walk of life, every standard of conduct, every establishment in the whole broad range of culture.

For the first time since 1776 the true and authentic voice of revolution was raised in the U.S.A. This should be understood. Unless the significance of this basic movement is perceived it is easy to trivialize what has been happening. This is what Robert Bly understands and records in *The Light Around the Body*, from which the segment "Those Being Eaten by America" is drawn. This is chips-down reality, regardless of whether or not it may seem to us that the standard-bearers of revolution are capable or likely to achieve their revolutionary end. It can be remarked that in England two hundred years ago many thought Patrick Henry was merely guilty of disorderly conduct, and Nicholas II did not for a moment believe that any of the chaotic radical movements had the capability of really ruling his country.

But what Dan Berrigan stands for with his civil disobedience is the same thing which Mohandas Gandhi stood for in India. Berrigan is earnestly and sincerely trying to create a revolution in this country which will change the whole ethical and moral basis of our life. And this is what the Weathermen are about, as well. Let us say that they started originally as a small group of energetic Columbia students who were seeking an issue and finally found one, almost accidentally. But this should not blind us to the fact that from this small, almost trivial beginning they emerged through the dynamic of conflict to a full-blown revolutionary position markedly resembling that of the Narodnaya Volya (which carried out the assassination of Alexander II) in Russia — the same intense idealism, the same ultraist objectives, the same passionate morality. There is no more poignant document in this collection than Bernardine Dohrn's letter in which the Weathermen turn their backs on irrational violence and move toward Gandhiism and "life-style" revolution.

Whatever we may think about Berrigan, whatever we may imagine about the Weathermen, the emergence in our society of forces such as these is in itself a barometer of the social condition. The signal stands at "Changing Weather: Storms."

If we do not understand this we understand nothing about our country. We do not then understand Dr. Williamson and his frank letter to his son in the Tulane freshman class. Dr. Williamson does understand that revolution is abroad in the land. He is not against change but he hates revolution more than he loves his son and the violence of his feeling is another register of the temperature of the nation.

If revolution were only a toy of the youth or of part of the youth and of random segments of the population, it might be dismissed as an aberration. But run your eye down the selection of material in this section. Ernest van den Haag points to the fundamental challenge to government implied in "Kill the Pigs." If the society's basic mechanism for maintaining its own orderly function is under attack, and on the verge of breaking down, then this, in itself, means that the social system is unraveling. This is the theme of my own contribution to the national debate, for not only is the mechanism breaking down but the very symbol of the state, the flag, is endangered from *both* right and left.

There is not space within the confines of an orderly selection to present examples of the feedback into our society of the individual challenges, the specific manifestations of the deterioration of the system. Robert Hatch represents one challenge — that of the system's capability for self-destruction, its tearing apart of the very land which makes up the nation; and Harold Hofstad gives us an equally profound example — the introduction into the most peaceful and peaceable countryside of the most deadly and dangerous implements of destruction. Small wonder that Stanley Kunitz calls the "Order of the State" that "pack of scoundrels tumbling through the gate." It is not without significance, it seems to me, that so many of our poets having traversed the fields of imagism, mysticism and randomism now speak sharply, clearly, fiercely, specifically.

The nation is embattled. That seems plain and it brings with it inevitably the struggle for justice, for human dignity, for truth, for the rights of the people against their government and for the rights of all against the privileges of the few.

Nowhere has the cutting edge of conflict been more sharp than on the frontiers of the press, the frontiers of free speech both spoken and written. As always the fiercest struggle comes for the rights of the minority — for conservatives to present their views before a liberal or radical Harvard audience, for "ethnics" (and Indians, as well) to be treated as full citizens.

These issues were dramatically illuminated in the struggle which emerged between press and government over publication of the Pentagon Papers. Nothing in the papers (and they were amazingly important) was as vital as the struggle for the right to publish and the right of the people to know. As in all conflict, truth is an early casualty and those with the power to control the levers of information inevitably and invariably use it in their own interest, opening the valves to what they regard as useful, narrowing them shut for the painful, the embarrassing, the revelatory. Only one who has seen this process carried to its ultimate in, for example, the Soviet Union (as I have) can fully appreciate what occurs when full government control is applied. It produces, to be sure, an image of a world which bears little resemblance to the real world, not much more real, for example, than that which Potëmkin built for Catherine amid the real misery of the Ukraine.

The true depth of the American revolution can be measured by its involvement of morals and personal relations. This is how we know that the revolution is in so many ways more profound than the crises of 1861 or 1929. When Gloria Steinem speaks for the total equality of men and women, when Bella Abzug demands that the apparatus of the state be compelled to bring even-handed justice and living conditions for men and women, we know that the issues have sunk into the roots of the human condition.

All of this makes up America in the 1970's. If we wish to examine the revolution at work in that milieu most excruciatingly affected, we turn to Woodstock, to Rainbow Farm, to Lennon and the end of the dream. Woodstock was the single most powerful experience of youth culture at the edge of the 1970's, just as Altamont, its antithesis, signaled the end of the dream. But the end of what we might call the children's crusade of our times did not end the movement. It went on to Rainbow Farm, to the commune, to a dozen other manifestations. For what is involved here is not a one-shot emotional binge. It was not simply a craze, a new kind of pop culture which would rise in a day and burn itself out with the manufacture of records and gimmickry, but the profound stirring and shaking of the whole moral basis on which society had expected its young people to live. Woodstock was a call to a new brotherhood of morality and honesty, or love and good will (oh, I know it was raddled with dope and all the rest — but this is what it *really* was into). It turned its back on hypocrisy, on "the system" — whether represented by family, by the job escalator, the suburban syndrome, the success psychosis, the conventional platitudes or whatever.

Rainbow Farm, with all its dropout connotations, its agony over existence, the frozen water, the shut-in winter of the cabin, the mess, the hang-ups, represents the first stage of experimental creation of a new moral order — the effort to end the cant of conventional sexual relations, the cant of dress, of values. Like any revolution it bears within itself the seeds of its own disintegration. But it also bears within itself the seeds of the new revolution which has not yet taken shape but which will certainly emerge out of the ashes of Woodstock, the Weathermen and Rainbow Farm.

All of this is in America today — survival in an environment once friendly but now hostile; injustice to those not of the majority (women, Indians, homosexuals, ethnics, prisoners, students); the right to print freely, speak freely, think freely, to tell the truth. Drugs. Sex. New life. All of this is America today and these are its voices.

Embattled Nation

Those Being Eaten by America

*No American poet has spoken more strongly on the "American disease"
than Robert Bly. In addition to his own work he has anthologized the
work of his contemporaries, both American and foreign, and translated
several poets, including the brilliant Russian poet, Andrei Voznesensky.
This work comes from his collection, The Light Around the Body,
published in 1970.*

The cry of those being eaten by America,
Others pale and soft being stored for later eating

And Jefferson
Who saw hope in new oats

The wild houses go on
With long hair growing from between their toes
The feet at night get up
And run down the long white roads by themselves

The dams reverse themselves and want to go stand
    alone in the desert

Ministers who dive headfirst into the earth
The pale flesh
Spreading guiltily into new literatures

That is why these poems are so sad
The long dead running over the fields

The mass sinking down
The light in children's faces fading at six or seven

The world will soon break up into small colonies of
the saved

Letter to the Weathermen

In the autumn of 1970 when he himself was still a fugitive from justice, moving about the country in defiance of FBI agents seeking to arrest him on charges growing out of the disruption of the Catonsville, Maryland, draft board offices, the Reverend Daniel Berrigan, S.J., wrote this letter to the Weathermen, who were also in the underground and being hunted on a series of charges growing out of various acts of violent defiance committed in the preceding months. The "letter" was actually placed on tape so that the Weathermen would know by Berrigan's voice that it was genuine and not a provocation. It is present here in slightly excerpted form.

Dear Brothers and Sisters,

This is Dan Berrigan speaking. I want to say what a very deep sense of gratitude I have that the chance has come to speak to you across the underground.

The cold-war alliance between politics, labor, and the military finds many Americans at the right end of the cornucopia. What has not yet risen in them is the question of whose blood is paying for all this, what families elsewhere are being blasted, what separation and agony and death are the other side of that coin of the realm — the connections are very hard to make, and very few come on them, and many can hardly imagine that all being right with America means that very much must go wrong elsewhere. How do we get such a message across to others? It seems to me that that is one way of putting the very substance of our task. This determination to keep talking with all who seek a rightful place in the world or all who have not yet awakened to it, this, I think, is the revolution, and the United States perversely and negatively knows it, and this is why we are in trouble.

Undoubtedly the FBI comes after people like me with guns because deeper than their personal chagrin and their corporate machismo, which is a kind of debased esprit de corps since they always get their man, there was that threat that the Panthers and the Vietnamese had learned so well as a reality. The threat is a very simple one because we are making connections, political connections, religious and moral connections, connections with prisoners and Cubans and Vietnamese, and these connections are forbidden under the policies which J. Edgar Hoover is greatly skilled both in enacting and in enforcing. They know by now what we are about, they know we are serious. And they are serious about us.

By and large the public is petrified of you. There is a great mythology surrounding you — much more than around me. You come through in public as another embodiment of the public nightmare which is menacing and sinister and senseless and violent: a spin-off of the public dread of Panthers and Vietcong, of Latins and Africans, and the poor of our country, of all those expendable and cluttering and clamorous lives who have refused to lie down and die on command or to perish at peace with their fate, or to exist in the world as suppliants and slaves.

But in a sense, of course, your case is even more complicated because your choice to rebel is not the passionate consequence of the stigma of slavery. Yours is a choice. It's one of the few momentous choices in American history. Your no could have been a yes, and the society realizes it because you had everything going for you.

The society, I think, was traumatized. What to do with Vietcong or Panthers had never been a very complicated matter, after all. We jailed them or shot them down or brought in the National Guard. But what to do with you — this indeed was one hell of a question. There was no blueprint and no answer. And yet this question, too, was not long in being answered, as we learned at Kent State. And now we know that even if those lives are white and middle-class, they are going to be in the same gunsights.

I'm trying to say that when people look about them for lives to run with and when hopeless people look for hope, the gift we can offer others is so simple a thing as hope. As they said about Che, as they say about Jesus, some people, even to this day, he gave us hope. So that my hope is that you see your lives in somewhat this way, which is to say I hope your lives are about something more than sabotage. I'm certain they are.

I hope you see your lives as Che saw his, that is to say mainly as teachers of the people, conscious as we must be of the vast range of human life that still awaits liberation and education and consciousness. If I'm learning anything it is that nearly everyone is in need of this and therefore in need of us, whether or not they realize it.

How shall we speak to our people, to the people everywhere? We must never refuse, in spite of their refusal of us, to call them our brothers. I must say to you as simply as I know how, if the people are not the main issue, there is simply no main issue and you and I are fooling ourselves also, and the American fear and dread of change has only transferred itself to a new setting.

This, I think, is where a sensible, humane movement operates on several levels at once if it is to get anywhere. So it is saying communication yes, organizing yes, community yes, sabotage yes — as a tool. That is the conviction that took us where we went. And it took us beyond, to this night.

My hope is that affection and compassion and nonviolence are now common resources once more and that we can proceed on that assumption, the assumption that the quality of life within our communities is exactly what we have to offer. I think a mistake in SDS's past was to kick out any evidence of that as being weakening or reactionary or counterproductive. The mark of inhuman treatment of humans is a mark that also hovers over us. It is the mark of a beast, whether its insignia is the military or the movement.

No principle is worth the sacrifice of a single human being. That's a very hard statement. At various stages of the movement some have acted as if almost the opposite were true, in that we get purer and purer. More and more people have been kicked out for less and less reason. At one period of the past, way back, the result of such thinking was another of the religious wars, or wars of extinction. At another time it was Hitler; he wanted a ton of purity too. I think I'm in the underground because I want part of none of these, whatever name they go by, whatever rhetoric they justify themselves with.

When madness is the acceptable public state of mind, we're all in danger, all in danger for we are under the heel of former masters as under the heel of new ones.

Some of your actions are going to involve inciting and conflict and trashing, and these actions are very difficult for thoughtful people. But I came upon a rule of thumb somewhere which might be of some help to us: do only that which one cannot not do. Maybe it isn't very helpful, and of course it's going to be applied differently by the Joint Chiefs of Staff and the underground group of sane men and women. I think our realization is that a movement has historic meaning only insofar as it puts its gains to the side dictated by human dignity and the protection of life, even of the lives most unworthy of such respect. A revolution is interesting insofar as it avoids like the plague the plague it promised to heal. Ultimately if we want to define the plague as death, and I think that's a good definition, the healing will neither put people to death nor fill the prisons nor inhibit freedom nor brainwash nor torture its enemies nor be mendacious nor exploit anyone, whether women or children or blacks or the poor. It will have a certain respect for the power of the truth, which created the revolution in the first place.

We may take it, I think, as a simple rule of thumb that the revolution will be no better and no more truthful and no more populist and no more attractive than those who brought it into being. Which is to say we are not killers, as America would stigmatize us, and indeed as America perversely longs for us to be. We are something far different, we are teachers of the people who have come on a new vision of things.

Instead of thinking of the underground as temporary or exotic or abnormal, perhaps we are being called upon to start thinking of its implication as an entirely self-sufficient, mobile, internal revival community, so that the underground may be the definition of our future. What does it mean literally to have nowhere to go in America or to be kicked out of America? It must mean to us — let us go somewhere in America, let us stay here and play here and love here and build here, and in this way join not only those who like us are recently kicked out also, but those who have never been inside at all, the blacks and the Indians and Puerto Ricans and Chicanos, whose consciousness has gone far under the rock.

Next, we are to strive to become such men and women as may, in a new world, be nonviolent. If there's any definition of the new man, the man of the future, it seems to me that we do violence unwillingly, bar exception, as instrument, knowing that destruction of property is only a means and keeping the end as vivid and urgent and as alive to us as are the means so that the means are judged in every instance by their relation to the ends. I have a great fear of American violence, not only out there in the military and the diplomacy, in economics, in industry and advertising, but also in here, in me, up close among us.

But the history of the movement, in the last years, it seems to me, shows how constantly and easily we are seduced by violence, not only as to method but as to end in itself. With very little politics, very little ethics, very little direction, and only a minimum moral sense, if any at all, it might lead one to conclude in despair: the movement is debased beyond recognition, I can't be a part of it. Far from giving birth to the new man, it has only proliferated

the armed, bellicose, and inflated spirit of the army, the plantation, the corporation, the diplomat.

Yet it seems to me good, in public as well as in our own house,
to turn the question of violence back on the true creators and pur-
veyors of it, working as we do from a very different ethos and for
very different ends. I remember being on a television program
recently and having the whole thing thrown at me, and saying —
look, ask the question in the seats of power, don't ask it of me,
don't ask me why I broke the law, go ask Nixon why he breaks the
law constantly, ask the Justice Department, ask the racists. Obviously, but for Johnson and Nixon and their fetching ways, Catonsville would never have taken place and you and I would not be
here today, just as but for the same people SDS would never have
grown into the Weathermen or the Weathermen have gone
underground. In a decent society, normally functioning for its
people, all of us would be doing the things that decent men do for
one another.

The question now is what can we create. I feel at your side
across the miles, and I hope that sometime, sometime in this mad
world, in this mad time, it will be possible for us to sit down face
to face, brother to brother, sister to sister, and find that our hopes
and our sweat, and the hopes and sweat and death and tears and
blood of our brothers throughout the world, have brought to birth
that for which we began.

Thank you and shalom.

New Morning—Changing Weather

This declaration, signed by Bernardine Dohrn and the Weather Underground, was delivered December 6, 1970, to the office of Liberation News Service. It arrived special delivery, bearing stamps commemorating Tom Paine and Lucy Stone. The first page of the document was marked with a hand-painted rainbow and a red-lightning arrow, with a Vietnamese stamp showing a woman dressed in green, rifle over her shoulder, in the right-hand corner. The last sheet bore Miss Dohrn's fingerprint. The letter, presented in slightly excerpted form, shows the effect of Father Berrigan's views on the underground Weathermen as well as the dramatic impact of the townhouse explosion on Washington Square in which several members of the underground were killed and wounded while making bombs.

THIS COMMUNICATION does not accompany a bombing or a specific action. We want to express ourselves to the mass movement not as military leaders but as tribes at council. It has been nine months since the townhouse explosion. In that time, the future of our revolution has been changed decisively. A growing illegal organization of young women and men can live and fight and love inside Babylon. The FBI can't catch us; we've pierced their bullet-proof shield. But the townhouse forever destroyed our belief that armed struggle is the only real revolutionary struggle.

It is time for the movement to go out into the air, to organize, to risk calling rallies and demonstrations, to convince that mass actions against the war and in support of rebellions do make a difference. Only acting openly, denouncing Nixon, Agnew and Mitchell, and sharing our numbers and wisdom together with young sisters and brothers will blow away the fear of the students at

Kent State, the smack of the Lower East Side and the national silence after the bombings of North Vietnam.

The deaths of three friends ended our military conception of what we are doing. It took us weeks of careful talking to rediscover our roots, to remember that we had been turned on to the possibilities of revolution by denying the schools, the jobs, the death relationships we were "educated" for. We went back to how we had begun living with groups of friends and found that this revolution could leave intact the enslavement of women if women did not fight to end and change it, together.

And marijuana and LSD and little money and awakening to the black revolution, the people of the world. Unprogramming ourselves; relearning Amerikan history. The first demonstration we joined; the first time we tried to convince our friends. In the wake of the townhouse we found that we didn't know much about each other's pasts — our talents, our interests, our differences.

We had all come together around the militancy of young white people determined to reject racism and US exploitation of the third world. Because we agreed that an underground must be built, we were able to disappear an entire organization within hours of the explosion. But it was clear that more had been wrong with our direction than technical inexperience (always install a safety switch so you can turn it off and on and a light to indicate if a short circuit exists).

Diana, Teddy and Terry had been in SDS for years. Diana and Teddy had been teachers and both spent weeks with the Vietnamese in Cuba. Terry had been a community organizer in Cleveland and at Kent; Diana had worked in Guatemala. They fought in the Days of Rage in Chicago. Everyone was angered by the murder of Fred Hampton. Because their collective began to define armed struggle as the only legitimate form of revolutionary action, they did not believe that there was any revolutionary motion among white youth. It seemed like black and third world people were going up against Amerikan imperialism alone.

Two weeks before the townhouse explosion, four members of this group had firebombed Judge Murtagh's house in New York as an action of support for the Panther 21, whose trial was just beginning. To many people this was a very good action. Within the group, however, the feeling developed that because this action had not done anything to hurt the pigs materially it wasn't very important. So within two weeks' time, this group had moved from firebombing to antipersonnel bombs. Many people in the collective did not want to be involved in the large-scale, almost random bombing offensive that was planned. But they struggled day and night and eventually, everyone agreed to do their part.

At the end, they believed and acted as if only those who die are proven revolutionaries. Many people had been argued into doing something they did not believe in, many had not slept for days. Personal relationships were full of guilt and fear. The group had spent so much time willing themselves to act that they had not dealt with the basic technological considerations of safety. They had not considered the future: either what to do with the bombs if it had not been possible to reach their targets, or what to do in the following days.

This tendency to consider only bombings or picking up the gun as revolutionary, with the glorification of the heavier the better, we've called the military error.

After the explosion, we called off all armed actions until such time as we felt the causes had been understood and acted upon. We found that the alternative direction already existed among us and had been developed within other collectives. We became aware that a group of outlaws who are isolated from the youth communities do not have a sense of what is going on, can not develop strategies that grow to include large numbers of people, have become "us" and "them."

It was a question of revolutionary culture. Either you saw the youth culture that has been developing as bourgeois or decadent and therefore to be treated as the enemy of the revolution, or you saw it as the forces which produced us, a culture that we were a part of, a young and unformed society (nation).

In the past months we have had our minds blown by the possibilities that exist for all of us to develop the movement so that as revolutionaries we change and shape the cultural revolution. We are in a position to change it for the better. Men who are chauvinists can change and become revolutionaries who no longer embrace any part of the culture that stands in the way of the freedom of women. Hippies and students who fear black power should check out Rap Brown's *Die Nigger Die* and George Jackson's writings. We can continue to liberate and subvert attempts to rip off the culture. People become revolutionaries in the schools, in the army, in prisons, in communes, and on the streets. Not in an underground cell.

Because we are fugitives, we could not go near the movement. That proved to be a blessing because we've been everywhere else. We meet as many people as we can with our new identities; we've watched the TV news of our bombings with neighbors and friends who don't know that we're Weatherpeople. We are often afraid but we take our fear for granted now, not trying to act tough. What we once thought would have to be some zombie-like discipline has turned out to be a yoga of alertness, a heightened awareness of activities and vibrations around us — almost a new set of eyes and ears.

Even though we have not communicated about ourselves specifically before this, our actions have said much about where our heads are at. We have obviously not gone in for large-scale material damage. Most of our actions have hurt the enemy on about the same military scale as a bee sting. But the political effect against the enemy has been devastating. The world knows that even the white youth of Babylon will resort to force to bring down imperialism.

The attacks on the Marin County Courthouse and the Long Island City Jail were because we believe that the resistance and political leadership that is growing within the prisons demands immediate and mass support from young people. For all the George Jacksons, Afeni Shakurs and potential revolutionaries in these jails, the movement is the lifeline. They rebelled expecting massive support from outside.

Demonstrations in support of prison revolts are a major responsibility of the movement, but someone must call for them, put out the leaflets, convince people that it is a priority. We are so used to feeling powerless that we believe pig propaganda about the death of the movement, or some bad politics about rallies being obsolete and bullshit. A year ago, when Bobby Seale was ripped off in Chicago and the movement didn't respond, it made it easier for the pigs to murder Fred Hampton. Now the Puerto Ricans have been killed by the pigs in the New York jails, in retaliation for the prisoner rebellion. What we do or don't do makes a difference.

It will require courage and close families of people to do this organizing. Twos and threes is not a good form for anything — it won't put out a newspaper, organize a conference on the war, or do an armed action without getting caught. Our power is that together we are mobile, decentralized, flexible and we come into every home where there are children who catch the music of freedom and life.

The women and men in jails are POWs held by the United States. When an Amerikan pilot is shot down while bombing North Vietnamese villages, he is often surrounded by thousands of people who have just seen their family and homes destroyed by the bombs he was delivering. Yet the man is not attacked and killed by the Vietnamese but is cared for as a prisoner. Nixon is now waging a last-ditch moral crusade around the treatment of those Amerikan war criminals to justify all his impending atrocities.

The demonstrations and strikes following the rape of Indochina and the murders at Jackson and Kent last May showed real power and made a strong difference. New people were reached and involved — and the government was put on the defensive. This month the bombings could have touched off actions expressing our fury at double-talking Laird and his crew — war research and school administrators and traveling politicians are within reach of our leaflets, our rallies, our rocks. Women's lib groups can find in Nguyen Thi Binh a sister for whom there is love and support here. Her proposals for peace must be explained and Bloody Dick's plans to use more bombers to replace the GIs who are refusing to fight exposed as the escalation and genocide it is. Vietnamization Indianization limited duration protective reaction suppressive fire horseshit. It seems that we sometimes forget that in Vietnam strong liberated women and men live and fight. Not as abstract guerrilla fighters, slugging it out with US imperialism in Southeast Asia, but as people with values and loves and parents and children and hopes for the future.

People like Thai, a fighter in the People's Liberation Armed Forces who was in Hue during Tet and at Hamburger Hill a year later, or Than Tra, an organizer in the mass women's organization and the students' movement in the cities, who had not seen her lover in nine years. They traveled for a month to come to Cuba to meet with us, to sing and dance and explain how it is in Vietnam. There is nothing brutal or macho about guns and bombs in their hands.

We can't help thinking that if more people knew about them, the antiwar movement would never have allowed Nixon and Agnew to travel to so many cities during the past election with only the freaks at Kansas State and the people of San Jose to make our anger at his racism known to the world.

The hearts of our people are in a good place. Over the past months, freaks and hippies and a lot of people in the movement have begun to dig in for a long winter. Kent and Augusta and Jackson brought to all of us a coming of age, a seriousness about how hard it will be to fight in Amerika and how long it will take us to win. We are all beginning to figure out what the Cubans meant when they told us about the need for new men and new women.

People have been experimenting with everything about their lives, fierce against the ways of the white man. They have learned how to survive together in the poisoned cities and how to live on the road and the land. They've moved to the country and found new ways to bring up free wild children. People have purified themselves with organic food, fought for sexual liberation, grown long hair. People have reached out to each other and learned that grass and organic consciousness-expanding drugs are weapons of the revolution. Not mandatory for everyone, not a gut-check, but a tool — a Yaqui way of knowledge. But while we sing of drugs the enemy knows how great a threat our youth culture is to their rule, and they employ their allies — the killer drugs (smack and speed) — to pacify and destroy young people. No revolution can succeed without the youth, and we face that possibility if we don't meet this threat.

People are forming new families. Collectives have sprung up from Seattle to Atlanta, Buffalo to Vermont, and they are units of people to trust each other both to live together and to organize and fight together. The revolution involves our whole lives; we aren't part-time soldiers or secret revolutionaries. It is our closeness and the integration of our personal lives with our revolutionary work that will make it hard for undercover pigs to infiltrate our collectives. It's one thing for pigs to go to a few meetings, even meetings of a secret cell. It's much harder for them to live in a family for long without being detected.

One of the most important things that has changed since people began working in collectives is the idea of what leadership is. People — and especially groups of sisters — don't want to follow academic ideologues or authoritarians. From Fidel's speeches and Ho's poems we've understood how leaders grow out of being deeply in touch with movements. From Crazy Horse and other great Indian chiefs we've learned that the people who respect their tribe and its needs are followed freely and with love. The Dakotas laughed at the whites' appointing one man to be chief of all the

Dakota tribes, as if people wouldn't still go with whichever leader they thought was doing the right thing!

Many of these changes have been pushed forward by women both in collectives with men and in all-women's collectives. The enormous energy of sisters working together has not only transformed the movement internally, but when it moves out it is a movement that confuses and terrifies Amerika. When asked about the sincerity of Madame Binh's proposals, Ky says, "Never trust a woman in politics." The pigs refuse to believe that women can write a statement or build a sophisticated explosive device or fight in the streets. But while we have seen the potential strength of thousands of women marching, it is now up to revolutionary women to take the lead to call militant demonstrations, to organize young women, to carry the Viet Cong flag, to make it hard for Nixon and Ky to travel around the country ranting about POWs the same day that hundreds of women are being tortured in the prisons of South Vietnam.

It's up to us to tell women in Amerika about Madame Binh in Paris; about Pham Thi Quyen, fighter in the Saigon underground wife of Nguyen Van Troi; about Madame Nguyen Thi Dinh, leader of the first South Vietnamese People's Liberation Armed Forces unit uprising in Ben Tre in 1961; about Celia Sanchez and Haydee Santamaria who fought at Moncada and in the Havana underground; about Bernadette Devlin and Leila Khaled and Lolita Lebrun; and about Joan Bird and Afeni Shakur and Mary Moylan here.

We can't wait to organize people until we get ourselves together any more than we can act without being together. They must go on at the same time. None of these changes that people are going through are rules and principles. We are in many different regions of the country and are building different kinds of leaders and organizations. It's not coming together into one organization, or paper structure of factions or coalitions. It's a New Nation that will grow out of the struggles of the next year.

A Doctor's Letter to His Son

Dr. Paul Williamson is a McComb, Mississippi, physician. He wrote this letter to his son in the autumn of 1970 as the son was about to enter Tulane University at New Orleans. He then published his letter in a small medical newsletter which he edits. The letter was reprinted from the medical publication and received wide national attention.

Dear Nathan:

Of course, you know that your mother and I love you deeply. There are limits to that love. Let me discuss one with you today.

You are going to Tulane. We are proud and happy for you. There are, however, awkward things that must be discussed. College kids over the nation are "protesting."

They use many beautiful phrases. What it often amounts to is a contest with the duly constituted authorities of the United States government. The only term that could apply is revolution. People are quite rightly shot in revolutions.

I suppose there is the legal differentiation between a peaceful demonstration and breaking windows. One graduates into the other by such indifferent degrees it is difficult to say where one ends and the other begins.

The duly constituted authorities have been merciful beyond belief — far too merciful, I think — with students. Obviously, this patience is nearing an end. Snap, I have seldom heard of a student being shot at his study desk. When he goes in the open and contests the ground with the National Guard, he may very likely be shot — and very rightly.

Let us take, for example, the sweet little girl in Kent, Ohio. I feel nothing but sorrow that a beautiful young girl of great mental attainments be killed. Yet, Snap, if she had been studying — doing what her parents were paying for her to accomplish — would she have died?

She was helping contest the ground with duly constituted US authorities. In this case, I back the US. I think it rather remarkable that they didn't shoot two hundred more. In this case, the girl was a revolutionary and she got exactly what a revolutionary should expect.

The same, Snap, would be true of you. If you care to challenge the US government, this is your affair. If you get killed doing it, this is your affair. You see, there are constitutional ways to change the US government and I agree that it desperately needs changing. However, if you choose to try to change it by revolution, expect to get shot. Mother and I will grieve but we will gladly buy a dinner for the National Guardsman who shot you. You see, son, they pretty-up in definition all the things you might want to do. When brought to its basics, it is still just revolution.

I am sorry for the colored boys who were killed at Jackson. But, son, I know a lot more about this than will ever be printed in national news media. There was sniper fire the night before as well as the night the police fired back. The students were given fifteen minutes' warning to clear the area before the police fired. I thought the duly constituted authorities were most gentle to take only two. If you take part in something like this and get shot, Mama and I will still back the US.

It may sound like great martyrdom to give your life for an ideal. Indeed, it may be when you are old enough to judge ideals. Trying to whip the National Guard or the Army appeals to me as damned foolishness. Snap, I have been shot and it hurts like hell. It's funny, but you don't think of ideals over the pain.

Now use your head, son. Remember this country is getting tired of student demonstrations which lead to revolution. The

National Guard can shove in a couple of clips and clean Tulane. I think they ought to when students disturb the peace and destroy property.

One thing of which you have probably not thought: Tulane is a nonprofit corporation belonging to the public, which means one brick is yours. The National Guard is a public organization, which means that one bolt on one rifle may have been paid for with your tax.

It seems awfully foolish for you to pay for the bolt that snaps the cartridge home which kills you. It seems even more foolish to tear down the bricks you own.

When I went to Oklahoma City University, I always thought of it as my university. Ann and I probably own one bit of cement between the bricks. Believe me, sir, I was very careful of that bit of cement.

I, too, had ebullient spirits but I used them for more practical purposes.

Have you ever considered how many co-eds there are to be kissed? This is a much more worthy purpose than absorbing a bullet and not nearly so painful.

Think of these things.

Love,

DAD

Kill the Pigs

Ernest van den Haag, one of the most thoughtful of national conservative commentators and a frequent contributor to the National Review, *set down this analysis of the American condition at the turn of the year, 1970–71.*

THE PARAMOUNT DUTY of government is to supply law and order so that citizens are secure in their lives and lawful pursuits. A minority may protest that the law and order provided do not do justice; but the majority must think otherwise in a democracy, else it would not consent. Certainly justice should be more, but it cannot be less, anywhere, than law and order. Hence the government's first task.

Pontius Pilatus, then, was in duty bound to sentence to death one he thought innocent if, on reasonable evidence, he thought that the maintenance of law and order required no less. Herman Melville poignantly affirmed the governor's duty when, writing toward the end of his life, he had the guiltless sailor Billy Budd accept the death sentence imposed by Captain Vere — who knew him innocent — but plausibly believed that Billy had to die, to daunt incipient mutiny. The ship of state sails on, its ropes and pulleys groaning, but its crew safe. Justice to the individual gave way to law and order, the paramount need of society, which governments exist to satisfy.

Mankind has made great material progress since Rome ruled and Melville wrote. We now can afford a less oppressive order, protected only by confining those actually guilty of violating it — without judicial sacrifice of known innocence. But our governments — federal, state and local — have been grossly remiss: 97 per cent of reported crimes go altogether unpunished now. Because the risk has become so small, and the reward considerable, crime rises every year: it pays.

As yet habit, moral scruple, and overestimation of the risk keep the great majority of citizens law-abiding. More saliently aggrieved groups, raging for "justice," already discount the government's ability to enforce order.

They are still small, but armed and sworn to "kill the pigs" and to overthrow the Republic. They owe their viability and their money to "liberals," and to college students, who sustain them in guilty sympathy with the grievances of the black and the poor (students thereby gratify their own need for a cause and a community, so frustrated by our undemanding and unresponsive ways of keeping the young green until they fester).

Democracy, however, cannot endure when armed private groups proposing violence are tolerated: Italian and German democracy were murdered by the turbulent groups they suffered. Nor, patently, can these groups readily be destroyed after they have grown into a "present danger."

As they realize that their government does not protect them from the ferocity of criminals and gangs, the citizens long for an authority to do so. Nothing has emerged to satisfy this legitimate longing in legitimate ways. New Yorkers have elected Rockefeller four times, Lindsay twice. Poverty declined. Welfare rolls rose. So did taxes. Yet crime rates increased faster each term, and the proportion of crimes punished fell, while that of citizens victimized grew.

In these circumstances policemen are accused of taking bribes, and of lawlessly fighting those who lawlessly fight them. Neither act can be justified; yet both can be explained. The unmanageable procedures, the irrelevant and unenforceable laws cherished by inept governments produce corruption. The beleaguered policeman's instinct of self-preservation seems sounder than that of those who deplore his struggle to survive and serve — instead of endeavoring to correct the conditions which produce his illegal outbursts.

The Flag Is in Trouble

Harrison E. Salisbury recorded this view of the state of the nation in The Many Americans Shall Be One, *published in spring 1971.*

THERE HAS BEEN a lot of talk lately about the flag. The flag is in trouble and this, if nothing else, is as clear a sign as we need of the intensity of the crisis which grips our country.

I am an old-fashioned man. I love the American flag, love to see it flying, get a thrill out of the colors although for many years I have been much too sophisticated to let on to that. This is George M. Cohan stuff; square. I admit it.

But, of course, that is what the flag is about, for it has no meaning whatever except as the symbol of the country which it represents. When we fight to possess the flag, we are fighting, in truth, for the soul of the country. Today, the flag is no longer the very sign of unity, of oneness, of the Americanness of us all. There are those who cringe when they see the decal on the car window and others who wave the flag violently in the face of their opponents. There are those who hoist it upside down and those who make of it a designer's mod toy.

It was not always so.

When I was a child in Minneapolis, my father got me up at 5:30 A.M., never later than six, on Memorial Day and the Fourth of July. In the stillness of the not-yet-awakened morning, with the sun just slanting through the tall elms outside, we tiptoed up to the attic, dusty, cobwebbed, with its smell of old furniture, medicines from my grandfather's medical cabinets, mothballs, moldering leather, ancient papers. We would rummage back into a dark cubbyhole and carefully pull out the great flag on its heavy oak pole. This we would carry, myself holding the brass-bound end, into the front attic room. We pried open the small window — it was always jammed — then we carefully projected the pole out the window, setting it to fit snugly and securely into the iron stanchion on the floor. After we unfurled the flag I ran down the back staircase into the alley and around to the front of the house to see how it looked. It looked splendid! It always did.

It was the regret of my childhood that we had no small brass cannon, like that in *The Swiss Family Robinson*, to salute the flag. It was another regret that we had no flagpole on the lawn as did some of our neighbors.

During Liberty Loan parades in World War I, in which, as a schoolboy, I participated proudly, it was intoxicating to be one of the multitude that carried the great outspread flag down the center of Nicollet Avenue receiving the tossed silver dollars, quarters, dimes, and even crumpled blanket-style dollar bills. On Arbor Day parades I proudly marched as color guard, shoulder to shoulder with my classmate Isadore Pass, who had the honor of carrying the flag because his grades were all A's and my report card showed two or three B's.

The salute to the flag (I believe it was invented in World War I and there have been some changes in its wording since) was then a simple, heartfelt experience with no posturing, no legionnairisms, no clasping of hand over heart, no touching up, just holding ourselves as straight at attention as small boys' spines could do and the explosive ring-out: "One nation, *indivisible*, with *liberty* and *justice* for *all!*" We shouted it. And at the end we flung our hand out to the flag. Our chests throbbed. We believed it. I still do. Profoundly. Which is not to say that the flag and the love of country which it symbolizes were not vilely distorted in World War I. Within the city of Minneapolis where I grew up, we, myself as a child among hate-sodden adults, turned savagely upon all

who believed differently from ourselves. We used the flag as a
vehicle of our intolerance just as some do today.

I was born and raised in a patriotic, chauvinistic, Bull Moose
Republican family. I supported Teddy Roosevelt with his Big
Stick and Manifest Destiny, his bully-for-you, Rough Rider na-
tionalism with all my heart. I grew up looking at the map of the
world (all red for the Empire on which the Sun Never Set), longing that it could be all green like the United States. Americans
were better than anyone else. The doctrine was unquestioned.
White Americans, I suppose, although blacks were so few in my
growing up that we children counted their favor a special privilege. It was different, of course, with Indians. I was raised on the
frontier doctrine that "the only good Indian is a dead Indian."

At the age of seven I was all for war (World War I) and wore a
Charles Evans Hughes button (although really I supported T.R.).
I zealously proclaimed Woodrow Wilson a "yellow dog" because
he "promised to keep us out of war" and I was for fighting side by
side with the gallant English Tommies and French Poilus to re-
venge the poor children of Belgium, their hands chopped off by
the Kaiser's Uhlans. When we entered the war I hated the "pros"
— a "pro" being a pro-German. You didn't have to use the full
phrase. Everyone knew what a "pro" was. The "good Germans"
whom you could not quite trust changed their names or said they
wished they could. The German conductor of the symphony orchestra was driven from his post; pacifist and antiwar candidates
like the father of Charles A. Lindbergh were rotten-egged, tarred
and feathered, ridden out of town, and worse. Ordinary Germans
were made to "kiss the flag" and mumble patriotic oaths. Not that
this won them acceptance. Their saloons were emptied, their
stores boycotted, even the most wondrous store in town, Holtzer-
man's German toy shop.

When the war was over the K.K.K. came in. Not against the
blacks. There were not enough of them to make a credible target.
Against the Catholics, mostly, and to a lesser extent, against the

small Jewish community. But mostly, of course, against anyone who was disliked, who did not conform, or who had the savage misfortune to get in their way.

It was very thrilling and very patriotic and my schoolmates and I secretly chalked K.K.K. on the slattern fences of the alleys through which we walked to school.

The K.K.K. rode under the flag. No Confederate banner in those days. Certainly not in the North. The fire and brimstone still smoldered and any northern political candidate in trouble "waved the bloody shirt" just as southern demagogues "hollered nigger" (and still do). Late as it was, the Civil War veterans were an honored and respected element in northern society. They were the GAR, the Grand Army of the Republic, a name to thrill a boy's bones. No amorphous catchall "veterans organization." No tawdry drunks. No raucous conventions. No bonus and pension cadgers. The original undiluted Grand Army of the Republic. The "boys in blue" who saved the Union. My heroes. Everybody's heroes. Memorial Day was their day and theirs alone. My old great-uncle, the survivor of Andersonville, tottered down to Nicollet Avenue each May 30 with his fellow survivors and the fine line of men in blue swept up the avenue, flags flying bravely, uniforms worn but neat, whiskers and mustaches white and flourishing, steps firm on that day. But soon the number of marchers began to dwindle and more and more rode — not marched — up the avenue. The GAR marched to "Old Glory" and "The Battle Hymn of the Republic."

The flag was all-embracing. Unimpeachable. The IWW agitators (it was years before I learned that the initials did not actually mean "I Won't Work!") who stood on soapboxes in Gateway Square and harangued the hoboes, the transient workers who harvested the wheat, felled the timber, worked the mines, and maintained the railroads of those days, preached their cause under the flag. So did the Salvation Army and the Volunteers of America.

The flag was not lightly used. The rules for its display were strict. No legions of toughs wrapped themselves in flags as a protection or distinction for making cause against fellow Americans. No radicals or iconoclasts carved the flag into odd patterns or embraced some strange device to set themselves apart. The red flag might appear. But it flew beside the Stars and Stripes, proud, no doubt, to be in such company.

All of which is by way of making clear my dissent from those who employ the flag as a symbol of *their* particularity — whatever the nature of that particularity. The flag is our country. God knows we are, always have been, and hopefully always will be a nation of diversity. In that is our strength. But we must have a symbol under which we can all rally. If we now take *the* symbol, the epitome of that America which in the words of the pledge is "one nation, indivisible, with liberty and justice for all," if we take this symbol and make of it an antisymbol, on the one hand, or, on the other, a symbol of pseudopatriotism, of a flaunted, better, higher patriotism than that of our neighbors, or of a cause which exploits the *divisibility* of America and proclaims liberty for some and justice only as a few understand it — then we do, indeed, fall victim to national schizophrenia, tearing at the very core of our being, wounding all, twisting and distorting all that is dear, in greater or lesser measure, to the hearts of flag-bearers and anti-flag-bearers alike.

I do not take lightly those who spurn the flag or those who seek to make of it a protective shield to conceal hatred and ignorance of the principles for which it stands.

To Kill a Mountain

Robert McConnell Hatch, the retired Episcopal bishop of western Massachusetts, has known Canaan Mountain for half a lifetime. In 1971 the mountain was threatened with destruction for power generation.

FOR YEARS I HAD gone to Canaan Mountain on Saturdays with my friend Jack Farr to explore and to hike through the surrounding forest. For both of us it was an opportunity to enter a world of immense natural beauty, freed from the pressures of our work and from the clatter and turmoil of the cities where we lived. We became very dependent on these Saturdays in the woods. If we missed one, the following week dragged insufferably. We went throughout the year, snowshoeing in the winter months. It was like repairing to a fountain of youth every Saturday morning and driving home that night after a ten- or twelve-mile hike feeling positively young again, recharged in body and spirit. The mountain and its environs became one of the focal points in our lives.

In addition to Canaan Mountain itself there are several lower ridges and outcrops that are nameless, but one bears the name of Crissey Mountain and has the distinction of being the highest point in the town of Norfolk. A number of ponds are scattered through the forest, none of them large, some supporting families of beaver and muskrat, one inhabited by otters, all occupied in summer by Canadian geese, wood ducks and black ducks.

The summits and shoulders of the ridges are matted with hair grass (*Deschampsia*), resembling the grassy balds on summits in the southern Appalachians. They are fringed with scrub oak and afford far-reaching views. Oaks and maples and birch, beech and hemlock predominate on the slopes and in the valleys. In some spots the hemlocks reach massive proportions, having stood unmolested for more than a century. Throughout the forest are tangles of mountain laurel.

The forest harbors a few reminders of human history. In its recesses one strumbles across occasional tree-choked cellar holes and tumbled-down walls. On one November afternoon Jack and I discovered three graves in a stand of ancient pines and maples, all sunken nearly a foot below ground level.

There are some excellent walks in the forest. Dirt roads and bridle trails probe many parts of it, but the best walks involve bushwhacking. Crissey Mountain commands a surprising western view that reveals hardly a sign of human habitation — only a few very distant buildings. Canaan Mountain fronts on a western skyline embracing Bear Mountain and the Taconic Range. There is a precipitous bluff rising over a pond that is one of the most inviting places in all New England to while away a warm afternoon, especially in laurel season.

It is a forest for all seasons. To be sure, nothing can compare with a day in June when the laurel is in flower or an October morning when the hillsides blaze with the blood red and yellow, russet and dark crimson. But all seasons are good, and some of our most memorable trips were made on snowshoes in the heart of winter. Long views through the forest are possible then and snowshoes can be quiet. Consequently winter is the season when we have seen the most deer — family groups of two or three does and their yearlings, or a buck freed of his antlers, wintering in a hemlock grove.

At first we went to Canaan Mountain for exercise, for a change of pace, for a respite from the daily grind. But soon we found that we were coming because we loved the mountain and the forest. We loved it for its wildness and most of all for the fact that it was unblemished by man. It was a miracle that such an unspoiled tract could still exist in one of the most overbuilt parts of America.

Finally Jack bought a house on Undermountain Road where Wangum Lake Brook tumbles down Canaan Mountain before threading westward to the Hollenbeck River. The view from his porch takes in a valley hemmed by hills and sprinkled with trim old farmhouses, suggesting the more picturesque valleys still left in Vermont — or those that once existed in many parts of Connecticut. To gaze down that valley from Jack's porch is to glimpse what Connecticut was like a hundred or even two hundred years ago.

Jack and his family lived there about a year in peace. They believed this would be their home for the rest of their lives and that nothing would change it. The proximity of the forest promised such protection.

It was a fool's paradise. The blow was struck by an organization known as Northeast Utilities. Their proposal embraced such a grandiose piece of devastation that it taxed credibility. Their target was Canaan Mountain. A reservoir, encompassing 750 acres, would be diked up near the summit; a pipeline would imprison Deming Brook, one of the main tributaries of Wangum Lake Brook; a second reservoir of 750 acres would inundate most of Wangum Lake Brook Valley; and 250-foot swathes would be slashed through the forest to make way for power lines in all directions. The complex would be called a pumped-storage facility. Water would be pumped from the lower reservoir to that on Canaan Mountain whenever extra power was available. From there it would be released to provide hydroelectric power during periods of peak demand.

A dam 1700 feet long and 100 feet high would rise directly in front of Jack's house.

The utility's proposal for Canaan Mountain embodies an issue that is facing all of us today. Either we save the more beautiful parts of our country for recreation in its broadest sense, or we succumb to a complete take-over by industry. The issue of Canaan Mountain is no more pointed than that involving every polluted river, every community befouled by poisoned air, every remaining scrap of scenic beauty that is threatened by another multilane superhighway. The issue, in fact, is everywhere.

A host of people are fighting to save the mountain's life. They have pointed out that there exist more desirable and efficient ways of generating power and that there is no actual need to violate the landscape with pumped-storage facilities. Alternatives may cost more, but Americans must face the fact that we cannot save our environment without some cost and that a salvaged and beautified country which our children can enjoy and love is far more precious than the dollars we might save today.

Less Than a Megadeath

The Reverend Harold F. Hofstad is pastor of Concordia Lutheran Church, Edmore, North Dakota, not far from the missile installations of which he wrote in 1971.

"LESS THAN A megadeath." That's what the report would read if everyone in North Dakota died in atomic war. So when defense planners talk about thirty, forty, fifty megadeaths, this sounds rather comforting — like it would be getting off easy.

I drive these roads past the missile installations — the Minutemen — and call them "my country cemeteries." That's what they look like, all fenced in and spread so evenly, every seven miles in all directions. Nobody I know has ever been inside the fences. At night they light up, and the glare shines over the prairies like dawn in the distance. I suppose they have to keep saboteurs at bay.

The stories go around that some people have seen the insides of those underground silos. One fellow says that the one on his land is all full of water from seepage. All rusted out. Last year they tried to fire some over near a neighboring town. They say that nothing worked. I find myself thinking, "That's the only good thing about them — they don't work."

How many are there? Nobody claims to know, except maybe the Russians and our Department of Defense. And they won't tell. Nobody knows exactly what would happen if they were fired; we try not to think about it anyway. Someplace on the other side of the world there would be the end of the world . . . megadeaths of people going to work or fixing supper or just finishing with the washing. Nobody knows.

Of course, we know we wouldn't use them first. That's important. They are strictly a "second strike" force — I think they call it retaliatory. But then, I find myself thinking that it really doesn't matter. People would be just as dead no matter who fires first.

They said these were hard sites, and that means they wouldn't be damaged except by a direct hit. That's important, too, especially because people wondered how we could possibly spend so much money on them in the first place. But now they tell us they really aren't that safe from attack. A first strike could knock out enough of them to take away our winning hand.

So now it's ABM — the ace up the sleeve. Of course, it's strictly defensive again. All it would do is fire off a bunch of interceptor rockets and blast the invaders from the skies. Comforting thought (to the Canadians especially).

But then I find myself wondering: "How come?" Could they really send enough missiles to knock out all of these we already have ready to fire? Wouldn't it be sort of like trying to hit a swarm of bees with a shotgun? Only direct hits would count. Or do they have enough missiles to blanket the area with a continuous sheet of fire — one hundred miles wide and at least fifty miles the other way?

And who are "they" anyway? The Russians? The Chinese? The Martians? It would take one thousand missiles and one thousand atomic fireballs to even start to get them all at once. Is that what the ABM installation is saying to us?

All of a sudden, while nobody was looking, we got to be Prime Target Area. Ground Zero for whoever might want to challenge our poker hand. Why don't they protect some cities? Why not work on the bigger megadeaths in New York or Los Angeles or Chicago?

No, I think to myself, this ABM sure doesn't look good for us less-than-one-megadeath North Dakotans. It looks like somebody knows something that nobody talks about. That is, of course, that we are expendable.

Well, we don't like to be cynical about it, but we know why they picked us. It was our location. Fine location for firing over the Pole. And we're pretty sure that the cheap land helped, too — it didn't cost them any $500,000 an acre, as it would in some places.

So we are the "chosen people" up here, I guess. Chosen because of our fine location, our cheap land and the cheap cost in mega-deaths.

And now, with ABM coming in, it looks like the defense people have already run us on their slide rules, and the answer still comes up the same — "cheap." Cheap land and cheap people.

So I think about these things. But there's only one feeling that keeps creeping up the back of my neck and makes the hair stand up stiff. You know what that is? It's the terrible thought that I don't know which "theys" I don't trust more — the ones in Russia or China or Wherever, or the ones with the slide rules who put this whole crazy business together.

The System

This poem is from Stanley Kunitz's collection The Testing Tree, *published in 1971.*

That pack of scoundrels
tumbling through the gate
emerges
as the Order of the State.

Rights and
Human Dignity

For Freedom of Speech

Professor Archibald Cox, representing the President and Fellows of Harvard University, made this plea attempting to quiet the crowd at a teach-in on Indochina sponsored by Young Americans for Freedom and Harvard Young Republicans on March 26, 1971.

MY NAME IS Archibald Cox. I beseech you to let me say a few words in the name of the President and Fellows of this university on behalf of freedom of speech. For if this meeting is disrupted — hateful as some of us may find it — then liberty will have died a little and those guilty of the disruption will have done inestimable damage to the causes of humanity and peace.

Men and women whose views aroused strong emotions — loved by some and hated by others — have always been allowed to speak at Harvard — Fidel Castro, the late Malcolm X, George Wallace, William Kuntsler, and others. Last year, in this very building, speeches were made for physical obstruction of university activities. Harvard gave a platform to all these speakers, even those calling for her destruction. No one in the community tried to silence them, despite intense opposition.

The reason is plain, and it applies here tonight. Freedom of speech is indivisible. You cannot deny it to one man and save it for others. Over and over again the test of our dedication to liberty is our willingness to allow the expression of ideas we hate. If those ideas are lies, the remedy is more speech and more debate, so that men will learn the truth — speech like the teach-in here a few weeks ago. To clap down or shout down a speaker on the ground that his ideas are dangerous or that he is telling a lie is to license all others to silence the speakers and suppress the publications with which they disagree. Suppose that speech is suppressed here tonight. Have you confidence that all who follow the example will be as morally right as they suppose themselves to be? History is filled with examples of the cruelty inflicted by men who set out to suppress ideas in the conviction of their own moral righteousness. This time those who have talked of disruption have a moral purpose, and may indeed be right in their goals and objectives. But will others be equally right when they resort to the same tactics? The price of liberty to speak the truth as each of us sees it is permitting others the same freedom.

Disruptive tactics seem to say, "We are scared to let others speak for fear that the listeners will believe them and not us." Disruptive tactics, even by noise alone, start us on the road to more and more disruption, and then to violence and more violence, because each group will come prepared the next time with greater numbers and ready to use a little more force until in the end, as in Hitler's Germany, all that counts is brute power.

And so I cling to the hope that those of you who started to prevent the speakers from being heard will desist. You have the power to disrupt the meeting, I am quite sure. The disciplinary action that will surely follow is not likely to deter you. But I hope that your good sense and courage in doing what's right will cause you to change your minds — to refrain from doing grievous and perhaps irretrievable harm to liberty.

Answer what is said here with more teach-ins and more truth, but let the speakers be heard.

A Definition of Objectivity

The question of the objectivity of the press and other media — indeed, of the whole concept of "objectivity" — came under increasing challenge in the 1970's. The question from critics of both left and right was: "Objective for whom?" These remarks by Thomas Winship, executive editor of the Boston Globe, were made in a debate of the question before the American Society of Newspaper Editors in Washington, D.C., April 15, 1971.

I'D LIKE TO GIVE *my* definition of objectivity. Objectivity is what we gave Senator Joe McCarthy before that group of great reporters — Murrey Marder, Phil Potter, Don Irwin and a couple of others — took their gloves off and before Ed Murrow's famous TV show.

It is what we gave cancer-producing cigarettes before the Surgeon General's report.

That's my working definition of *objectivity* for this debate. I say it's spinach and to *hell* with it.

But relax, nobody needs to worry about the public even now getting *objective* news. A recent poll shows that:

99.8 per cent of newspapers and TV are owned by millionaires.

99.5 per cent of millionaires think alike. Everything they believe is objective.

99.7 per cent of newspapers think what their owners think.

99 per cent of us editors wouldn't be here if we didn't agree with what the owners of our papers think.

So, the American people can always be sure of *objective* news. And we know that the reason this debate is on the ASNE dance card this year is that since Agnew yipped at us, many editors have been more *objective* than ever. (I call it a quiet backslide.)

Let's see how this objective journalism has been serving us.

It let Joe McCarthy ravage the reputations of thousands of Americans for too long without challenge.

It let the most unexplained war in history go on far too long before the challenge came.

It let industrial wastage almost clobber to death the face of America. Ralph Nader and Rachel Carson blew the whistle — not our great newspapers.

Yet, when newspapers *do* a superb crusading job, they win the Pulitzer Prize for it. This is not objective journalism, yet all the traditionalists think it's great stuff. This shows how utterly ridiculous the term "objectivity" is.

We all know the formula of the objectivity cult:

First — Report what the government official says, no matter what he says. Hell, he should know. He has all the facts, hasn't he?

Second — Give "both sides," even though most stories today are so complicated they can't be reduced to just two sides.

Third — Don't *explain* too much. That's "advocate" stuff.

Fourth — Quote only official sources. No one ever got in trouble that way.

Fifth — Beware of what the reporter thinks. He might lay open to public question the official line.

Objectivity is such a nice *trip* for an editor. Every morning he swallows his little objectivity pill. It turns him off from that paranoia over those long-haired kids out in his city room . . . those kids who whisper dirty talk over the water cooler — like "Nader," "Hanoi," "Panther."

I say these brainy kids in our city rooms are the best thing that ever happened to the newspaper business. They are our salvation. Attracting really bright young people to the business is the most compelling reason why I am so fed up with this objectivity double talk. For objectivity in today's climate is a code word that connotes playing it safe, covering up and superficiality.

If you gents buy the line of our honorable scaredy-cats, you kiss good-bye to the best new recruits to our muscle-bound trade.

The kids send such a strong waft of fresh air through our newsrooms.

They *write* better than we do.

They *know* more than we do.

They are more *honest* than we are.

They want to give the system a good college try.

They think the newspaper is *still* one of the most effective instruments for social change.

Certainly activist reporters are hard to handle. But what counts in the credibility issue is what gets in the paper. That's what we pay editors for. And, by God, socially concerned young men and women are susceptible to good editing. They can be taught to be responsible and fair, if only editors will stay out of the executive dining room and the country club long enough to teach them and keep them interested.

Dump the silly code words — objectivity and advocate journalism. Worry instead about fairness, credibility and professionalism. Worry about digging out and printing more of the truth.

TV and radio have all but liberated newspapers to concentrate upon improving society.

Editors and publishers who dare grab this new mantle will stay in business, increase profits, and best of all, lure to their newspapers the most effective young people of this and future generations.

Editors and publishers who continue to preoccupy themselves with objectivity jazz and the other code words will have as much luck keeping the establishment press afloat as they will selling Nixon as a folk hero to anyone under thirty-five.

The Government and the Press

This affidavit on the real nature of the relationship between the government and the press, particularly with respect to confidential and classified materials, was submitted to the US District Court in New York City, June 18, 1971, by Max Frankel, chief of the Washington Bureau of the New York Times, *in support of the effort by the* Times *to resist a government effort to halt by court injunction the publication of the Pentagon Papers.*

THE GOVERNMENT's unprecedented challenge to the *Times* in the case of the Pentagon Papers, I am convinced, cannot be understood, or decided, without an appreciation of the manner in which a small and specialized corps of reporters and a few hundred American officials regularly make use of so-called classified, secret and top-secret information and documentation. It is a cooperative, competitive, antagonistic and arcane relationship.

Without the use of "secrets" that I shall attempt to explain in this affidavit, there could be no adequate diplomatic, military and political reporting of the kind our people take for granted, either abroad or in Washington, and there could be no mature system of communication between the government and the people. That is one reason why the sudden complaint by one party to these regular dealings strikes us as monstrous and hypocritical — unless it is essentially perfunctory, for the purpose of retaining some discipline over the federal bureaucracy.

Presidents make "secret" decisions only to reveal them for the purposes of frightening an adversary nation, wooing a friendly electorate, protecting their reputations. The military services conduct "secret" research in weaponry only to reveal it for the purpose of enhancing their budgets, appearing superior or inferior to a foreign army, gaining the vote of a congressman or the favor of a contractor. High officials of the government reveal secrets in the search for support of their policies, or to help sabotage the plans and policies of rival departments. Middle-rank officials of government reveal secrets so as to attract the attention of their superiors or to lobby against the orders of those superiors. Though not the only vehicle for this traffic in secrets — the Congress is always eager to provide a forum — the press is probably the most important.

In the field of foreign affairs, only rarely does our government give full public information to the press for the direct purpose of simply informing the people. For the most part, the press obtains significant information bearing on foreign policy only because it has managed to make itself a party to confidential materials, and of value in transmitting these materials from government to other branches and offices of government as well as to the public at large. This is why the press has been wisely and correctly called the fourth branch of government.

I turn now in an attempt to explain, from a reporter's point of view, the several ways in which "classified" information figures in our relations with government. The government's complaint against the *Times* in the present case comes with ill grace because government itself has regularly and consistently, over the decades, violated the conditions it suddenly seeks to impose upon us — in three distinct ways:

First, it is our regular partner in the informal but customary traffic in secret information, without even the pretense of legal or formal "declassification." Presumably, many of the "secrets" I cited above, and all the "secret" documents and pieces of information that form the basis of the many newspaper stories that are attached hereto, remain "secret" in their official designation.

Second, the government and its officials regularly and customarily engage in a kind of ad hoc, de facto "declassification" that normally has no bearing whatever on considerations of the national interest. To promote a political, personal, bureaucratic or even commercial interest, incumbent officials and officials who return to civilian life are constantly revealing the secrets entrusted to them. They use them to barter with the Congress or the press, to curry favor with foreign governments and officials from whom they seek information in return. They use them freely, and with a startling record of impunity, in their memoirs and other writings.

Third, the government and its officials regularly and routinely misuse and abuse the "classification" of information, either by imposing secrecy where none is justified or by retaining it long after the justification has become invalid, for simple reasons of political or bureaucratic convenience. To hide mistakes of judgment, to protect reputations of individuals, to cover up the loss and waste of funds, almost everything in government is kept secret for a time and, in the foreign policy field, classified as "secret" and "sensitive" beyond any rule of law or reason. Every minor official can testify to this fact.

The Pentagon Papers

Judge Murray I. Gurfein, on June 19, 1971, upheld in US District Court for the Southern District of New York the right of the New York Times to publish the Pentagon Papers. This right had been challenged by Attorney General John Mitchell, seeking an injunction to prevent further publication of the Pentagon materials. It was Gurfein's decision which was ultimately upheld by the US Supreme Court in its landmark opinion a few days later. This is his decision, slightly excerpted.

ON JUNE 12, June 13 and June 14, 1971, the *New York Times* published summaries and portions of the text of two documents — certain volumes from a 1968 Pentagon study relating to Vietnam and a summary of a 1965 Defense Department study relating to the Tonkin Gulf incident. The United States sues to enjoin the *Times* from "further dissemination, disclosure or divulgence" of materials contained in the 1968 study of the decision-making process with respect to Vietnam and the summary of the 1965 Tonkin Gulf study.

The government contends that the documents still unpublished and the information in the possession of the *Times* involves a serious breach of the security of the United States and that the further publication will cause "irreparable injury to the national defense."

The articles involved material that has been classified as Top-Secret and Secret, although the government concedes that these classifications are related to volumes rather than individual documents and that included within the volumes may be documents which should not be classified in such high categories. My finding with respect to the testimony on security will be adverted to below.

1. This case is one of first impression. In the researches of both counsel and of the court nobody has been able to find a case remotely resembling this one where a claim is made that national security permits a prior restraint on the publication of a newspaper. The *Times* in affidavits has indicated a number of situations in which classified information has been "leaked" to the press without adverse governmental or judicial action. It cites news stories and the memoirs of public officials who have used (shortly after the events) classified material in explaining their versions of the decision-making process. They point out that no action has ever been taken against any such publication of "leaks." The government on the other hand points out that there has never been an attempt to publish such a massive compilation of documents, which is probably unique in the history of "leaks." The Vietnam study had been authorized by Secretary of Defense McNamara, continued under Secretary Clifford and finally delivered to the present Secretary of Defense Laird. The White House was not given a copy. The work was done by a group of historians, including certain persons on contract with the government. It is actually called a "history." The documents in the Vietnam study relate to the period from 1945 to early 1968. There is no reference to any material subsequent to that date. The Tonkin Gulf incident analysis was prepared in 1965, six years ago. The *Times* contends that the material is historical and that the circumstance that it involves the decision-making procedures of the government is no different from the descriptions that have emerged in the writings of diarists and memoirists. The government on the other hand contends that by reference to the totality of the studies an enemy might learn something about United States methods which he does not know, that references to past relationships with foreign governments might affect the conduct of our

relations in the future and that the duty of public officials to advise their superiors frankly and freely in the decision-making process would be impeded if it was believed that newspapers could with impunity publish such private information. These are indeed troublesome questions.

This case, in the judgment of the court, was brought by the government in absolute good faith to protect its security and not as a means of suppressing dissident or contrary political opinion. The issue is narrower — as to whether and to what degree the alleged security of the United States may "chill" the right of newspapers to publish. That the attempt by the government to restrain the *Times* is not an act of attempted precensorship as such is also made clear by the historic nature of the documents themselves.

2. The *Times* contends that the government has no inherent power to seek injunction against publication and that power of the court to grant such an injunction can be derived only from a statute. The government has asserted a statutory authority for the injunction. The government contends, moreover, that it has an inherent right to protect itself in its vital functions and that hence an injunction will lie even in the absence of a specific statute.

There seems little doubt that the government may ask a federal district court for injunctive relief even in the absence of a specific statute authorizing such relief.

That, however, is only the threshold question. Assuming the right of the United States and, indeed, its duty in this case to attempt to restrain the further publication of these documents, the government claims and the *Times* denies that there is any statute which proscribes such publication. The argument requires an analysis of the various sections contained in Chapter 37 of Title 18 of the US Criminal Code entitled "Espionage and Censorship."

It will be noted that the word "publication" does not appear in this section. The government contends that the word "communicates" covers the publication by a newspaper of the material interdicted by the subsection. A careful reading of the section would indicate that this is truly an espionage section where what is prohibited is the secret or clandestine communication to a person not entitled to receive it where the possessor has reason to believe that it may be used to the injury of the United States or the advantage of any foreign nation. This conclusion is fortified by the circumstance that in other sections of Chapter 37 there is specific reference to publication.

Similarly, in Section 797, one who publishes photographs, sketches, etc., of vital military and naval installations or equipment is subject to punishment. And finally, in Section 798, which deals with "Disclosure of Classified Information," there is a specific prohibition against one who "publishes" any classified information. This classified information is limited to the nature, preparation, or use of any code, cipher, or cryptographic system of the United States or any foreign government; or the design, construction, use, maintenance or repair of any device, apparatus or appliance used or prepared or planned for use by the United States or any foreign government for cryptographic or communication intelligence purposes; or the communication intelligence activities of the United States or any foreign government; or obtained by the processes of communications of any foreign government, knowing the same to have been obtained by such processes.

The government does not contend, nor do the facts indicate, that the publication of the documents in question would disclose the types of classified information specifically prohibited by the Congress. Aside from the internal evidence of the language in the various sections as indicating that newspapers were not intended by Congress to come within the purview of Section 793, there is Congressional history to support the conclusion. Section 793 derives from the original espionage act of 1917.

It would appear, therefore, that Congress, recognizing the constitutional problems of the First Amendment with respect to free press, refused to include a form of precensorship even in wartime.

In 1957 the report of the United States Commission on Government Security, in urging further safeguards against publication of matters affecting national security, recognized that "any statute designed to correct this difficulty must necessarily minimize constitutional objections by maintaining the proper balance between the guarantee of the First Amendment, on one hand, and required measures to establish a needed safeguard against any real danger to our national security."

The injunction sought by the government must, therefore, rest upon the premise that in the absence of statutory authority there is inherent power in the Executive to protect the national security. It was conceded at the argument that there is constitutional power to restrain serious security breaches vitally affecting the interests of the nation. This court does not doubt the right of the government to injunctive relief against a newspaper that is about to publish information or documents absolutely vital to current national security. But it does not find that to be the case here. Nor does this court have to pass on the delicate question of the power of the President in the absence of legislation to protect the functioning of his prerogatives — the conduct of foreign relations, the right to impartial advice and military security, for the responsibility of which the Executive is charged — against private citizens who are not government officials. For I am constrained to find as a fact that the in camera proceedings at which representatives of the Department of State, Department of Defense and the Joint Chiefs of Staff testified did not convince this court that the publication of these historical documents would seriously breach the national security. It is true, of course, that any breach of security will cause the jitters in the security agencies themselves and indeed in foreign governments who deal with us. But to sustain a preliminary injunction the government would have to establish not only irreparable injury, but also the probability of success in the litigation itself. It is true that the court has not been able to read through the many volumes of documents in the history of

Vietnam, but it did give the government an opportunity to pinpoint what it believed to be vital breaches to our national security of sufficient impact to contravert the right of a free press. Without revealing the content of the testimony, suffice it to say that no cogent reasons were advanced as to why these documents except in the general framework of embarrassment previously mentioned, would vitally affect the security of the nation. In the light of such a finding the inquiry must end. If the statute were applicable (which I must assume as an alternative so that this decision may be reviewed by an appellate court) it is doubtful that it could be applied to the activities of the *New York Times*. For it would be necessary to find as an element of the violation a willful belief that the information to be published "could be used to the injury of the United States or to the advantage of any foreign nation." That this is an essential element of the offense is clear.

I find that there is no reasonable likelihood of the government successfully proving that the actions of the *Times* were not in good faith, which is here irreparable injury to the government. This has been an effort on the part of the *Times* to vindicate the right of the public to know. It is not a case involving an intent to communicate vital secrets for the benefit of a foreign government or to the detriment of the United States.

3. As a general matter we start with the proposition that prior restraint on publication is unconstitutional.

Yet the free press provision of the First Amendment is not absolute. The First Amendment concept of a "free press" must be read in the light of the struggle of free men against prior restraint of publication. From the time of Blackstone it was a tenet of the founding fathers that precensorship was the primary evil to be dealt with in the First Amendment. Fortunately, upon the facts adduced in this case there is no sharp clash such as might have appeared between the vital security interest of the nation and the compelling constitutional doctrine against prior restraint. If there be some embarrassment to the government in security aspects as remote as the general embarrassment that flows from any security breach we must learn to live with it. The security of the nation is not at the ramparts alone. Security also lies in the value of our free institutions. A cantankerous press, an obstinate press, a ubiquitous press must be suffered by those in authority in order to preserve the even greater values of freedom of expression and the right of the people to know. In this case there has been no attempt by the government at political suppression. There has been no attempt to stifle criticism. Yet in the last analysis it is not merely the opinion of the editorial writer, or of the columnist, which is protected by the First Amendment. It is the free flow of information so that the public will be informed about the government and its actions.

These are troubled times. There is no greater safety valve for discontent and cynicism about the affairs of government than freedom of expression in any form. This has been the genius of our institutions throughout our history. It has been the credo of all our Presidents. It is one of the marked traits of our national life that distinguish us from other nations under different forms of government.

For the reasons given the court will not continue the restraining order which expires today and will deny the application of the government for a preliminary injunction. The temporary restraining order will continue, however, until such time during the day as the government may seek a stay from a judge of the Court of Appeals for the Second Circuit.

The Father of Our Country

Vine Deloria, Jr., is a Standing Rock Sioux, author of Custer Died for Your Sins *and* We Talk, You Listen. *He wrote this essay for Washington's Birthday, 1971.*

THE LITTLE CHILDREN stare at a picture of George of the blue eyes and white hair and seek a connection between that apparition and the statement "Father of Our Country." Seek no further, little brown-eyed, brown-skinned ones. George *is* the father of your country.

But George and Company did not spring full-blown from Hydra's head — although Indians sometimes wonder. Someone had to prepare the way for them. Someone had to help them get rid of the French. If George Washington is the father of this country because he defeated the English, then logic impels one to conclude that the men of the Iroquois are the grandfathers of this country.

George, prior to 1776, was a foreigner in America. He was an Englishman by birth and allegiance. The English, from the time they planted themselves on this shore until 1759, were waging a desperate struggle with the French for control of the North American continent. It is an established fact (at least in Indian country) that the English could not have succeeded in ousting the French if they had not had the assistance of the Iroquois Confederacy.

The league of the Iroquois was composed of six tribes: the Mohawks, the Oneidas, the Onondagas, the Cayugas, the Senecas and the Tuscarora. Actually, the Iroquois were fighting the French without the aid of the British during the 1680's and the 1690's — and doing a pretty good job of it. Thus, it may be said that the Iroquois kept the French at bay until the English were strong enough to fight alongside the Confederacy.

In 1754, what is called in American history books "The French and Indian War" (conveniently ignoring the fact that the Iroquois sided with the English — George and Company) broke out. In the first major action of that war, Washington and his Virginian militiamen were forced to surrender to the Indians and their French allies. He went back for help. A year later he and his militiamen returned, accompanied by the English general Edward Braddock and 2500 British regulars. Once again the Indians and their French allies taught the British some New World military tactics.

It wasn't until the English obtained the good offices of the Delaware chief, Tedyuskung (whose tribes were under the protection of the Iroquois Confederacy), and a Moravian missionary, that the English were able to negotiate a peace treaty with the Indian allies of the French, and thereby secure peace on that front.

The Iroquois played an even greater role in the French and English War when the theater of action was in their own country. Alvin M. Josephy, Jr., in his book, *The Indian Heritage of America*, writes: ". . . [the Iroquois] gave both direct and indirect aid to the British. Their geographical position lay athwart the principal routes connecting eastern Canada with the French positions in the Ohio Valley and Louisiana, and this fact hobbled French strategy, movements and command. At the same time, the Iroquois controlled the water routes leading from the St. Lawrence to the heart of the English colonies, and when the French tried to use them, some of the Iroquois joined the British forces in halting them. An important British victory was won at Fort William Henry, near Lake George, when a Mohawk sachem named Hendrick (of all things), responding to an appeal from his friend, Sir William Johnson, England's agent among the Iroquois, led several hundred warriors in helping the British turn back a French invasion force."

The Iroquois, being of unforked tongue, maintained their loyalty to the English long after George and Company had turned their red coats in for blue. Four of the six tribes sided with the English in the Revolutionary War. (Two remained neutral.) The colonists had to call in their old enemy, the French, and other Indian tribes to defeat the Iroquois and the English.

However, the Iroquois got their oar in when it came to laying the philosophical foundations of the new country of America. Ben Franklin noted in 1754 that, "It would be a strange thing if six capital nations of ignorant savages [???] should be capable of forming a scheme for such a union, and be able to execute it in such a manner as that it has subsisted ages and appears indissoluble; and yet that a like union should be impracticable for ten or a dozen English colonies, to whom it is more necessary and must be more advantageous, and who cannot be supposed to want an equal understanding of their interests."

Josephy writes again: "In time, the structure of the league had an indirect influence not only on the union of the colonies, but on the government of the US as it was constituted in 1789. In such forms as the methods by which Congressional, Senate and House conferees work out bills in compromise sessions, for instance, one may recognize similarities to the ways in which the Iroquois league functioned."

Thus, little brown-eyed, brown-skinned ones, don't worry: One way or another Americans have an Iroquois Indian in their ancestry.

Who Speaks for the Ethnics?

The question of the role of the "ethnics" in American society came strongly to the fore at the turn of the 70's with rising feeling on the part of first-, second- and third-generation Poles, Italians, Slavs, Irish and other ethnic groups that they were being treated as second-class citizens. These feelings were exacerbated by racial conflict, strongly tinged with economic and social competition, and the emergence of a "hard-hat" minority, largely ethnic, in opposition to "longhairs." Barbara Mikulski, a young Polish-American and a member of a Baltimore community organization, spoke out for the ethnics in autumn 1970.

THE ETHNIC AMERICAN is forgotten and forlorn. He is infuriated at being used and abused by the media, government and business. Pejorative epithets such as "pigs" and "racists" or slick, patronizing labels like the "silent majority" or "hard-hats" are graphic examples of the lack of respect, understanding and appreciation of him and his way of life.

The Ethnic Americans are forty million working-class Americans who live primarily in fifty-eight major industrial cities like Baltimore and Chicago. Our roots are in central and southern Europe. We have been in this country for one, two or three generations. We have made a maximum contribution to the USA, yet received minimal recognition.

The ethnics came to America from the turn of the century through the twenties, until we were restricted by prejudicial immigration quotas — sixty-five thousand Anglo-Saxons to three hundred Greeks. We came looking for political freedom and economic opportunity. Many fled from countries where there had been political, religious and cultural oppression for one thousand years.

It was this working class which built the great cities — constructed the skyscrapers, operated the railroads, worked on the docks, factories, steel mills and in the mines. Though our labor was in demand, we were not accepted. Our names, language, food and cultural customs were the subject of ridicule. We were discriminated against by banks, institutions of higher learning and other organizations controlled by the Yankee patricians. There were no protective mechanisms for safety, wages and tenure. We called ourselves Americans. We were called "wop," "Polack" and "hunky."

For our own protection, we formed our own institutions and organizations and clung together in our new neighborhoods. We created communities like "Little Italy" and "Polish Hill." The ethnic parish church and the fraternal organizations like the Polish Womens' Alliance and the Sons of Italy became the focal points of our culture.

These neighborhoods were genuine "urban villages." Warmth, charm and zesty communal spirit were their characteristics. People knew each other. This was true not only of relatives and friends but of the grocer, politician and priest. The people were proud, industrious and ambitious. All they wanted was a chance to "make it" in America.

Here we are in the 1970's, earning from five to ten thousand dollars per year. We are "near poor" economically. No one listens to our problems. The President's staff responds to our problems by patronizingly patting us on the head and putting pictures of construction workers on postage stamps. The media stereotype us as gangsters or dumb clods in dirty sweat shirts. The status of manual labor has been denigrated to the point where men are often embarrassed to say they are plumbers or tugboat operators. This robs men of pride in their work and themselves.

The Ethnic American is losing ground economically. He is the victim of both inflation and anti-inflation measures. Though wages have increased by 20 per cent since the mid-sixties, true purchasing power has remained the same. He is hurt by layoffs due to cutbacks in production and construction. Tight money policies strangle him with high interest rates for installment buying and mortgages. He is the man who at forty is told by the factory bosses that he is too old to be promoted. The old job is often threatened by automation. At the same time, his expenses are at their peak. He is paying on his home and car, probably trying to put at least one child through college.

In pursuing his dream of home ownership, he finds that it becomes a millstone rather than a milestone in his life. Since FHA loans are primarily restricted to "new" housing, he cannot buy a house in the old neighborhood. He has no silk-stocking lawyers or fancy lobbyists getting him tax breaks.

He believes in the espoused norms of American manhood like "A son should take care of his mother" and "A father should give his children every opportunity." Yet he is torn between putting out sixty dollars a month for his mother's arthritis medication or paying for his daughter's college tuition.

When the ethnic worker looks for some modest help, he is told that his income is too high. He's "too rich" to get help when his dad goes into a nursing home. Colleges make practically no effort to provide scholarships to kids named Colstiani, Slukowski or Klima.

The one place where he felt the master of his fate and had status was in his own neighborhood. Now even that security is being threatened. He wants new schools for his children and recreation facilities for the entire family — not just the token wading pool for preschoolers or the occasional dance for teen-agers. He wants his street fixed and his garbage collected. He finds that the only things being planned for his area are housing projects, expressways and fertilizer factories. When he goes to City Hall to make his problems known, he is either put off, put down or put out.

Liberals scapegoat us as racists. Yet there was no racial prejudice in our hearts when we came. There were very few black people in Poland or Lithuania. The elitists who now smugly call us racists are the ones who taught us the meaning of the word: their bigotry extended to those of a different class or national origin.

Government is further polarizing people by the creation of myths that black needs are being met. Thus the ethnic worker is fooled into thinking that the blacks are getting everything.

Old prejudices and new fears are ignited. The two groups end up fighting each other for the same jobs and competing so that the new schools and recreation centers will be built in their respective communities. What results is angry confrontation for tokens, when there should be an alliance for a whole new agenda for America. This agenda would be created if black and white organized separately in their own communities for their own needs and came together to form an alliance based on mutual issues, interdependence and respect. This alliance would develop new strategies for community organization and political restructuring. From this, the new agenda for America would be generated. It could include such items as "new towns in town," innovative concepts of work and creative structures for community control.

What is necessary is to get rid of the guilt of phony liberals, control by economic elitists and manipulation by selfish politicians. Then, let us get on with creating the democratic and pluralistic society that we say we are.

How Fair Was My Newark!

Probably nowhere in America was the urban crisis more severe, more endemic, more advanced than Newark. Benjamin Kluger, a New York advertising man, grew up in Newark's Ironbound section and in this restropective examination of his birthplace catches the poetry and tragedy of urban change in America in the spring of 1971.

How SERENE and ethnically ordered it all was. The Brahmins in Forest Hill; the more successful latter-day Americans assimilating in Vailsburg; the Italians in the Branch Brook section; the Ginsbergs and Horowitzes and a smattering of Schmidts and McCloskeys in Clinton Hill; the achieving Jews in Weequahic (the cradle of Portnoy); the neighborly Italian-Irish-German-Polish-Jewish amalgam of the Ironbound; stainless Roseville, pure North Newark; and the Negroes, safely penned up, shooting dice, razoring each other, eating peanuts and watermelon, whiling away the years killing cockroaches and clubbing rats in their warrens off Springfield and South Orange Avenues just above the courthouse where Lincoln sits.

How fair was my city.

Memories of growing up in the Ironbound . . .

The oleaginous Passaic winding past the factories, as sacred to the true Down Necker as the Ganges is to the Hindu. Jim Gaven catching, Ed Hershdorfer at first base and Red Mandell playing shortstop for the East Side Separates. The funeral processions preceded by Joe Basile's somberly pounding Italian band headed down Ferry Street toward Our Lady of Mt. Carmel Church. Fa-

ther Murphy and his adoring flock at St. James. The relay races
on Fridays in the gymnasium of the Lafayette Street School.
Clean-swept porches and ferociously tended gardens, Polish
dances, Jewish holidays, German picnics, Italian feast days, Irish
excursions up the Hudson or down to Keansburg. Venturing up-
town, the commercial splendors of Broad Street, City Hall with
its newly elected politicos taking their seats in the flower-bedecked
commission chamber. The leisurely walk from Lincoln Park to
Washington Park, Gutzon Borglum's Wars of America, the im-
pregnable façade of Public Service, the Newark Public Library
with its first overpowering offerings of Thomas Wolfe, T. S. Eliot
and James Joyce. The festive white crowds thronging Broad and
Market on Saturday night, on their way to see Jimmy Cagney or
Jean Harlow, or meeting one another amid the amenities of the
Essex House or the Robert Treat . . . scarcely an ebony speck
in all that shining mass. And absolute safety and well-being from
the gates of the iron foundries in deepest Down Neck to the pris-
tine portals of the surburbs.

Imamu Amiri Baraka, what have you done to my city?

Imamu Amiri Baraka. What arrogance, what effrontery!
Wasn't just plain simple LeRoi Jones good enough? What transforms an American black boy into a tribal chieftain? Was it possible that a black lad on Charlton Street or wherever in his en-
clave, or one fleeing the repressions of the South, had a drastically
different vision of the beneficences of growing up in Newark?

Say, what is it like to have black skin, anyway? Or what did it
feel like in those days? Puzzlement, at first, doubt, resentment, a
presentiment of fear, helplessness, despair, searing humiliations
day after day, utter inferiority, an occasional thrust of pride at the
exploits of an irrepressible brother, Jack Johnson, Harry Wills, Bo-
jangles, Cab Calloway, Duke Ellington, Joe Louis, Jackie Robinson. Anyhow, this was Newark, in the USA, the land of freedom,
North America, the Western Hemisphere, the world, the universe,
the mind of God. One just had to believe and make the effort;

where else could he go? A fellow rubbed his rabbit's foot and prayed for the best.

But there were disquieting clues to the future. The never-ending epithets: nigger, jigaboo, spade, coon, blooch, sambo. Relatives were never lawyers or doctors, engineers or architects, but sandwich men, numbers runners, errand boys, garbage haulers, jailbirds. Year by year the houses grew shabbier, the alleyways dirtier, the feeling of abandonment sharper. Inside the wall was wracking poverty; outside it, unyielding hate. Until the ultimate awareness struck: white was life and black was death, and this skin you wore, blatant and immutable, like the blotches of a leper, doomed you forever to a fifth-rate existence amid the realms of infinite possibility.

So we come to a new age in Newark. Certainly there is some justification for action — but this havoc, this ruin? To walk the streets of one's youth and see block after block of riot-scarred buildings. To hear the curses and threats against Whitey. To be glared at by swaggering bucks wearing berets and bandoleers. To feel menaced by the maniacal clutch for life, for bread, for fullness by semislaves who had burst their fetters, the defiant and the delinquent, the straight and the twisted, the bold and the timid, the pushers and the shooters, the ambitious and the gifted, all heaving themselves up with passion and violence after the long sleep in their ghetto. To listen to the ultramilitants, the irrevocably alienated, mouthing mad dreams of separateness, revolution, secession, the establishment of an independent Africa-in-America with my beloved metropolis as its capital.

Come back, you self-immersed ethnics with your murderous bigotries, you priests in the parishes where love never took hold, you masters of swag and boodle at City Hall who turned your backs on the future. Come back, you captains of the precincts who were always willing to unleash your boys to open up a few black skulls, you landlords milking your ratholes of slum houses, you teachers with an aversion to helping the little woollyheads onto a seat at the banquet table. Come back, you champions of liberty and justice scrambling for your cars, buses and trains before night comes down. Come back, you entrepreneurs in your big offices and stores with nary a lick or a promise for the young LeRois or Clarabelles eager to earn a few dollars and to fling open a window on a brighter prospect. Shoeshine boy on Market Street? Sure. Porter at the Pennsylvania Station? Why not. Janitor at the "Pru"? Of course. Elevator operator at New Jersey Bell? Just sign the application. But that's all, nigger, not a step further — no job, no encouragement, no education, no career, no money, no chance, no hope.

How fair was my city. Who will free it from its agony?

Return, O lost, and by the wind grieved, ghosts, come back again.

Women and Men

The First Problem

The Women's Liberation movement in America has deep roots into the heart of the nineteenth century and its first flowering with the success of the suffragettes in winning the woman's vote. The contemporary Women's Lib movement emerged as a full-scale political entity in 1970 with a broad-spectrum demand for not only legal equality but also social and physical equality of men and women. Gloria Steinem put the case eloquently to the Harvard Law Review banquet in 1971.

THE FIRST PROBLEM for all of us, men and women, is not to learn, but to unlearn. We are filled with the popular wisdom of several centuries just past, and we are terrified to give it up. Patriotism means obedience, age means wisdom, woman means submission, black means inferior: these are preconceptions imbedded so deeply in our thinking that we honestly may not know that they are there.

Whether it's woman's secondary role in society or the paternalistic role of the United States in the world, the old assumptions just don't work anymore.

Part of living this revolution is having the scales fall from our eyes. Every day, we see small obvious truths that we had missed before. Our histories, for instance, have generally been written for and about white men. Inhabited countries were "discovered" when the first white male set foot there, and most of us learned more about any one European country than we did about Africa and Asia combined.

We need Women's Studies courses just as much as we need Black Studies. We need courses on sexism and American law just as much as we need them on racism. The number of laws that discriminate against women is staggering. At least to women.

"Anonymous," as Virginia Woolf once said bitterly, "was a woman."

If we weren't studying white paternalistic documents, after all, we might start long before Charlemagne in history, or Blackstone in law. More than five thousand years before, in fact, when women were treated as equals or superiors. When women were the gods, and worshiped *because* they had the children. Men didn't consider childbearing a drawback, and in fact imitated that envied act in their ceremonies. It was thought that women bore fruit when they were ripe, like trees.

When paternity was discovered — a day I like to imagine as a gigantic light bulb over someone's head, as he says, "Oh, *that's* why" — the idea of ownership of children began. And the possibility of passing authority and goods down to them. And the origin of marriage — which was locking women up long enough to make sure who the father was. Women were subjugated, the original political subjugation and the pattern which others were to follow, as the means of production. They were given whatever tasks the men considered odious, and they became "feminine," a cultural habit which has continued till today.

When other tribes or groups were captured, they were given the least desirable role: that of women. When black people were brought to these shores as slaves, for instance, they were given the legal status of wives; that is, chattel. Since then, our revolutions have followed, each on the heels of the other.

I don't mean to equate women's problems with the sufferings of slavery. Women lose their identities: black men lose their lives. But, as Gunnar Myrdal pointed out more than thirty years ago, the parallel between women and blacks — the two largest second-class groups — is the deepest truth of American life.

"We suffer from the same myths — childlike natures, smaller brains, naturally passive, lack of objectivity (Harvard Law School professors are still peddling that), inability to govern ourselves, identity as sex objects, supernatural powers — usually evil — and special job skills. We're great at detail work for instance, as long as it's poorly paid, but brain surgery is something else.

When we make a generalization about women, it helps if we substitute black, or Chicano or Puerto Rican. Then we see what we are saying.

The truth is that women are so much more durable than men at every stage of life, so much less subject to diseases of stress, for instance. Childbearing shouldn't mean child-rearing. Motherhood is not all-consuming, nor is fatherhood a sometime thing. In fact, there are tribes in which the fathers rear the children, and the famous mother instinct turns out to be largely cultural.

The problem is achieving a compassionate balance, something this society has not done. It's clear that most American children suffer from too much mother and too little father.

Women employees in general lose no more time from work than men do, even including childbirth. They change jobs less, since they have less chance of trading upward, and tend to leave only after long periods of no promotion — thus benefiting male employees by financing their retirement plans.

Women don't want to imitate the male pattern of obsessive work ending up with a heart attack and an engraved wrist watch. We want to humanize the work pattern, to make new, egalitarian life-styles.

We are not more moral, we are only less corrupted by power. But we haven't been culturally trained to feel our identity depends on money, manipulative power or a gun.

From now on, no man can call himself liberal, or radical, or even a conservative advocate of fair play, if his work depends in any way on the unpaid or underpaid labor of women at home, or in the office. Politics doesn't begin in Washington. Politics begins with those who are oppressed right here.

And maybe, if we live this revolution every day, we will put a suitable end to this second five-thousand-year period: that of patriarchy and racism. Perhaps we have a chance for a third and new period — one of humanism.

Women

Bella S. Abzug, representative of New York's Nineteenth Congressional District, wrote this article for Women's Liberation Day, August 26, 1971.

I AM ONE of those rare creatures, a congress*woman*, and that may explain why I was invited recently to appear on a Bob Hope TV comedy show as part of an all-female variety act. I turned it down, of course, because I see nothing funny about the scarcity of women political leaders in our country. In fact, I think it is a national scandal.

Women members of Congress are not only scarce. They appear to be a vanishing species. Ten years ago there were 19 women in Congress — 17 representatives and 2 senators. Today, out of 435 members of the House, only 11 are women, and we're down to just 2 in the Senate.

There are no women on the Supreme Court or in the President's cabinet. There are no women governors. President Nixon has appointed just one woman ambassador — to Barbados. Of some 10,000 top jobs in the Nixon administration ($26,000 annual salaries and up), only 150 are held by women.

And so it goes. The freeze-out of women from political power is almost total, and it is one of the ironies of history that ever since women won the vote (fifty-one years ago today), they have been using it almost exclusively to elect men to office.

We're going to change that. Last month in Washington several hundred women from all parts of the country met to organize the

National Women's Political Caucus. The movement which we
have started is catching on in cities and states all across the US.

Women are a majority of the population. We are 53 per cent of
the electorate. As a matter of right, as a matter of simple justice,
we should be fully represnted in the political power structure in
all branches of government, at all levels. Women have learned
that discrimination exists not only because of century-old prejudices but also because it is profitable.

When we consider that more than 31 million women work for a
living (most of them because they have to), it is clear that industry has saved billions of dollars by shortchanging its women employees.

Women either are segregated into the lowest-paying drudge
jobs or, if they do get good jobs, they are paid less. In 1969, the
average American woman who worked full time earned only $60
for every $100 earned by the average man. Black, Puerto Rican,
Chicano and Asian women — the most heavily concentrated in
low-wage, low-skill jobs — earned less than half that.

Even a high degree of education and training does not assure a
woman equality of treatment. A woman college graduate typi-
cally makes about $6,694 a year. That's roughly the same income
earned by a man with an eighth-grade education.

The situation is deteriorating. Compared with men, women are
making less today than they did in 1955 and, as in Congress, their
numbers are decreasing in the professions. Women account for
only 9 per cent of all full professors, 7 per cent of physicians, 3 per
cent of lawyers, 1 per cent of federal judges.

Only by getting women in large numbers into positions of political power and leadership in government can this blatant discrimination end. With political power, women can secure approval of
the Equal Rights Amendment and its complementary Women's
Equality Act.

We can guarantee enforcement of antidiscrimination orders issued by the Equal Employment Opportunity Commission, a government watchdog that currently exists without teeth.

We can end the state's myriad antiabortion laws that have condemned literally millions of American women to back-alley, dangerous, degrading, illegal operations.

We can set up a nationally funded system of child-care centers to provide facilities for the four million youngsters of preschool age who have working mothers. We can change the tax laws to allow working women the right to deduct the full cost of a housekeeper or nursery for her children. That is surely as legitimate a working expense as a businessman's lunchtime martinis.

Women, on the whole, bring special qualities of humanism, compassion, and creativity to society, and these are the qualities that our nation most desperately needs right now. If we had several hundred women in Congress, not just a dozen, would we still have men dying in Vietnam? I think not. But if anyone disagrees, let's put it to the test. Starting in 1972.

What It Means to Be a Homosexual

Homosexuality as a social and political force has no antecedents in America prior to the late 1960's. Thus, the movement for political and social acceptance of homosexuality and homosexuals burst forth in the central vortex of the general movement for a new moral ethic in American society. Merle Miller, the prominent writer, proclaimed his homosexual philosophy in a significant article published by the New York Times Magazine *in January 1971, presented here in excerpted form.*

EDWARD MORGAN FORSTER was a very good writer and a very gutsy man. In the essay "What I Believe," he said:

> *I hate the idea of causes, and if I had to choose between betraying my country and betraying my friend, I hope I would have the guts to betray my country. Such a choice may scandalize the modern reader, and he may stretch out his patriotic hand to the telephone at once and ring up the police. It would not have shocked Dante, though. Dante places Brutus and Cassius in the lowest circle of Hell because they had chosen to betray their friend Julius Caesar rather than their country Rome.*

It took courage to write those words, just as it does, at times, for anyone else to repeat them . . .

Forster was not a man who rolled with the tide. I met him twice, heard him lecture several times, was acquainted with several of his friends, and knew that he was a homosexual, but I did not know that he had written a novel, *Maurice*, dealing with homosexual characters, until it was announced last November. On top of the manuscript he wrote, "Publishable — but is it worth it?" . . .

Is it worth it? Even so outspoken a man as Forster had to ask himself that question. It is one thing to confess to political unorthodoxy but quite another to admit to sexual unorthodoxy. Still. Yet. A homosexual friend of mine has said, "Straights don't want to know for sure, and they can never forgive you for telling them. They prefer to think it doesn't exist, but if it does, at least keep quiet about it" . . .

Is it true? Is that the way it is? Have my heterosexual friends, people I thought were my heterosexual friends, been going through an elaborate charade all these years? . . .

When I was a child in Marshalltown, Iowa, I hated Christmas almost as much as I do now, but I loved Halloween. I never wanted to take off the mask; I wanted to wear it everywhere, night and day, always. And I suppose I still do. I have often used liquor, which is another kind of mask, and, more recently, pot.

Then, too, I suppose if my friends have been playing games with me, they might with justice say that I have been playing games with them. It took me almost fifty years to come out of the closet, to stop pretending to be something I was not, most of the time fooling nobody.

But I guess it is never easy to open the closet door . . . James Owles, president of Gay Activists' Alliance, a militant, nonviolent organization concerned with civil rights for homosexuals, says: "We don't give a damn whether people like us or not. We want the rights we're entitled to."

I'm afraid I want both. I dislike being despised, unless I have done something despicable, realizing that the simple fact of being homosexual is all by itself despicable to many people . . .

Nobody seems to know why homosexuality happens, how it happens, or even what it is that does happen. Assuming *it* happens in any one way. Or any thousand ways. We do not even know how prevalent it is . . . .

In the 1950's, McCarthy found that attacking homosexuals paid off almost as well as attacking the Communists, and he claimed they were often the same . . .

The great fear is that a son will turn out to be homosexual. Nobody seems to worry about a Lesbian daughter; nobody talks about it anyway. But the former runs through every level of our culture . . .

I should add that not all mothers are afraid that their sons will be homosexuals. Everywhere among us are those dominant ladies who welcome homosexuality in their sons. That way the mothers know they won't lose them to another woman . . .

Is homosexuality contagious? Once again, nobody seems to know for sure . . .

I know this. Almost the first words I remember hearing, maybe the first words I choose to remember hearing, were my mother's, saying, "We ordered a little girl, and when you came along, we were somewhat disappointed" . . .

Not until college did I read that Oscar Wilde's mother started him down the garden path by letting his hair grow and dressing him as a little girl. As Oscar said, "Children begin by loving their parents; as they grow older they judge them; sometimes they forgive them" . . .

As a child I wanted to be the girl my mother had had in mind — or else the all-American boy everybody else so admired. Since sex changes were unheard of in those days, I clearly couldn't be a girl; so I tried the other. I ate carloads of Wheaties, hoping I'd turn into another Jack Armstrong, but I still could neither throw nor catch a baseball. I couldn't even see the thing . . .

After finishing my first successful novel, *That Winter,* which became a best seller, I decided there was no reason at all why I couldn't be just as straight as the next man. I might not be able to play baseball, but I could get married.

Pëtr Ilich Tchaikovsky had the same idea . . .

Pëtr Ilich's marriage lasted only two weeks. My own lasted

longer and was not quite so searing an experience, but it could not have succeeded . . .

Most members of the Gay Liberation Front appear to believe that Marxism is the answer, which is odd because in Communist China homosexuals are put in prisons for brainwashing that are called "hospitals for ideological reform" . . .

I was fourteen when I happened on a book called *Winesburg, Ohio*. I don't know how. Maybe it was recommended by the librarian, a kind and knowing woman with the happy name of Alice Story. Anyway, there at last, in a story called "Hands," were the words I had been looking for. I was not the only sissy in the world: "Adolf Myers was meant to be a teacher . . . In their feeling for the boys under their charge such men are not unlike the finer sort of women in their love of men."

Sherwood Anderson's story ended unhappily. Of course. How else could it end? . . .

I must have read "Hands" more than any story before or since. I can still quote it from beginning to end. "They had intended to hang the schoolmaster, but something in his figure, so small, white, and pitiful, touched their hearts and they let him escape."

Naturally. If you were *that way*, what else could you expect? Either they ran you out of town or you left before they got around to it. I decided on the latter. I once wrote that I started packing to leave Marshalltown when I was two years old, which is a slight exaggeration . . .

Laws discriminating against homosexuals will almost surely be changed. If not this year, in 1972; if not in 1972, in 1976; if not in 1976 . . .

Private acceptance of homosexuals and homosexuality will take somewhat longer. Most of the psychiatric establishment will continue to insist that homosexuality is a disease, and homosexuals, unlike the blacks, will not benefit from any guilt feelings on the part of liberals. So far as I can make out, there simply aren't any such feelings. On the contrary, most people of every political persuasion seem to be too uncertain of their own sexual identification to be anything but defensive. Fearful. And maybe it is contagious. Prove it isn't.

I have never infected anybody, and it's too late for the head people to do anything about me now. Gay is good. Gay is proud. Well, yes, I suppose. If I had been given a choice (but who is?), I would prefer to have been straight. But then would I rather not have been me? Oh, I think not, not this morning anyway. It is a very clear day in late December, and the sun is shining on the pine trees outside my studio. The air is extraordinarily clear, and the sky is the color it gets only at this time of year, dark, almost navy blue. On such a day I would not choose to be anyone else or anyplace else.

Youth and
the New Life-Styles

Woodstock

So far as youth culture in America is concerned, Woodstock, the gigantic pilgrimage of young people to the rock music festival at Woodstock, New York, in the summer of 1969 is the high-water mark. Somewhere in the vicinity of five hundred thousand young people made the pilgrimage. They demonstrated for the first time to themselves (and to the nation) the nature of their freeform life-style with its emphasis on camaraderie, open relationships, antiprudery, good will, honesty, good temper (and also attachment to pot and stronger drugs). The impact of Woodstock on the thought and philosophy of both younger and older America is still to be assessed. Joni Mitchell memorializes the experience (and idealizes it) in her song, "Woodstock."

I came upon a child of God;
He was walking along the road
And I asked him, "Where are you going?"
This he told me: "I'm going down to Yasgur's Farm,
Gonna join in a rock and roll band.
I'm gonna camp out on the land
And try 'n' get my soul free."
We are stardust, we are golden
And we got to get ourselves back to the garden
Caught in the devil's bargain
And we got to get ourselves back to the garden.
"Can I walk beside you?
I have come here to lose the smog
And I feel to be a cog in something turning.

Maybe it is just the time of year,
Or maybe it's the time of man.
I don't know who I am,
But life is for learning."
    We are stardust, we are golden
    And we got to get ourselves back to the garden
    Caught in the devil's bargain
    And we got to get ourselves back to the garden.
Time we got to Woodstock
We were half a million strong
And everywhere was song and celebration
And I dreamed I saw the bombers
Riding shotgun in the sky,
Turning into butterflies above our nation.
We are stardust, billion year old carbon
And we got to get ourselves back to the garden.

Rainbow Farm

The commune movement arose almost directly out of the Woodstock ecstasy. It represented a concrete attempt to institutionalize the brotherhood and life-style of Woodstock; to create within the broad confines of the "system" a way of life which incorporated the Woodstock ideal. In philosophical essence there is little if any difference between the commune of 1970 and that of 1840, when a similar wave of idealism sent many Americans in search of a more perfect social order. Rainbow Farm is an impression of a fairly typical commune on the eastern seaboard. This anonymous account by a member of Rainbow Farm tells of its experiences during the harsh winter of 1970–71. It is presented here slightly excerpted.

AFTER THE WINTER, the brown muddy ground looked defeated and dead, incapable of supporting life, beaten finally by five months of snow in the cruelest season of the century. It was late in April before we could walk in the fields back of the two-hundred-year-old farmhouse (lately and somewhat haphazardly refurbished) in which we had lived out the winter; and for two weeks or more after that, the mud was almost as thick as the snow had been. During most of May, we burned the last of our winter's wood in the Ashley stove every night, and every drizzle threatened to become a spring snowstorm.

What first came through the winter's snow was not a crocus or a hemlock top, but the right armrest of an old gray overstuffed chair we had left upturned under an apple tree in early December. Then, through the kitchen window, we saw the top of an old cement mixer that had been irretrievably locked in the snow. Soon old rakes, buckets and sections of stovepipe began turning up. The winter had been confining in many ways, but the reappearance of these forgotten possessions made our own long snowy spell in Vermont seem more of an imprisonment than we had noticed at the time.

When the snow started falling in November, six of us were living here under an uneasy truce: friends in a house more than a family in its home. The permanent collection of people had settled out from the summer's bunch of crashers without particular plan.

As the snow level rose, our world became increasingly small. The road periodically disappeared. Much of every day was spent pushing by muscle or pulling by Jeep our own cars or those of our visitors — mostly neighboring communards. Half of our house was closed for the winter (the rooms with no insulation or heat), and on the coldest days, when it was 20 below, we stayed huddled together around the two stoves. We got to know each other some, and we watched the icicles grow.

We also got to know our firewood. We had cut it all by hand (with a small chainsaw and a two-man crosscut), hauled it from the woods to various collecting stacks, chopped it into usable chunks and thrown it into the fires. Almost all of the wood in the first year on the farm was of dead or fallen trees (much of it blighted elm — the hardest to split), and not all of it burned very well. One old oak seemed to be composed of negative wood: the brighter it burned, the more it seemed to draw heat from every corner of the room.

The sun grew distant and passed by us only briefly. We fed our fires and ourselves, talked, and sat watching the snowy fields, like voyagers on an ancient ship, pushing deeper and deeper into the Arctic. The winter finally began to define us. Locked in by the snow, what visitors we received sometimes overwhelmed us, or we overwhelmed them. There were old friends from former lives, and new ones from familiar and unfamiliar places. We talked about revolution, and, although we felt ourselves to be part of the movement, we were at a loss to say where we were on the continuum of politics. We were intensely involved this winter (as were many people in the cities) with what someone euphemistically called "the politics of personal liberation"; but we were sure we'd find ourselves in Washington in May.

Not much went smoothly. The wind blew the heat out of the house; one of the woodsheds collapsed under the snow, burying five cord of cut logs; axe handles broke every other day; the chickens stopped laying. We got into endless uncollective rounds of messing up and cleaning up the house, scooping up piles of dog and cat shit, and hassling about money. We struggled happily and unhappily about our differences in age and experience, male and female roles, gayness and straightness, powertripping and dependency. There were wonderful times when we skied or snowshoed across the vast snowfields, or found calm ways of being together and feeling good. In March the snow was still high, but the birds began coming back and the dogs began going out, and winter began moving away. We felt that it had been a seventh member of our commune, and we had struggled with it not to triumph or defeat, but to some new understanding of who we are and what in the world we're doing at the end of a dirt road beneath three hills in Vermont.

There is a list tacked to the wall in the kitchen:

Morning Work:
Feed and water: pigs, goat, dogs, cats, chickens, bees (until they get it on themselves).
Collect eggs.
Water seedlings in flats.
Empty trash and compost.
Wash dishes and clean up kitchen.
Fire up cookstove, chop and carry in wood, empty ashes.
Put records back in alphabetical order.

That all gets done, usually, by the first person up.

There is another list with projected plans for the (short) building and growing season:

> Build dog pen.
> Clear old barn site and build barn.
> Reconstruct stone walls.
> Finish sauna.
> Finish attic rooms.
> Convert woodshed to workshop and build new woodshed.
> Get in winter's wood.
> Do planting, etc., etc.
> Put clapboarding on outside wall of kitchen.
> Raise X thousands of dollars.

Since the list went up several weeks ago, only the kitchen clapboarding has been completed; other projects are under way on the ground, or in our heads. The dog pen, for instance, is finished in everything but the fencing ($150 worth of Sing-Sing quality walls). The dogs roamed free for most of the fall and winter. Then, when the winter was almost over, they ran and mortally wounded a pregnant doe, and as a pack they became dangerous to wild and domestic animals. They have behaved badly: charges against them now stand at murder of one kitten, chickenslaughter in the second degree, deerslaughter in the first degree, conspiracy to kill more deer, attempted murder of a goat (two overt acts), conspiracy to do in two guinea hens, and common nuisance.

When the pen is finished, we'll begin work on the barn. Like archeologists on a dig, we are excavating the ancient site of a barn which burned down long ago. We'll rebuild its stone foundation, level the ground enclosed, and raise a new building according to the old dimensions.

It still amazes us that as much gets done as *does* get done; by choice and inclination, work is very loosely organized and the days are structured subtly in our heads and not in formal ways. We are all middle-class freaks, with the predictable attitudes about work, and we have found that it is not only the Man's work that alienates us. Tensions arise over sex roles in work, competence and incompetence, goal orientation and process orientation. We're alternately lazy and compulsive, overachieving and bored. Some projects are fun and rewarding: we make our own home brew (with malt, water, yeast, a handful of rice, and a touch of coconut) and our first batch of dandelion wine is sitting in our "brewery" corner by the cookstove. The garden is the best work of all; we have plowed, harrowed, and tilled more than half an acre, and the rows are filling up with an enormous assortment of vegetable seeds and seedlings that may or may not be ready to eat by the time the short growing season (120 days, maybe) ends. We'll freeze and can as much as we need to get through the winter with as little dependency on the A&P as possible.

It's hard for any one of us to believe that the green expanses of field and forest in our valley were white and barren less than a month ago. Spring exploded with unexpected extravagance, and life forced its way through the land with a natural poetry that put the things we read in school to shame. But with the buds came the first summer trippers.

Our friends are mostly like ourselves: urban dropouts of one, two, or three years' duration in country communes. We've become close to only a few "local" young people, friendly with several more, and at odds with one or two.

Living our lives communally is a choice that we once made and now cannot abandon. We live with the exhilarations and the ambiguities of the style. The ideal of sturdy pioneers living on the land to escape the city's "values" rubs against the reality of our individual needs. We brought our dogs, our stereos, our rugs, and our political posters; we left behind the possibilities of tropical fish, American Express visits, *Playboy* magazine, ranch houses, and 2.4 kids. We're neither political heroes nor rugged vagabonds, famous farmers nor footloose freaks.

One day during the winter, Great-aunt Beatrice came here to

visit her grandniece, who is in our family; she stayed for a week. She is forty years older than the oldest "young" person here. We didn't need to change our style while she was here: we took our communal saunas, kept our doors open, did our usual things that might freak out uptight parents. Aunt Bea was not freaked. On the last day of Aunt Bea's visit, a great many visitors came to the farm; one thing led to another, and we found ourselves partying on the roof of the porch under a hot spring sun as the snow melted beneath us. We had forgotten that Aunt Bea was in the kitchen, until we saw her start down the path to the cars, her cane slipping in the soft snow. A friend from her town in Connecticut was driving her back home. She waved to us on the roof, and we climbed down to wish her good-bye. We were embarrassed at the sudden scene, but when her car pulled away we went back up to the roof and didn't think about her again that day.

Waiting for My Friend

Of the plagues of the 1970's none was more pervasive than drugs. Addiction spread like a dirty stain out of the ghettos and into the middle and upper class; out of the metropolises into rural and small-town America; away from the Mother Country and into the distant armed forces. It was everywhere. Sandy Smith knows drugs, knows addiction. He is a former addict and now a writer. In this sketch of the spring of 1971 he paints a swift vignette of the reality of addiction.

SALLY J., AGED FOURTEEN years, school dropout and a dropout of life itself.

When I last saw Sally she was standing on the corner of 141st Street and Seventh Avenue "waiting for my friend!" The friend would prove to be a "john" or "trick."

Sally, from a broken home, member of a family of six who are welfare recipients, a mother who is a hopeless alcoholic (causing her common-law husband to leave her stranded with the care of six illegitimate children), disillusioned early in life, has turned to narcotics. The narcotics have caused her to in turn go into the streets for the money to support a habit that runs seventy dollars a day.

A child of fourteen attempting to obtain that amount of money each and every day, seven days a week, is in more than a little trouble.

Billy Joe, aged eight, hooked on heroin. Not a broken home — it was never once together. A mother who has known seven different men in her lifetime of "loving" and has borne seven different children, one fathered by each.

Billy Joe has not the obligation of getting out each day to try and obtain the money to support his habit. A man is "taking care" of him. The man, a sexual deviate, who was responsible for getting the boy hooked in the first place and who supported his habit, was jailed only two weeks ago. The charges that sent him to prison are not sufficient to hold him there for life, although that should be the case.

So it is that there are two prostitutes — one male and the other female — although the boy is not to be held responsible for his own prostitution. Neither can the girl-child be held responsible for her actions since she is as yet of such a tender age. The one is aware, however, of what it is that she is doing. The boy has no real knowledge of what is happening to him.

These are not simply rare and isolated cases. Similar circumstances and activities are going on daily in the black communities of the nation. Drugs are forcing girls and boys not yet old enough to be able to give legal consent to many vile acts. They are being preyed upon by sick persons and supplied the death-dealing heroin by others who are themselves sick-minded, too.

On the corners alongside these children are the older, professional prostitutes and hustlers who encourage these youngsters to continue in the degradation to which they have been committed. Having the young in juxtaposition to themselves allows for the worn-out hags to be available to the "johns" that come around looking for the "young stuff" and are not able to find them. The young provide a sort of insurance for the old. The young are told to "sell it, baby; why give it away to some young cat that is not going to be around to support you when the baby comes or to give a damn about you once you are in trouble!"

These older men and women care not a whit for the many young lives they are helping to snuff out or are sending into a life of shame, bad health, death or the merry-go-round of the country's jails. "I need a dollar to get next to my next fix, baby, and all is fair in this game!"

The drugs are first of all being brought into this country under the very eyes of the world's most populated and well-trained police agencies, both federal and local. We, the American public, are also guilty of contributing to the fall of the young, in that we daily pay the taxes to support the politicians and lawmakers.

Why is it a country so strong as ours, which was able to seal up the entire Mexican border in order to stop the flow of marijuana into our states, cannot stop the ever-growing tidal wave of the narcotic epidemic we are undergoing?

I can see no reason why I, as a citizen, should continue to elect men and women who are not making the main concern of those offices be the complete halt to all drug trafficking.

There must be a stop put to our young people's being forced into prostitution and other crime because of the dread disease, narcotic addiction; this to the delight of the sick-minded and to the disgrace of us all, along with the loss of life.

John Lennon Remembers

If there was a single religion of youth culture in the late 60's and early 70's it was the Beatles. The breakup of the Beatles was certain evidence of the end of an era, the failure of a dream. The greatest of the Beatle gods was John Lennon and his goddess was Yoko Ono. In this interview with Jann Wenner of Rolling Stone, *conducted in December 1970, and published early in 1971, Lennon tells how the dream turned to nightmare.*

"Yer Blues"— was that deliberately meant to be a parody of the English blues scene?

Well, a bit. I'm a bit self-conscious — we all were a bit self-conscious and the Beatles were super self-conscious people about parody of Americans which we do and have done.

I know we developed our own style but we still in a way parodied American music.

What was your experience with heroin?

It just was not too much fun. I never injected it or anything. We sniffed a little when we were in real pain. We got such a hard time from everyone, and I've had so much thrown at me, and at Yoko, especially at Yoko. We took "H" because of what the Beatles and others were doing to us. But we got out of it.

What is your concept of pain?

I don't know what you mean, really.

On the song "God" you start by saying: "God is a concept by which we measure our pain . . ."

Well, pain is the pain we go through all the time. You're born in pain. Pain is what we are in most of the time, and I think that the bigger the pain, the more God you look for.

There is a tremendous body of philosophical literature about God as a measure of pain.

I never heard of it. You see, it was my own revelation. I don't know who wrote about it, or what anybody else said, I just know that's what *I know.*

Yoko: He just felt it.

John: Yes, I just felt it. It was like I was crucified, when I felt it. So I know what they're talking about now.

Always the Beatles were talked about — and the Beatles talked about themselves — as being four parts of the same person. What's happened to those four parts?

They remembered that they were four individuals. You see, we believed the Beatles myth, too. I don't know whether the others still believe it. We were four guys . . .

What was your feeling when Brian died?

The feeling that anybody has when somebody close to them dies. There is a sort of little hysterical, sort of hee, hee, I'm glad it's not me or something in it, the funny feeling when somebody close to you dies.

I knew that we were in trouble then. I didn't really have any misconceptions about our ability to do anything other than play music and I was scared. I thought, "We've fuckin' had it."

You said you quit the Beatles first.

Yes.

How?

I said to Paul, "I'm leaving."

Paul said something or other about the Beatles doing something, and I kept saying "No, no, no" to everything he said. So it came to a point where I had to say something, of course, and Paul said, "What do you mean?"

I said, "I mean the group is over, I'm leaving."

So that's what happened. So, like anybody when you say divorce, their face goes all sorts of colors. It's like he knew really that this was the final thing; and six months later he comes out with whatever.

Do you think you're a genius?

Yes, if there is such a thing as one, I am one.

When did you first realize that?

When I was about twelve. I used to think I must be a genius, but nobody's noticed. I used to wonder whether I'm a genius or I'm not, which is it? I used to think, well, I can't be mad, because nobody's put me away; therefore, I'm a genius. A genius is a form of madness, and we're all that way, you know, and I used to be a bit coy about it.

If there is such a thing as genius — which is what . . . what the fuck is it? — I am one, and if there isn't, I don't care. I used to think it when I was a kid, writing me poetry and doing me paintings. I didn't become something when the Beatles made it, or when you heard about me, I've been like this all me life. Genius is pain too.

You say that the dream is over. Part of the dream was that the Beatles were God or that the Beatles were the messengers of God, and of course yourself as God . . .

Yeah. Well, if there is a God, we're all it.

When did somebody first come up to you about this thing about John Lennon as God?

I can't remember it exactly happening. We just took that position. I mean, we started putting out messages. Like "The Word Is Love" and things like that. I write messages, you know. See, when you start putting out messages, people start asking you, "What's the message?"

How did you first get involved in LSD?

A dentist in London laid it on George, me and wives, without telling us, at a dinner party at his house. He just put it in our coffee or something. He didn't know what it was; it's all the same thing with that sort of middle-class London swinger, or whatever.

They had all heard about it, and they didn't know it was different from pot or pills and they gave us it. He said, "I advise you not to leave," and we all thought he was trying to keep us for an orgy in his house.

It was insane going around London. When we went to the club we thought it was on fire and then we thought it was a première, and it was just an ordinary light outside. We thought, "Shit, what's going on here?" We were cackling in the streets, and people were shouting, "Let's break a window," you know, it was just insane. We were just out of our heads. When we finally got on the lift we all thought there was a fire, but there was just a little red light. We were all screaming like that, and we were all hot and hysterical, and when we all arrived on the floor, because this was a discotheque that was up a building, the lift stopped and the door opened and we were all [John demonstrates by screaming].

I had read somebody describing the effects of opium in the old days and I thought, "Fuck! It's happening," and then we went to the Ad Lib and all of that, and then some singer came up to me and said, "Can I sit next to you?" And I said, "Only if you don't talk," because I just couldn't think.

This seemed to go on all night. I can't remember the details. George somehow or another managed to drive us home in his mini. We were going about ten miles an hour, but it seemed like a thousand and Patty was saying let's jump out and play football.

God, it was just terrifying, but it was fantastic. I did some drawings at the time, I've got them somewhere, of four faces saying, "We all agree with you!" I gave them to Ringo, the originals. I did a lot of drawing that night. And then George's house seemed to be just like a big submarine, I was driving it, they all went to bed, I was carrying on in it, it seemed to float above his wall which was eighteen foot and I was driving it.

When you came down what did you think?

I was pretty stunned for a month or two. The second time we

had it was in L.A. We were on tour in one of those houses, and the three of us took it, Ringo, George and I. We were in the garden, it was only our second one and we still didn't know anything about doing it in a nice place and cool it. Then they saw the reporter and thought, "How do we act?" We were terrified waiting for him to go.

Peter Fonda came, and that was another thing. He kept saying (in a whisper), "I know what it's like to be dead," and we said, "What?" and he kept saying it. We were saying, "For Christ's sake, shut up, we don't care, we don't want to know," and he kept going on about it. That's how I wrote, "She Said, She Said" — "I know what's it's like to be dead." It was a sad song, an acidy song I suppose. "When I was a little boy" . . . you see, a lot of early childhood was coming out, anyway.

So LSD started for you in 1964: how long did it go on?

It went on for years. I must have had a thousand trips.

Literally a thousand, *or a couple of hundred?*

A thousand. I used to just eat it all the time.

I never took it in the studio. Once I thought I was taking some uppers and I was not in the state of handling it, I can't remember what album it was, but I took it and I just noticed . . . I suddenly got so scared on the mike. I thought I felt ill, and I thought I was going to crack. I said I must get some air. They all took me upstairs on the roof and then it dawned on me I must have taken acid. I said, "Well I can't go on, you'll have to do it and I'll just stay and watch." You know I got very nervous just watching them all. I was saying, "Is it all right?" And they were saying, "Yeah." They had all been very kind and they carried on making the record.

The other Beatles didn't get into LSD as much as you did?

George did. In L.A. the second time we took it, Paul felt very out of it, because we are all a bit slightly cruel, sort of "we're taking it, and *you're* not." But we kept *seeing him,* you know. We couldn't eat our food, I just couldn't manage it, just picking it up with our hands. There were all these people serving us in the house and we were knocking food on the floor and all of that. It was a long time before Paul took it. Then there was the big announcement.

Right.

So, I think George was pretty heavy on it; we are probably the most cracked. Paul is a bit more stable than George and I.

Did you have many bad trips?

I had many. Jesus Christ, I stopped taking it because of that. I just couldn't stand it.

You got too afraid to take it?

It got like that, but then I stopped it for I don't know how long, and then I started taking it again just before I met Yoko. Derek came over and . . . you see, I got the message that I should destroy my ego and I did, you know. I was reading that stupid book of Leary's; we were going through a whole game that everybody went through, and I destroyed myself. Bit by bit over a two-year period, I had destroyed me ego.

I didn't believe I could do anything. I just was nothing. I was shit. Then Derek tripped me out at his house after he got back from L.A. He sort of said, "You're all right," and pointed out which songs I had written. "You wrote this," and "You said this" and "You are intelligent, don't be frightened."

The next week I went to Derek's with Yoko and we tripped again, and she filled me completely to realize that I was me and that's it's all right. That was it; I started fighting again, being a loudmouth again and saying, "I *can* do this, fuck it, this is what I want, you know, I want it and don't put me down." I did this, so that's where I am now.

At some point, right between Help *and* Hard Day's Night, *you got into drugs and got into doing drug songs?*

A Hard Day's Night I was on pills, that's drugs, that's bigger drugs than pot. Started on pills when I was fifteen, no, since I was seventeen, since I became a musician. The only way to survive in

Hamburg, to play eight hours a night, was to take pills. The wait-
ers gave you them — the pills and drink. I was a fucking dropped-
down drunk in art school. *Help* was where we turned on to pot
and we dropped drink, simple as that. I've always needed a drug
to survive. The others, too, but I always had more, more pills,
more of everything because I'm more crazy probably.

*How do you think that affected your conception of the music?
In general.*

It was only another mirror. It wasn't a miracle. It was more of a
visual thing and a therapy, looking at yourself a bit. It did all
that.

Why can't you be alone without Yoko?

I can be, but I don't wish to be.

There is no reason on earth why I should be without her. There
is nothing more important than our relationship.

You say you write songs because you can't help it?

Yeah, creating is a result of pain, too. I have to put it somewhere, and I write songs.

*How are you going to keep from going overboard on things
again?*

I think I'll be able to control meself. "Control" is the wrong
word. I just won't get involved in too many things, that's all. I'll
just do whatever happens. It's silly to feel guilty that I'm not
working, that I'm not doing this or that, it's just stupid. I'm just
going to do what I want for meself and for both of us.

*You say on your record that "The freaks on the phone won't
leave me alone, so don't give me that brother, brother."*

Because I'm sick of all these aggressive hippies or whatever
they are, the "Now Generation," being very uptight with me.
Either on the street or anywhere, or on the phone, demanding my
attention, as if I owed them something.

I'm not their fucking parents, that's what it is. They come to
the door with a fucking peace symbol and expect to just sort of
march around the house or something, like an old Beatle fan.

They're under a delusion of awareness by having long hair, and that's what I'm sick of. They frighten me, a lot of uptight maniacs going around, wearing fuckin' peace symbols.

What do you think of Manson and that thing?

I don't know what I thought when it happened. A lot of the things he says are true; he is a child of the state, made by us, and he took their children in when nobody else would. Of course, he's cracked all right.

What do you think rock and roll will become?

Whatever we make it. If we want to go bullshitting off into intellectualism with rock and roll then we are going to get bull- shitting rock intellectualism. If we want real rock and roll, it's up to all of us to create it and stop being hyped by the revolutionary image and long hair. We've got to get over that bit. That's what cutting hair is about. Let's own up *now* and see who's who.

Why do you think it means so much to people?

Because the best stuff is primitive enough and has no bullshit. It gets through to you, it's beat, go to the jungle and they have the rhythm. It goes throughout the world and it's as simple as that, you get the rhythm going because everybody goes into it. I read that Eldridge Cleaver said that blacks gave the middle-class whites back their bodies, and put their minds and bodies together. Something like that. It gets through; it got through to me, when I was fifteen. Rock and roll then was real, everything else was unreal. You recognize something in it which is true, like all true art. Whatever art is, readers. O.K. If it's real, it's simple usually, and if it's simple, it's true. Something like that.

What was it in your music that turned everyone on at first? Why was it so infectious?

We didn't sound like everybody else. We didn't sound like the black musicians because we weren't black and we were brought up on an entirely different type of music and atmosphere.

The cripples.

Wherever we went on tour, in Britain and everywhere we went, there were always a few seats laid aside for cripples and people in wheelchairs. Because we were famous, we were supposed to have epileptics and whatever they are in our dressing room all the time. We were supposed to be sort of "good," and really you wanted to be alone. You don't know what to say, because they're usually saying "I've got your record," or they can't speak and just want to touch you. It's always the mother or the nurse pushing them on you. They themselves would just say hello and go away, but the mothers would push them at you like you were Christ or something, as if there were some aura about you which would rub off on them. It just got to be like that and we were very sort of callous about it. It was just dreadful: you would open up every night, and instead of seeing kids there, you would just see a row full of cripples along the front. It seemed that we were just surrounded by cripples and blind people all the time, and when we would go through corridors, they would be all touching us and things like that. It was horrifying.

It didn't astound you at that point that you were supposed to be able to make the lame walk and the blind see?

It was the "in" joke that we were supposed to cure them. It was the kind of thing that we would say, because it was a cruel thing to say. We felt sorry for them, anybody would, but there is a kind of embarrassment when you're surrounded by blind, deaf and crippled people.

The bigger we got, the more unreality we had to face; the more we were expected to do until, when you didn't sort of shake hands with a mayor's wife she would start abusing you and screaming and saying, "How dare they?"

This complete craziness is surrounding you, and you're doing exactly what you don't want to do with people you can't stand — the people you hated when you were ten. And that's what I'm saying in this album — I remember what it's all about now you fuckers — fuck you! That's what I'm saying, you don't get me twice.

Would you take it all back?

What?

Being a Beatle.

If I could be a fuckin' fisherman I would. If I had the capabilities of being something other than I am, I would. It's no fun being an artist. You know what it's like, writing, it's torture. I read about Van Gogh, Beethoven, any of the fuckers. If they had psychiatrists, we wouldn't have had Gauguin's great pictures. These bastards are just sucking us to death; that's about all that we can do, is do it like circus animals.

I resent being an artist, in that respect, I resent performing for fucking idiots who don't know anything. They can't feel. I'm the one that's feeling, because I'm the one that is expressing. They live vicariously through me and other artists, and we are the ones . . .

One of my big things is that I wish to be a fisherman. I know it sounds silly — and I'd sooner be rich than poor, and all the rest of that shit — but I wish the pain was ignorance or bliss or something. If you don't know, man, then there's no pain; that's how I express it.

What do you think the effect was of the Beatles on the history of Britain?

I don't know about the "history"; the people who are in control and in power, and the class system and the whole bullshit bourgeoisie is exactly the same, except there is a lot of fag middle-class kids with long, long hair walking around London in trendy clothes, and Kenneth Tynan is making a fortune out of the word "fuck." Apart from that, nothing happened. We all dressed up, the same bastards are in control, the same people are runnin' everything. It is exactly the same.

We've grown up a little, all of us; there has been a change and we're all a bit freer and all that, but it's the same game. Shit, they're doing exactly the same thing, selling arms to South Africa, killing blacks on the street, people are living in fucking poverty, with rats crawling over them. It just makes you puke, and I woke up to *that* too.

The dream is over. It's just the same, only I'm thirty, and a lot of people have got long hair. That's what it is, man, nothing happened except that we grew up, we did our thing — just like they were telling us. You kids — most of the so-called "Now Generation" — are getting a job. We're a minority, you know, people like us always were, but maybe we are a slightly larger minority because of maybe something or other.

You don't really believe that we are headed for a violent revolution?

I don't know; I've got no more conception than you. I can't see . . . eventually it'll happen, like it will happen — it has to happen; what else can happen? It might happen now, or it might happen in a hundred years, but . . .

Having a violent revolution now might just be the end of the world.

Not necessarily. They say that every time, but I don't really believe it, you see. If it is, O.K., I'm back to where I was when I was seventeen and at seventeen I used to wish a fuckin' earthquake or revolution would happen so that I could go out and steal and do what the blacks are doing now. If I was black, I'd be all for it; if I were seventeen I'd be all for it, too. What have you got to lose? Now I've got something to lose. I don't want to die, and I don't want to be hurt physically, but if they blow the world up, fuck it, we're all out of our pain then, forget it, no more problems!

You say on the record, "I don't believe in the Beatles."

Yeah. I don't believe in the Beatles, that's all. I don't believe in the Beatles myth. "I don't believe in the Beatles" — there is no other way of saying it, is there? I don't believe in them whatever they were supposed to be in everybody's head, including our own heads for a period. It was a dream. I don't believe in the dream anymore.

II
THE WORLD

ONE COULD NOT SPEAK OF a single world in an age when it took months for news to travel from London to New York and nearly as long from Moscow to Paris. Nor even in a world where a week's travel spanned the Atlantic and three times that period the Pacific. But the jet aircraft, the satellite, instantaneous global television and image transmission have made it a single world and the technological network has spawned a unitary spirit and mood which not even the repressive and restrictive barriers of dictatorial governments can effectively compartment.

The world has always been one. This is a knowledge shared by poets and philosophers but seldom acknowledged by politicians and ordinary citizens. It has not *seemed* one. Today it does and with the immediacy of communication and of travel we quickly find that war is no nation's monopoly. It is no accident that we now live in an age of World Wars. The catastrophes swiftly surge over national boundaries and encompass the globe. When a Russian physicist's appeal against injustice can in a matter of hours be published simultaneously in Bombay, Bangkok and Birmingham, it is plain that there is no such thing as a "domestic political question" no matter how jealously a bureaucratic state may strive to perpetuate its monopoly over the affairs of its subjects. Injustice shared becomes injustice universally perceived. Repression, oppression, evil, man's inhumanity, the ambition of tyrants, the fear of the weak, the courage of the rebel — these become universal. We share the courage of Bernadette Devlin as she cries: "Dare to Struggle, Dare to Win." She speaks not only for the Catholic

Irish. She speaks for us all — for ghetto black, for Attica victim, for Russian mathematicians confined to the insane asylums of the KGB.

Each of us sees his experience as unique and personal. We cry against the evil which oppresses us — possibly the surveillance of the FBI or, it may be, the ravages of the Pakistani hussars in East Bengal. Then we listen to the poets — we listen to Ted Hughes writing from England:

> Then everybody wept,
> Or sat, too exhausted to weep,
> Or lay, too hurt to weep,
> And when the smoke cleared it became clear
> That this had happened too often before
> And was going to happen too often in future.

Of what is he writing? Can this be tiger cages in Saigon or the prison *isalator* in Yaroslavl? William Irwin Thompson in *At the Edge of History* suggests that poets sense what the history of the future shall be; that their imagination previsions the world to come; that men consciously or unconsciously shape their conduct to fit the dreams which the poets' vision has conjured. Perhaps Hughes writes not about a specific land, a specific sequence of events. Perhaps he sings the universal condition of mankind.

A peasant in the fields of Vietnam asks the simple question: "When does peace come?" Does he ask for himself alone or for the Catholics of Belfast and the inmates of San Quentin? Are not all of us, poets, peasants and people, eternally echoing the basic thesis of John Donne? Are we not beginning to experience more perceptively that indeed we are each of us part of the main?

It was possible only a few years ago to travel into the heart of Asia and find there lands and peoples who moved still on the kind of time which has regulated Asia for more millenniums than any of us can count. In the depths of central Asia men lived, essentially, as they had in the twelfth century when Genghis Khan was beginning his conquests. But today on those distant steppes and deserts nuclear weapons, electronic communications and surveillance ganglia have brought the most advanced — and dangerous — fruits of twentieth-century knowledge into the oldest landscape man knows. To be sure there are on earth here and there little pockets of humanity which have not yet been hooked up. But their number shrinks and with technological interconnection, emotional and ideological interconnection and interpenetration spreads and deepens.

Aleksandr Solzhenitsyn writes: "Blow the dust off the clock. Your watches are behind the times. Throw open the heavy curtains which are so dear to you — you do not even suspect that the day has already dawned outside."

To whom is he speaking? The anachronistic, repressive forces in Washington, the ignorant, posturing colonels of Greece or the lumpen bureaucrats of Moscow who suppress his novels and shunt the body of Nikita Khrushchev off to a distant corner of the Novodevichye Cemetery, fearful that even in death the spirit of this irrepressible man might touch off shock waves with which their gray minds and sterile policies could not cope.

We are coming into an age in which nations are becoming truly aware of their shared life on this planet — when questions begin to arise: Why should the life of the peasant in the Khuzistan snuff out at the age of thirty, disease-raddled, hunger-emaciated, when the agricultural millionaire of California grows enough food to feed a hundred thousand people and make a mint of money? If it is true (and it is) that the world does not possess sufficient natural resources to bring eight hundred million or one billion Chinese up to the living standard of the USA or even Russia — then what shall we answer the Chinese (and the Indians, the Persians, the Arabs, the Latin Americans) when they ask for equity in the division of the world's riches?

These are the questions of which the world of the 1970's is compounded. What is the difference between injustice in Haiti or injustice in Greece and that in our own small town? The distance that separates Haiti or Greece from New York is less than that which separated New York from Albany less than one hundred years ago. The same restless dreams torment us all and we are beginning to perceive that no tyranny is too small, too remote, too petty or too complex to pass by without notice.

For Peace

Crow's Account of the Battle

Ted Hughes, whose wife was Sylvia Plath, may be the most brilliant poet in the world today. He lives in England but his eyes and ears know no national boundaries. Crow, published in 1971, knows no nationality, no time. It is universal, and as Crow looks on the world he sees battle.

There was this terrific battle.
The noise was as much
As the limits of possible noise could take.
There were screams higher groans deeper
Than any ear could hold.
Many eardrums burst and some walls
Collapsed to escape the noise.
Everything struggled on its way
Through this tearing deafness
As through a torrent in a dark cave.

The cartridges were banging off, as planned,
The fingers were keeping things going
According to excitement and orders.
The unhurt eyes were full of deadliness.
The bullets pursued their courses
Through clods of stone, earth and skin,
Through intestines, pocket-books, brains, hair, teeth
According to Universal laws
And mouths cried "Mamma"
From sudden traps of calculus,

Theorems wrenched men in two,
Shock-severed eyes watched blood
Squandering as from a drain-pipe
Into the blanks between the stars.
Faces slammed down into clay
As for the making of a life-mask
Knew that even on the sun's surface
They could not be learning more or more to the point.
Reality was giving its lesson,
Its mishmash of scripture and physics,
With here, brains in hands, for example,
And there, legs in a treetop.
There was no escape except into death.
And still it went on — it outlasted
Many prayers, many a proved watch,
Many bodies in excellent trim,
Till the explosives ran out
And sheer weariness supervened
And what was left looked round at what was left.

Then everybody wept,
Or sat, too exhausted to weep,
Or lay, too hurt to weep.
And when the smoke cleared it became clear
This had happened too often before
And was going to happen too often in future
And happened too easily
Bones were too like lath and twigs
Blood was too like water
Cries were too like silence
The most terrible grimaces too like footprints in mud
And shooting somebody through the midriff
Was too like striking a match
Too like potting a snooker ball

Too like tearing up a bill
Blasting the whole world to bits
Was too like slamming a door
Too like dropping in a chair
Exhausted with rage
Too like being blown to bits yourself
Which happened too easily
With too like no consequences.

So the survivors stayed.
And the earth and the sky stayed.
Everything took the blame.

Not a leaf flinched, nobody smiled.

Letter from a Saigon Prison

Three monks, Bikkhu Thich Nguyen Nhu (Prison Badge No. 57283), Dang Van Hung (Prison Badge No. 60376) and Nguyen Hong Long (Prison Badge No. 60638) smuggled this letter out of a Saigon jail December 21, 1970. The monks represented some five hundred prisoners of various religions, mostly imprisoned for refusing to bear arms.

FROM THE DARK, narrow and filthy cells, we five hundred imprisoned monks in South Vietnam urgently send this call for peace to all goodwill people working to stop the war in Vietnam.

We consider this our duty, firstly, because we have opposed this inhuman war by nature since the beginning, and secondly, because we are suffering all kinds of ill-treatment solely because we refuse to bear arms against our brothers.

We are monks and Taoists belonging to the great and popular religions of Vietnam such as Buddhism, Caodaism and Dao Dua; but above all, we are followers of the greatest and most popular religion in Vietnam, and we believe throughout the world, that is, the religion of Peace. We prefer imprisonment to murder and our ideal reflects that of the majority of the Vietnamese people, especially the peasants, who suffer the heaviest calamities in this war.

Since 1960, at the onset of this war, thousands of our monks and Taoists have courageously chosen the prison as nonviolent fighters for Peace. As the war escalates, our hardships multiply. Many of us have been killed in insecure areas, withered miserably in the cells and "tiger cages," and waited hopelessly for more than five years behind the bars.

The South Vietnamese authorities do not recognize the conscientious objector's status of our religious vocation. Before May 1970 we were prosecuted at the Front Court-Martial as political prisoners with the maximum penalty without revocation. After that date, the Front Court-Martial being judged anticonstitutional by the Supreme Court, we were brought before the military court as simple soldiers convicted of "civil disobedience" and "disobedience to higher orders."

With the same so-called offense, we are sentenced again and again, and shuffled from the induction center to the prison through the court, and we become perpetual prisoners. The purpose of the government is to terrorize us and to demoralize those peace-loving young men who want to follow our examples by refusing and abandoning the war.

On November 1 and December 1, 1970, we celebrated two ten-day fastings to denounce the above injustice.

We demand:

1. That those monks and Taoists who have been sentenced by the anticonstitutional Front Court-Martial must be set free or rejudged before a civil court;

2. That those monks and Taoists who have completed their terms of "civil disobedience" must be released from prison to return to their pagodas.

To demonstrate to the government our determination against the war, our love for peace, and our defense of religious freedom, fifty persons from among us have opposed the forceful draft and lifelong imprisonment imposed on our monks and Taoists by self-destroying our eyes, limbs, and fingers. These people want to make themselves unfit for manslaughter for life as a sacrifice to their religious ideal. We are ready to go up to hara-kiri and self-immolation to awake the government to its religious oppression. We voluntarily give up a part of or the whole of our bodies rather than inflict a damage on the lives of our brothers.

On this occasion of Christmas and New Year, we raise this call

for Peace to inform the public about the injustice we are undergoing, to give witness to peace-loving people the faith that love and
peace will overcome hatred and war. At last, we solemnly burn
the incense, close our hands, and pray for all a PEACEFUL
HAPPY NEW YEAR. We cannot have any happiness unless we
have Peace. Please have the kindness to pray with us.

Personal Freedom

A Letter from
Aleksandr Solzhenitsyn

In November 1969, nearly a year before he was awarded the Nobel Prize for literature, Aleksandr Solzhenitsyn was expelled from the Union of Soviet Writers in an action, ostensibly initiated by the local union chapter in rural Ryazan, where he maintained his residence, but actually incited by high personalities in the Soviet government. The expulsion was a symbolic act of censure and also a practical repression, since it is difficult and sometimes impossible for a Soviet writer who does not belong to the union to be published. Solzhenitsyn replied to the union in a letter of November 12, 1969, which was published throughout the world — except in Russia.

To the Secretariat of the Union of Soviet Writers:

Shamelessly trampling underfoot your own statutes, you have expelled me in my absence, as at the sound of a fire alarm, without even sending me a summons by telegram, without even giving me the four hours I needed to come from Ryazan and be present at the meeting. You have shown openly that the RESOLUTION preceded the "discussion." Was it less awkward for you to invent new charges in my absence? Were you afraid of being obliged to grant me ten minutes for my answer? I am compelled to substitute this letter for those ten minutes.

Blow the dust off the clock. Your watches are behind the times. Throw open the heavy curtains which are so dear to you — you do not even suspect that the day has already dawned outside. It is no longer that stifling, that somber, irrevocable time when you expelled Akhmatova in the same servile manner. It is not even that timid, frosty period when you expelled Pasternak, whining

abuse at him. Was this shame not enough for you? Do you want
to make it greater? But the time is near when each of you will
seek to erase his signature from today's resolution.

Blind leading the blind! You do not even notice that you are
wandering in the opposite direction from the one you yourselves
announced. At this time of crisis you are incapable of suggesting
anything constructive, anything good for our society, which is
gravely sick — only your hatred, your vigilance, your "hold on
and don't let go."

Your clumsy articles fall apart; your vacant minds stir feebly —
but you have no arguments. You have only your voting and your
administration. And that is why neither Sholokhov nor any of
you, of all the lot of you, dared reply to the famous letter of Lydia
Chukovskaya, who is the pride of Russian publicistic writing. But
the administrative pincers are ready for her: how could she allow
people to read her book [*The Deserted House*] when it has not
been published? Once the AUTHORITIES have made up their mind
not to publish you — then stifle yourself, choke yourself, cease to
exist, and don't give your stuff to anyone to read!

They are also threatening to expel Lev Kopelev, the front-line
veteran, who has already served ten years in prison although he
was completely innocent. Today he is guilty: he intercedes for
the persecuted, he revealed the hallowed secrets of his conversation with an influential person, he disclosed an OFFICIAL SECRET.
But why do you hold conversations like these which have to be
concealed from the people? Were we not promised fifty years
ago that never again would there be any secret diplomacy, secret
talks, secret and incomprehensible appointments and transfers,
that the masses would be informed of all matters and discuss
them openly?

"The enemy will overhear" — that is your excuse. The eternal,
omnipresent "enemies" are a convenient justification for your
functions and your very existence. As if there were no enemies
when you promised immediate openness. But what would you do

without "enemies"? You could not live without "enemies"; hatred, a hatred no better than racial hatred, has become your sterile atmosphere. But in this way a sense of our single, common humanity is lost and its doom is accelerated. Should the Antarctic ice melt tomorrow, we would all become a sea of drowning humanity, and into whose heads would you then be drilling your concepts of "class struggle"? Not to speak of the time when the few surviving bipeds will be wandering over a radioactive earth, dying.

It is high time to remember that we belong first and foremost to humanity. And that man has distinguished himself from the animal world by THOUGHT and SPEECH. And these, naturally, should be FREE. If they are put in chains, we shall return to the state of animals.

OPENNESS, honest and complete OPENNESS — that is the first condition of health in all societies, including our own. And he who does not want this openness for our country cares nothing for his fatherland and thinks only of his own interest. He who does not wish this openness for his fatherland does not want to purify it of its diseases, but only to drive them inward, there to fester.

A. SOLZHENITSYN

12 November 1969

An Open Letter to Pravda

After Aleksandr Solzhenitsyn won the Nobel Prize for literature in October 1970, his close friend, Mstislav Rostropovich, the cellist, wrote a letter of protest to Pravda *and other Soviet papers against the government's campaign of calumny. It has never been published in Russia.*

OPEN LETTER to the chief editors of the newspapers *Pravda, Izvestia, Literaturnaya Gazeta,* and *Sovetskaya Kultura.*

Esteemed Comrade Editor:

It is no longer a secret that A. I. Solzhenitsyn lives a great part of the time in my house near Moscow. I have seen how he was expelled from the Writers' Union — at the very time when he was working strenuously on a novel about the year 1914. Now the Nobel Prize has been awarded to him. The newspaper campaign in this connection compels me to undertake this letter to you.

In my memory this is already the third time that a Soviet writer has been given the Nobel Prize. In two cases out of three we have considered the awarding of the prize a "dirty political game," but in one (Sholokhov) as a "just recognition" of the outstanding world significance of our literature.

If in his time Sholokhov had declined to accept the prize from hands which had given it to Pasternak "for Cold War considerations" I would have understood that we no longer trusted the objectivity and the honesty of the Swedish academicians. But now it happens that we selectively sometimes accept the Nobel Prize with gratitude and sometimes curse it.

And what if next time the prize is awarded to Comrade Kochetov [Vsevolod Kochetov, Soviet author and hard-line editor]? Of course it will have to be accepted!

Why, a day after the award of the prize to Solzhenitsyn, in our papers appeared a strange report of correspondent "X" with representatives of the secretariat of the Writers' Union to the effect that the entire public of the country (that is evidently all scholars and all musicians, etc.) actively supported his expulsion from the Writers' Union?

Why does *Literaturnaya Gazeta* select from numerous Western newspapers only the opinion of American and Swedish newspapers, avoiding the incomparably more popular and important Communist newspapers like *L'Humanité, Lettre Française* and *L'Unità,* to say nothing of the numerous non-Communist ones?

If we trust a certain critic Bonosky [Philip Bonosky, an American Communist journalist], then how should we consider the opinion of such important writers as Böll, Aragon and François Mauriac?

I remember and would like to remind you of our newspapers in 1948, how much nonsense was written about those giants of our music, S. S. Prokofiev and D. D. Shostakovich, who are now honored.

For example:

> *Comrades D. Shostakovich, S. Prokofiev, V. Shebalin, N. Myaskovky and others — your atonal disharmonic music is organically alien to the people . . . formalistic trickery arises when there is an obvious lack of talent, but very much pretension to innovation . . . we absolutely do not accept the music of Shostakovich, Myaskovsky, Prokofiev. There is no harmony in it, no order, no wide melodiousness, no melody.*

Now, when one looks at the newspapers of those years, one becomes unbearably ashamed of many things. For the fact is that for three decades the opera *Katerina Izmailova* [of Shostakovich] was not performed, that S. Prokofiev during his life did not hear

the last version of his opera *War and Peace*, and his Symphonic
Concerto for Cello and Orchestra, that there were official lists of
forbidden works of Shostakovich, Prokofiev, Myaskovsky and
Khachaturian.

Has time really not taught us to approach cautiously the crush-
ing of talented people? And not to speak in the name of all the
people? Not to oblige people to express as their opinions what
they simply have not read or heard? I recall with pride that I did
not go to the meeting of cultural figures in the Central House of
Cultural Workers where B. Pasternak was abused and where I
was expected to deliver a speech which I had been "commis-
sioned" to deliver, criticizing *Doctor Zhivago*, which at that time
I had not read.

In 1948 there were lists of forbidden works. Now oral prohibi-
tions are preferred, referring to the fact that "opinions exist" that
the work is not recommended. It is impossible to establish where
this opinion exists and whose it is. Why for instance was Galina
Vishnevskaya [Mr. Rostropovich's wife] forbidden to perform in
her concert in Moscow the brilliant vocal cycle of Boris Tchaikovsky with the words of I. Brodsky [a dissident Leningrad poet]?
Why was the performance of the Shostakovich cycle to the words
of Sasha Chyorny obstructed several times (although the text had
already been published)? Why did difficulties accompany the
performance of Shostakovich's Thirteenth and Fourteenth Sym-
phonies?

Again, apparently, "there was an opinion." Who first had the
"opinion" that it was necessary to expel Solzhenitsyn from the
Writers' Union? I did not manage to clarify this question although I was very interested in it. Did five Ryazan writer-
musketeers really dare to do it themselves without a serious "opinion"?

Apparently the "opinion" prevented also my fellow citizens
from getting to know Tarkovsky's film *Andrey Rublyov*, which we
sold abroad and which I had the pleasure of seeing among enrap-

tured Parisians. Obviously it was "opinion" which also prevented publication of Solzhenitsyn's *Cancer Ward*, which was already set in type for *Novy Mir* [the leading Soviet literary journal]. So if this had been published here it would have been openly and widely discussed to the benefit of the author as well as the readers.

I do not speak about political or economic questions in our country. There are people who know these better than I. But explain to me please, why in our literature and art so often people absolutely incompetent in this field have the final word? Why are they given the right to discredit our art in the eyes of our people?

I recall the past not in order to grumble but in order that in the future, let's say in twenty years, we won't have to bury today's newspapers in shame.

Every man must have the right fearlessly to think independently and express his opinion about what he knows, what he has personally thought about, experienced, and not merely to express with slightly different variations the opinion which has been inculcated in him.

We will definitely arrive at reconstruction without prompting and without being corrected.

I know that after my letter there will undoubtedly be an *"opinion"* about me, but I am not afraid of it. I openly say what I think. Talent, of which we are proud, must not be submitted to the assaults of the past. I know many of the works of Solzhenitsyn. I like them. I consider he seeks the right through his suffering to write the truth as he saw it and I see no reason to hide my attitude toward him at a time when a campaign is being launched against him.

Moscow, 31 October, 1970

How They Taught Me I Was a Jew

Alla Rusinek was born and lived in the Soviet Union until November 1970, when she was permitted finally to emigrate to Israel. Thousands of protests like Alla's and continuous violent agitation on the part of Soviet Jews has finally compelled or persuaded Soviet authorities to permit an increasing number of Jews to emigrate to Israel.

You ask me how I came to the idea of leaving the Soviet Union and going to Israel. I think that though I heard about Israel only four years ago my whole life was the way to it. You can see it yourself.

I was born in Moscow in 1949 and was the most typical Soviet girl. I studied well, was a young Pioneer-Leninist. My classmates thought me very ambitious. But they were wrong. My family was very poor. Mother brought us up, two daughters, without a father and having a very low salary. We never had new clothes. I never thought about our poverty. I was sure that everybody lived this way, at least the families of engineers, because my mother was an engineer.

I gave all my time to my school, my Pioneer organization and later the Young Communist League — the Komsomol. I worked hard. And I was happy coming home late after school. According to Communist ideals "the individual must sacrifice his own personal interests for that of the socialist society at large." And I loved my country, my Soviet people.

My? Yes, I thought it was mine. But there was something that made me different from other people. I happened to be born a

Jew. I don't know what it meant but it was written in my identity card: *yevreika*. My Russian classmates insulted each other with this word. I saw it written in chalk on the walls of the houses. It was written very distinctly in my identity card and legalized by a round seal of the government. At the beginning of every school year the teacher asked everybody: "Your name and nationality." I answered in whispers.

Little by little I began to understand what it meant to be Jewish. In 1961 I was not admitted to a special English high school. In 1966 I was not admitted to the Institute of Foreign Languages. I thought it was my personal failure and couldn't understand why the examiner, looking at my identity card, said that I didn't speak good Russian.

Well, in other words I understood at last. They don't want me, I am a stranger, this is not my country. But where is a place for me? I began to be proud of being Jewish.

When I heard about Israel in 1967, about "an aggressive, capitalist state, an agent of US imperialism in the Middle East," I didn't fail to understand it was my home, my people, defending their young state. I understood that to be Jewish meant to belong to the Jewish nation with its history, culture, religion.

I began to study Hebrew. In some old books I learned the first facts about Jewish history: the Maccabees, the Warsaw ghetto. For the first time in my life I went to the synagogue, the only synagogue in Moscow, where I saw thousands of people who looked like me and thought like me. We sang Jewish songs, we danced Israeli dances. It was wonderful but it was dangerous. Secret police entered my life. I was expelled from the Komsomol, then I lost my job. They followed me, they searched me, they called me in for "frank talks" and threatened me. What did I think then about Communism? I didn't think. I was tired and frightened. For two years I applied for an exit visa and was refused. I applied alone. Mother had died after eight years of dreadful disease.

I was not alone in this struggle. There were thousands of us in Russia who came to the synagogue to sing. And among them was one, the most handsome boy in the Soviet Union at least. A year after we met at a Chanukah party we married. We were in a hurry, any of us could be arrested then in the summer of 1970. Most of our friends were arrested then in Leningrad and Riga. We didn't want to lose each other.

A week after our marriage I was informed that I had to leave the country within six days and alone.

Please, don't ask me what I felt. I don't remember. Perhaps I was in a deep shock. No, I didn't cry. His family paid for me the sum the Soviets demanded for "renunciation of Soviet citizenship" — nine hundred rubles [nearly one thousand dollars]. I never thought I owned such an expensive thing or I would have sold it and bought something nice. All these months I have hoped they would allow him to join me. We are husband and wife. One family. But he has not been allowed to leave.

You ask me what I think about Israel now that I live there. It is difficult to answer this question. It's the same as if you asked me what I thought about myself. I can't praise myself. Israel is me and I am Israel.

P.S. I have just learned today after my article was written that my husband has been granted permission to leave the Soviet Union and join me in Israel. I wish to express my thanks to everyone who has helped, and particularly to the American people.

A Last Letter

One of Yukio Mishima's last acts before committing seppuku or cere-monial suicide on November 25, 1970, was to mail this letter to his friend, Professor Ivan Morris, at Columbia University.

Dear Ivan:

This is my last letter to both of you. You showed me the most beautiful friendship and fulfilled my life by the most enjoyable relation; I am extremely grateful to you.

You might be one of very [few] persons who can understand my conclusion. Influenced by Yomei philosophy [seventeenth-century Confucianism], I have believed that knowing without acting is not sufficiently knowing and the acting itself does not require any effectiveness. In Japan, any genuine rightist's think-ing should result in Emperor and Death, anyway.

I would like to take liberty to ask you something, which I asked to Donald Keene, too. It is concerned with my novel *HOJO-NO-UMI*.

I wrote everything in it and I believe I expressed by it every-thing I felt and thought about all through my life.

I just finished the novel on the very day of my action in order to realize my BUNBU-RYODO [synthesis of cultural and warrior arts]. But one thing I am worried about is Knopf's attitude, that they became suddenly cold to Mr. Tanizaki since his death.

I do wish *HOJO-NO-UMI* would be introduced to readers all over the world, and actually the first two volumes are already under translation by Mr. Mike Gallagher. I would like to ask you to push Knopf to publish [the] whole four volumes, unless they might give up its publication [for] a cold commercial reason.

It was a most memorable trip to Korea with you. How enjoyable it was!

After thinking and thinking through four years, I [came] to wish to sacrifice myself for the old, beautiful tradition of Japan, which is disappearing very quickly day by day.

I do wish both of you'll have the happiest and healthiest life!

As always,
YUKIO MISHIMA

November 1970

Political Oppression

Letter from the Greek Underground

Eleftheros Anthropos is the nom de plume of a young member of the Greek underground who spent New Year's Eve, 1970, planting bombs at American installations.

I SPENT THIS NEW YEAR'S EVE planting bombs at three American targets in Athens.

I would have called anyone a lunatic who would have predicted this back in 1967 before the colonels backed by Americans took over our country. As our group waited, we received word that the bomb at the American military canteen at Omonia Square went off as did the one at the Congo Palace Hotel occupied by American military personnel. Our contact who passed near the third target at the set time reported back that there had been no explosion.

We had to make a difficult decision. This was the first time that one of our bombs had not gone off and we could not risk the police finding the mechanism intact. Someone had to go back. The youngest volunteered. We waited in the small hours of the morning, fearful that he might blow himself up as two others of another organization did outside the US Embassy in September, or that he might be caught and tortured, as hundreds have been, until he revealed everything. At dawn we heard his footsteps on the stairs. As he entered, he took from under his coat the detonator and the plastic explosive.

The day I was first approached by a member of EMA (Greek Militant Resistance) and asked to hide explosives was the day I had to face myself and could no longer seek refuge at the level of words. Before that day I had resisted my conscience with the arguments of cold reason: "How can I fight a well-organized modern army, how can I fight the junta which has behind it the whole power of the United States, how can I hide anything from the omnipotence of the CIA? It is absolutely illogical that a few men improvising primitive arms should dare to try to lift this dead weight of steel and concrete which has fallen on our country. Of course it is unacceptable to live under this dictatorship, to live without the basic freedoms, the basic respect for human beings, but I am impotent and one must face reality."

I tried another, more clever argument: "Why not concentrate on my career, become first a success without altogether denying my principles, and then reveal my ideas in the proper time and place? If all young people did the same, then a time would come when the junta would fall under the pressure of the new generation."

The result of this "reasonable thinking" was that I soon despised reason and despised myself. The truth was that I did not want to risk my personal well-being and security. When I decided to hide the bombs, I felt a sense of enormous relief, of liberation, for the decision to join the struggle was the natural consequence of my beliefs, of my whole life.

I might have remained passive if we did not have our Greek past, so many killed, so much pain, so many times having to build up from nothing. Perhaps I would have reacted differently if we had not so often been disillusioned by the powerful of the world trampling on our ideals. I felt a terrible personal responsibility toward the people who believed in ideals and suffered for them, both to those in the past and to those who today fill Greek prisons. I had the feeling I had betrayed them.

How did such a change occur in me, a person who had no inclination toward violence, and in others? That is really for the powerful of the world to answer, the Nixons and the Brezhnevs the generals and the diplomats, who play a separate game from the people of the world. They have alienated themselves from the real basis of human life which is the happiness of people.

I have studied American history and admired its great men from Lincoln to Roosevelt. I cried at Kennedy's death. We are sorry for what will fall on the American people; it is not their leaders who do the fighting in Vietnam nor who will suffer for what their leaders have gotten them into in Greece.

Though our strength is small, we will go on, contributing to the larger fight in the world where the will of the people opposes the leaders. Power can command, power can rule, but the soul of a people has a different kind of power which cannot be suppressed forever. The power machine of the Pentagon cannot understand this as it is not in its technological dictionaries.

Our history shows that freedom is born in pain. A price must be set on tyranny and the tyrants must pay the price.

Dare to Struggle, Dare to Win

On her emergence from English prison in autumn 1970, Bernadette Devlin, M.P., and Irish rebel leader, recorded her determination to: "Dare to Struggle, Dare to Win!"

WADING THROUGH A MASS of impressions formed in prison, not because it was prison but because for the first time in my life I had 117 consecutive days in which, against a clockwork background, all I had to do was survive and think, the single most important fact that I established in my mind can be best summed up in the battle cry, "Dare to Struggle — Dare to Win."

Caught up within the system of society that we are trying to destroy, we often lose sight of the reason why we are trying to destroy it.

If we reduce the situation to its simplest terms, we want to destroy the existing system because the people cannot live within it. I say "the people," meaning the mass of ordinary people as opposed to the few who at present control them, and who in order to do so create the "color problem," "religious problem," and the "race problem." Want then becomes a beating plea which in itself admits defeat. Therefore, I say, rather, "We will destroy the system."

In the eyes of respectable politicians, merchants, and liberals, I am immediately classified as an extremist. They prefer to use the word "change" rather than "destroy."

In prison every morning we filed out with our chamber pots to the yard toilet. Every time the governor came to the workroom we stood up and said "Sir." Those things are disconcerting to liberals, but they are the essential trappings of the prison system.

So, too, in society as a whole, the facts that our children sit in neat rows in school, the brightest at the back, our workers call the boss Sir, and women promise not only to love but to obey daily reinforce the system that creates high unemployment, slums, and "inferior races."

"Changing" the system asks only that our prisoners be allowed to use the lavatory, our slums be tidied up and workers better treated by their masters. Liberals dare to struggle. The people still cannot live because the people still have masters.

If we are serious — and I have never been more so — in our efforts to end the poverty, the greed, the hatred and fear within our society, then we must destroy the system that creates it, and build the Socialist Republic of Ireland. Our brothers wherever they find themselves, be it America, be it Russia, be it Czechoslovakia, must carry on the struggle by building the Socialist Republic of wherever they find themselves.

The essential lesson I learned in prison was that there were 18 working hours in every day and 7 days in every week. I was, in the judgment of the court, removed from society for 117 of these days. Over the past few years I have removed myself at intervals from the task of destroying the system. I saw it essentially as a task I believed necessary.

Today I realize that just as our present society is a way of life, so, too, is its destruction, and its destruction is my way of life. Prison was the last flattery I accept from the system I was born in. Yesterday I dared to struggle. Today I dare to win.

A Haitian Cri de Coeur

Sully Le-Preux is the nom de plume of a Haitian exile in New York who wrote this plea for his country in June 1971.

It has been the Mephisto Dance for about fourteen years. The ceaseless dance of death upon the misfortune of the Haitian people. Dance of blood, dance of fire.

Fourteen years of cry and rattle. Fourteen years of funeral obsequies celebrated in the secret of the bedroom, because the families of the victims dared not weep in public or show themselves at the church.

Fourteen years of silence and confinement, fear and despair, because whatever the grief was, you dared not sigh out, for the torturing chamber and the nailed coffin would have your last breath.

Fourteen years of horrifying misery, a whole people attending the agents of unavoidable death. Fourteen years of a living nightmare, spectacle of dismay, the burning of houses with families and visitors inside, breaking down doors at midnight, taking away in their pajamas husbands or fathers, brothers or sisters, who disappeared forever.

The most ridiculous and perhaps the most sanguinary chief of state of the "modern" world has died. Like most of those similar to him, he established his reign of destruction, with the help of the White House in Washington and the Pentagon, for the simple and comic reason that Communism has to be prevented or eliminated.

All the murders, all the massacres were justified by anti-Communism. Students protesting against despotism were killed in the streets by anti-Communist legions, while, conversely, Communist theoreticians occupied key positions in government and dined in the Palace. Starving people crying out their hunger were shot in the street by the anti-Communist gestapo.

It has been seen there what has never been seen anywhere. Haitians have seen things they are ashamed to say, things the remembering of which brings a taste of blood and vomit to the throat.

For how long will the dignity and freedom of the Latin American people be accounted a mere trifle in America's foreign policy, their rights laid supine in the United States's quest for security?

After Trujillo, Washington managed with its Marines in the Dominican Republic to impose Joaquin Balaguer. After Duvalier the Haitians will be gratified with the continuation of the "people's revolution," whose supreme result was misery and death, by handing the power to his grotesque son. Balaguer proclaimed two days of mourning for his best friend "Papa Doc" and aligned an army along the Haitian border; the USA aligned its ships loaded with Marines along the coast.

People of America, you have the privilege of being a great nation, the richest country of the world, which gives you the sacred responsibility to speak up and to protest, to help, not to destroy. Use this tremendous right toward dying people under oppression, use it to stop the US government from spoiling your prestige and disfiguring the magnificent concept of humanism and freedom which should characterize the spirit of your nation!

Old and worn are those strings played upon by dreadful despots, the music of which is cacophonous for everyone but Washington. To believe these confirmed liars screaming against Communism where there is no shadow of Communism is just childish or malignant! Everyone knows about that scream, when the people threaten to reverse the situation, but the Marines landed in the Dominican Republic to stop the people's revolution against torture and corruption. The Marines may now be ready to land in Haiti.

Haiti is the world's first black nation, since the African continent was shared like a cake by European colonialists, and the second independent country of this hemisphere. She is the only country of the world where the black slaves acquired their freedom in the field of battle and proclaimed their independence (from France) in 1804.

In July 1915, the people of Port-au-Prince, in an access of rage, seized the President and cut him to pieces. Their action followed the slaughter of more than two hundred political prisoners in the penitentiary. The US, under the pretext of bringing law and order, invaded Haiti and remained until 1934. The leader of the guerrilla warfare against the American occupation was captured by the Marines, crucified and machine-gunned publicly. This interference is shameful to the Haitian people, who were then left with an army of mercenaries receiving always their order from Washington, to do or undo governments in the country.

People of the USA, let it not happen again. Washington must withdraw its ships from the coast of Haiti. This little nation needs comprehension. The Haitian blood is mixed with your blood at Savannah and Pensacola in your fight for liberty and justice. Haiti's ultimate aspiration is for liberty and justice.

A Letter to Sartre

Vladimir Dedijer, the Yugoslav revolutionary and historian, spent 1970–1971 in the United States, teaching at American colleges and universities and studying the revolutionary evolution of mood, attitude and philosophy in the American nation. The American phenomenon has been extremely difficult for European leftists to analyze. Here he presents his observations in an open letter to his long-time friend and associate, Jean-Paul Sartre.

Dear Sartre:

What new, if anything, does the American New Left bring to us Europeans?

The beauty of the American New Left is its spontaneity. It was born not out of foreign agitation but out of the pains of its own society. In Europe we identify it often with students and the Black Panthers. In fact it is much more broadly based. It is a real Noah's Ark with all kinds of rebels. Here Ibsen's dream of permanent revolt (which we discussed last summer in Bergen) is coming true. We are witnessing not only an outburst of energy against a mighty empire but an effort to liberate man in all his repressive relationships: social, ethical, esthetical.

Events in America are again proving that no revolution repeats the forms of earlier ones. American realities do not conform to European dogma. The New Left has its own, constantly changing forms of struggle. It challenges everyone and everything. It has no leaders in the European sense. It is aware of the danger of manipulation and this is one of its great strengths. The American radicals are determined not to create a new Establishment that can become the master rather than a servant of the revolution. On my way to Brandeis the other morning, I saw a graffito on the wooden shack at the Porter Square train stop: *No man is good enough to be another man's master.*

We well know spontaneity is not enough. A revolution becomes reality only when the outburst of discontent produces its own ideology and organization. The most important phenomenon that I have observed recently is a marked effort of hard thinking among the American radicals to formulate a new ideology. Some of the best brains of America are deeply concerned with this problem. One should not be impatient.

No radical movement in the world has ever had to face an enemy that possesses such powers of destruction and surveillance. As testimony at recent trials has shown, the Establishment has taken pains to infiltrate revolutionary ranks. Obviously the openness of the radical groups — an openness that must seem to the two of us, old conspirators against Hitler during the days of Resistance, disconcertingly naive — makes the work of the undercover agents easier. But in the Widener Library I saw young men with Stepnyak's *Underground Russia,* the textbook of revolutionary work — the days of our grandfathers.

Let us, as Europeans, pay special respect to the internationalism of the New Left. These Americans oppose the war of their Establishment against Vietnam far more strongly than the French Communist party or the working class of France opposed the Indochina or the Algerian war or than the Russian working class opposed the invasion of Czechoslovakia. Did not the American radicals succeed in smoking out a President from the White House?

I am aware of the fact that the radicals here do have moments of lethargy. Nowhere are they more American than in their rapid shifts of moods. There are some prophets who would like to see these shifts in mood as proof that the movement is already declining. It is not. The strength of the Left grows primarily from the social and other contradictions of their own society. Roosevelt succeeded in diminishing social tensions by concessions to a part of the dispossessed. Today the reigning dictum is just the opposite. Racial injustices have increased, the richest country in the world is facing acute poverty not only among the people of color but whites as well. America is witnessing the rise of new intellectual proletarians, as in eastern Europe. There are thousands of the unemployed Ph.D.s.

Perhaps the Establishment may draw some lessons from these counterprofitable political tactics. But many signs indicate that social contradictions both in this country and the world on a longer perspective are going to deepen.

Vietnam is an organic outgrowth of structures and ideological elements of the American system. I am not a prophet of doom, but I envisage new Vietnams, although with different political and military strategy. Even such a man as Robert S. McNamara, now the president of the World Bank, is predicting "a wider social and political crisis which grows deeper with each decade and threatens to round off this century with years of unrest and turbulence" because of the increased gap between poor and rich nations, population explosions, etc.

The future of the world depends so much on the American New Left. Nowhere are the social contradictions deeper, and nowhere does a rebel have a greater opportunity to demonstrate the firmness of his convictions than here. Therefore it is the greatest country in the world.

Letter in a Bottle

Professor George Mangakis was arrested in July 1969, and tortured and imprisoned in Athens on charges of plotting to overthrow the "social order." This letter, slightly excerpted, reached the outside in 1971.

THE DIMENSIONS OF MY CELL are approximately ten feet by ten feet. You gradually become accustomed to this space, and even grow to like it, since, in a way, it is like a lair in which you lie hidden, licking your wounds. But in reality, its object is to annihilate you. On one side of it there is a heavy iron door, with a little round hole in the upper part. Prisoners hate this little hole; they call it the "stool pigeon." It is through this hole that the jailkeeper's eye appears every now and then — an isolated eye, without a face.

On the other side of my cell there is a little window, with bars. From this window you can see part of the city. And yet a prisoner rarely looks out the window. It is too painful. Its only use is to bring you some light. That is something I have studied very carefully. I have learned all the possible shades of light. I can distinguish the light that comes just before daybreak, and the light that lingers on after nightfall. This light, with its many variations, is one of the chief joys of the prisoner. It often happens that a certain shade of light coincides with your mood, with the spiritual needs of that particular moment.

Apart from the door and the window, my cell also has a temperature. That is another fundamental element of my life here. It is unbearably cold in winter and extremely hot in summer. I find this natural, even though it brings me great discomfort.

I live in this space, then, for endless hours of the day and night. It is like a piece of thread on which my days are strung and fall away, lifeless. This space can also be compared to a wrestling ring. Here a man struggles alone with the evil of the world.

.

I write these papers, and then I hide them. They let you write, but every so often they search your cell and take away your writings. They look them over, and after some time they return the ones which are considered permissible. You take them back, and suddenly you loathe them. This system is a diabolical device for annihilating your own soul. They want to make you see your thoughts through their eyes and control them yourself, from their point of view. It is like having a nail pushed into your mind.

.

My mind often goes back to the dead I have known and loved. In the vacuum of my cell, only concepts have substance. My cell is like a bottomless hole in the void. My most frequent visitor is my brother Yannis — he comes to me almost every day. He was killed in the war, but not in the act of killing others: he was a doctor. His regiment was afflicted with an epidemic of meningitis. He did not have time to cure himself. I have never been able to accept his death. I have simply managed, in time, to become reconciled to his absence. Now we are once again very close to each other. He has smiling, honey-colored eyes. He stays on for hours, and we sit there and think together. It used to be the same when he was alive.

.

There are moments when I sit in my cell thinking of what would be the best way to summarize my motives, those that made me end up in this cell and those that make me endure it. These motives are certainly not a belief in a single truth — not because we no longer have any truths to believe in but because, in our

world, we do not experience these truths as absolute certainties.
We are no longer as simple as that; we seek something more profound than certainty, something more substantial, something that
is naturally, spontaneously simple. I think, then, that the totality
of my motives in this connection could best be epitomized as
hope — in other words, the most fragile, but also the most spontaneous and tenacious form of human thought. A deeply rooted,
indestructible hope.

Yet I don't think that by saying this I am expressing myself as
concretely as I would wish. This hope takes shape only in certain
attitudes. During the past months, through all the prisons I've
known, I have often come across these attitudes. When I was
held at the police-station jails — those places of utter human degradation — I remember a girl who was locked in a cell next to
mine. She had been there for five months. She hadn't seen the
light of day once throughout that period. She had been accused
of helping her fiancé to do Resistance work. At regular intervals,
they would summon her for questioning and would try to make
her disown him, using cunning persuasion or brutal intimidation
alternately. If she disowned her fiancé, she would be set free. She
refused unflinchingly, to the very end, even though she knew that
her fiancé was dying of cancer and she would probably never see
him again. He died on the day of her trial. She was a pale, frail
girl, with a kind of nobility about her. Every evening she used to
sing in her cell in a soft, low voice. She would sing till dawn
about her love, in her sad voice. The girl's attitude is my hope.

I live with a number of ideas that I love. They fill my days and
my nights. To the treacherous uniformity of my stagnant hours, I
oppose this dialogue with my ideas. Now I have come to know
them better and to understand them better. I have actually experienced their significance. When I was being questioned, I discovered the essence of human dignity, in both its deepest and its
simplest sense. When I was court-martialed I hungered for jus-

tice, and when I was imprisoned I thirsted for humanity. The brutal oppression which is now stifling my country has taught me a great deal, among other things the value of refusing to submit. As I sit in my cell thinking about these things, I am filled with a strange power — a power which has nothing in common with the power of my jailkeepers. It is not expressed in a loud, insolent voice. It is the power of endurance — the power that is born of a sense of being right. That is how I face the relentless attack of empty days which has been launched against me. Each time, I repulse the attack at its very start. I begin my day by uttering the word "freedom." This usually happens at daybreak. I emerge from sleep, always feeling bitterly surprised to find myself in prison, as on the first day. Then I utter my beloved word, before the sense of being in prison has time to overpower me.

I think of my companions. The political prisoners I have come across in my various prisons. The ones who resisted and are now pacing across their cells, taking those three little jerky steps forward, then backward. They are all made of the same stuff, even though they may be very different persons in other respects. They all possess a very rare sensitivity of conscience. A truly unbelievable sensitivity.

I often ask myself what it was exactly that touched our consciences in such a way as to give us all an imperatively personal motive for opposing the dictatorship and enlisting in the Resistance, putting aside all other personal obligations and pursuits. One does not enlist in the Resistance — in that mortally dangerous confrontation with the all-powerful persecution mechanism of a dictatorship, where the chances of being caught are far greater than the chances of getting away with it, where arrest will result in the most unbearable and long-term suffering — one doesn't get involved in all this without some very strong personal motive. So strong, in fact, that it must literally affect the very roots of one's being — since it makes one decide to risk falling into the clutches

of the most appalling arbitrariness and barbarism, being reduced
from a human being to an object, a mere receptacle of suffering,
jeopardizing all the achievements and dreams of the lifetime and
plunging loved ones into the most terrible agonies and depriva-
tions.

I keep thinking, then, that this motive can be no other than the
deep humiliation which the dictatorship represents for you, both
as an individual and as a member of the people to whom you belong. When a dictatorship is imposed on your country, the very
first thing you feel, the very first day, is humiliation. You are being deprived of the right to consider yourself worthy of responsibility for your own life and destiny. This feeling of humiliation
grows day by day as a result of the oppressors' unceasing effort to
force your mind to accept all the vulgarity which makes up the
abortive mental world of dictators.

·

Morally speaking, the Resistance is the purest of all struggles.
As a rule, you join it only to follow the dictates of your conscience; it affords no other satisfaction except the justification of
your conscience. Not only is there no benefit to be expected from
this struggle but, on the contrary, you are endangering, or rather
you are exposing to a near certain catastrophe, whatever you may
have achieved until now with your labors, and you enter a way of
life that is full of anxiety and peril. You cannot expect immediate
praise, because you have to act secretly, in darkness and silence;
nor can you expect future praise, because under a dictatorship the
future is always uncertain and confused. There is only your conscience to justify you.

·

Another thing: we feel very European. This feeling does not
derive primarily from political opinions, even though it does end
up by becoming a fundamental political stand. It is a feeling that
grows out of the immediacy and the intensity that our cultural
values have acquired under dictatorship. Fortunately, these values, which have become our whole life and which help us to en-

dure our long nights and days, are not exclusively ours. We share them with all the peoples of Europe. Or rather the European people, for Europe is one single people. Here in prison we can affirm this with complete seriousness. Suffering helps us to get down to the essence of things and to express it with perfect simplicity. We see only the deeper meaning of Europe, not the foolish borders, the petty rivalries, the unfounded fears and reservations. We see ourselves simply as one people, as a whole. It may seem strange — though only at first glance — how intensely the Greeks felt they were Europeans the very first day of the dictatorship. Our values are the values of Europe. We created them together. We felt instinctively, at the time, that nobody but a European could understand the tragedy that was taking place in our country and feel about it the way we did. And we were right.

We turned in despair to Europe, and the people of Europe did not forsake us.

·

We often talk about the dignity of man. It is not an abstraction; it is a thing which I have actually experienced. It exists in our very depths, like a sensitive steel spring. It has absolutely nothing to do with personal dignity. Its roots lie much deeper. Throughout the nightmare of the interrogation sessions, I lost my personal dignity; it was replaced by pure suffering. But human dignity was within me, without my knowing it.

·

I have experienced the fate of a victim. I have seen the torturer's face at close quarters. It was in a worse condition than my own bleeding, livid face. The torturer's face was distorted by a kind of twitching that had nothing human about it. He was in such a state of tension that he had an expression very similar to those we see on Chinese masks; I am not exaggerating. It is not an easy thing to torture people. It requires inner participation. In this situation, I turned out to be the lucky one. I was humiliated. I did not humiliate others.

·

Our position as prisoners has many distinguishing features. One of them is that we sing, quite frequently. It may sound strange to people who don't know about prisons. But that's the way it is — and come to think of it, it is very natural. Singing is part of the unwritten instructions passed on by veteran prisoners to newly arrived ones: when the pain and anguish are too much for you, sing. We begin to sing precisely when the anguish becomes unbearable. On days that are free of anguish, we don't sing.

It has all become quite clear to me. It had to be this way. From the moment my country was humiliated, debased, it was inevitable that I should go underground. It was an inexorable spiritual imperative. My whole life had been leading me to that imperative. Since childhood, I was taught to gaze upon open horizons, to love the human face, to respect human problems, to honor free attitudes. At the time of the Second World War, I was an adolescent; I lived through the Resistance; it left its moral mark on me. Only I didn't know at the time how deep that mark was. It has now become clear that it was to be the most vital inspiration force in my life. At last I can explain many things that happened to me between then and now. And so when the dictatorship came, I was already committed to the Resistance, without knowing it.

I would like to write about a friendship I formed the autumn before last. I think it has some significance. It shows the solidarity that can be forged between unhappy creatures. I had been kept in solitary confinement for four months. I hadn't seen a soul throughout that period. Only uniforms — inquisitors and jail-keepers. One day, I noticed three mosquitoes in my cell. They were struggling hard to resist the cold that was just beginning. In the daytime they slept on the wall. At night they would come buzzing over me. In the beginning, they exasperated me. But fortunately I soon understood. I too was struggling hard to live through the cold spell. What were they asking from me? Something unimportant. A drop of blood — it would save them. I couldn't refuse. At nightfall I would bare my arm and wait for them. After some days they got used to me and they were no longer afraid. They would come to me quite naturally, openly. This trust is something I owe them. Thanks to them, the world was no longer merely an inquisition chamber. Then one day I was transferred to another prison. I never saw my mosquitoes again. This is how you are deprived of the presence of your friends in the arbitrary world of prisons. But you go on thinking of them, often.

.

During the months when I was being interrogated, alone before those men with the multiple eyes of a spider — and the instincts of a spider — one night a policeman on guard smiled at me. At that moment, the policeman was all men to me. Four months later, when the representative of the International Red Cross walked into my cell, once again I saw all men in his friendly face. When one day they finally put me in a cell with another prisoner and he began to talk to me about the thing he loved most in life — sailing and fishing boats — this man too was all men to me. It is true, then, that there are situations in which each one of us represents all mankind. And it is the same with these papers: I have entrusted them to a poor Italian prisoner who has just been released and who was willing to try to smuggle them out for me. Through him I hope they will eventually reach you. That man again is all men to me. But I think it is time I finished. I have raised my hand, made a sign. And so we exist. We over here in prison, and you out there who agree with us. So: *Freedom my love.*

The Keys of the Comandante

Yevgeny Yevtushenko, the Russian poet, visited Peru and Chile in the spring of 1971, where he wrote this appreciation of Che Guevara. The verse was originally composed in Spanish.

Our horses are walking to la Higuera*
To the left — the abyss,
            to the right — the abyss.

To think of you, Major,
            is not a heavy load.
Within me is a silent ache,
            resembling the earthquake.

I am filled with the creeks,
            of severe, hard rocks.
My nerves are tense
            as the bridle of a cowhand.

The rhythm of this poem
            is dictated by horseshoes,
stumbling against the stones
            of this deadly path.

For guerrilleros
            around here there are no
            monuments.

* The village where Che Guevara was killed.

Their monuments — rocks,
            with sad, human faces.
The clouds are motionless,

            like thoughts,
like thoughts
            of the Bolivian mountains.

Comandante your precious name
            they wish to sell so cheaply.

With your name industry wants to buy
            new customers.
Comandante: in Paris I saw your
            portrait on little pants called
            "hot."

Your pictures, Che,
            are printed on shirts
You plunged into the fire.
            They want to turn you into
            smoke.

But you fell,
            riddled by bullets,
            by poisonous smiles
not to become later
            merchandise for the consumer
            society.

"Where is the key
            to the school?"
The peasants give me no answer.

            I feel the smell of death.
The wall is white
            like the candle

of the boat
　　　　　left abandoned to its fate.

The silence is total.
　　　　　Only the buzzard flies.
Horse dung — the posthumous
chrysanthemums.

"Where is the key
　　　　　to the school?"
The peasants answer:
　　　　　"We don't know, sir,
　　　　　we don't know . . ."

Where is the key
　　　　　to the case of Che Guevara?

Where is the key
　　　　　to the future?

Fear of not finding it,
　　　　　panic grips me,
but the key is in our hands —
　　　　　of that I am certain
Boys: to shout promises
　　　　　and not to fulfill them,
　　　　　that's crap!

Our own stumbling has deceived the others.

To the left, boys,
　　　　　always to the left,
but not beyond the left
　　　　　of your own heart.

Comandante, your hands were severed
　　　　　in the square of Valle Grande,

Comandante, over your death
        the wild flowers and the guitars
        sing
But,
        The young do not surrender,
        the young, forward!
Ours are the hands of Che,
        they cannot be cut!

Nikita Sergeyevich Khrushchev

On September 13, 1971, Nikita Sergeyevich Khrushchev was buried in Moscow in a private ceremony at the Novodevichye Cemetery. The funeral address was given by Khrushchev's son, Sergei. An old Communist worker from the Donets, Nadezhda Dimanshtein, and Vadim Vasilyev, whose father and grandfather died in the purge of the 1930's, spoke briefly.

SERGEI KHRUSHCHEV:

We have no official meeting, no official speeches. Therefore I would simply like to say a few words about the man we are burying here, the man for whom we are shedding tears, and the sky is shedding tears with us.

I will not speak about him as a great statesman. On that subject a great deal was said in the last few days, with rare exceptions, by newspapers of the entire world, by all radio stations. It is not up to me to appraise the contributions made by Nikita Sergeyevich, my father. I have no right to do that. That will be done, and is already being done, by history.

The only thing I can say is that he left few people indifferent to him. There were those who loved him, there were those who hated him, but there were few who would pass by without looking in his direction.

Nor do I want to speak about him as my father at this family farewell, even though many people have come, because it is not easy for us to get used to the word "was." It is not easy.

We knew him in different ways, but he was one of us. He is in our hearts and he will remain in our hearts, in the hearts of his family, in the hearts of his many friends, and we do not want to give our hearts away. Because for me to speak would mean to say nothing.

But there is one thing I would like to say. We have lost someone who had every right to be called a man. Unfortunately, there are not many real people like him. That is actually all I wanted to say.

There are two others here who would like to say a few words, and I would like to ask Nadezhda Dimanshtein to try to push her way through if she can. She is an old revolutionary from the Donets Basin, a woman who helped make the Revolution, a Communist.

Nadezhda Dimanshtein:

Dear friends, dear comrades. It is a bitter honor for me to bid farewell to Nikita Sergeyevich on behalf of a group of Donets Communists. We remember Nikita Sergeyevich as an unbending proletarian, one who was to us, the younger people, an example of fortitude, of heroism, an example of unbending will, of unbending passion in defense of the party line.

We watched this man, in fighting for the party line, sweep away everything that was low, everything that served the personal interest. He was an example of a real party man, a real Bolshevik. He reared the broad masses of Donets Communists and proletarians. He reared huge numbers of people.

Later, for many of us who worked with him in the Moscow party organization, the meetings of the leadership of the Moscow city party committee constituted a real school of Bolshevism.

And that was the way we always saw him, a man who lived with the thoughts of the party's deeds, the deeds of our nation and of all mankind.

That image, comrades, will remain in the hearts of all those who had the fortune to work with Nikita Sergeyevich, all those who knew him, all those who saw him engaged in stubborn battles with our enemies, one who brought us up and led our party organization.

Let me say one last farewell to Nikita Sergeyevich on behalf of those who had the fortune to work under his leadership.

SERGEI KHRUSHCHEV:

On behalf of the younger Communists, if we can be called young, Vadim Vasilyev, a Communist and son of a purged Bolshevik, would now like to say a word. He knew Nikita Sergeyevich for many years and worked with him too.

VADIM VASILYEV:

Dear comrades. It is very bitter, very bitter for me to speak on this occasion, on this sad event in the life of our nation and of the entire world. It is not easy for me to speak.

Somewhere in the Taiga, the northern forest, are the graves of my father and my grandfather, who perished in the tragic year thirty-seven. It was Nikita Sergeyevich who restored honor and dignity to our dead relatives. It was deep respect for him that brought me here, and I grieve deeply for him, and with me my daughter and my wife.

SERGEI KHRUSHCHEV:

It looks as if we will pronounce no more speeches. Much could be said and it would take a long time, but it seems to me that there is no need. We have bade farewell to Nikita Sergeyevich. Let us now close this meeting. My only request to you is not to crowd and to move a bit to the side. Thank you, comrades.

Youth

IN A SENSE youth is what this anthology is about, because it has been youth, pre-eminently and particularly American youth, which has given this moment in history its particular pathos. The theme of youth runs through almost every selection, whether it be classified as Embattled Nation or The World. And this, if one stops to think, is only natural, for it is youth, with that passion for the "open truth" and that "fiery vehemence" of which Peter Marin speaks, which dares to raise the questions which the old and the middle-aged have tired of asking (or have long since forgotten even exist). It is youth which perceives that the Emperor is without clothes and asks about his nakedness. It is youth which hears the conflict between the lie of the politician and the principle of the Constitution. It is youth which throws off the pandered costume of Seventh Avenue and appears in the blue jeans of the working man or the castoffs of the World War II veterans. Youth has not yet learned to be afraid, to temper faith to the winds of expediency. If we can understand what youth is saying and why it is being said, then we can understand the nature of the crisis of our times.

Here we find youth speaking for itself and youth observed, quantified, poeticized, philosophized — and denounced. Youth is seen through the prism of young eyes and the sometimes distorted lens of the older generation (although age is not necessarily a distortion, for probably no one has captured the essence of the matter more clearly than George Wald in his famous talk at the Massachusetts Institute of Technology, March 4, 1969 — remarks which will be studied and quoted as long as men seek to understand what was happening at the bridge that linked the 1960's to the 1970's).

It is obviously artificial to compartmentalize these works, when youth so clearly serves as the crucible which holds it all — war, race, and the crimes of man against man wherever they may occur. Youth is the protagonist of our times. Youth is the conscience, the rebel, the arousing, disturbing force which stimulates the blunt and even bullying words of the Tooles and the Ottingers, those who insist that young people "should know their place," should not rock the boat, should sit quietly while their elders tell them how the world should be run. But youth will not be put down. It rejects the world into which it has been born and the faded image of the middle-aged. It sees war as a murderous force and while it can not easily imagine that force turned directly against itself it comes to understand this after Kent State.

The strength of Peter Marin's essay is his understanding of youth's search for the truth, for the meaning of life, the questions asked with open eyes and hopeful face, the lifting of the seashell to one's ear to listen for answers, the looking to the stars for light on the new path. The questing and the listening, the asking and the finding that, as Marin says, there are "no easy conclusions, no startling syntheses . . . only change in mood, a softening, a kind of sadness . . . a kind of city (of words) so natural, so familiar, that the other world, the one that appears to be will look by comparison, absurd and flat, limited and unnecessary."

It is summed up by Marks, who celebrates the coming of maturity, the end of adolescence and youth's certainty that it will inherit and, in fact, is at this very moment in the process of inheriting the earth. "Ah, yes, it's true, there were some really terrible things that went down in 1970. But just think of it — just think what a bright, strong light it took to cast such a dark shadow!"

This is the assurance of the meek who are bold enough to stand at the gateway to the promised land. Can they be right?

A Generation
in Search of a Future

Dr. George Wald, the Harvard biologist, delivered this address at the
"March 4" movement meeting at the Massachusetts Institute of Tech-
nology, March 4, 1969. It has been slightly excerpted.

ALL OF YOU KNOW that in the last couple of years there has been
student unrest breaking at times into violence in many parts of the
world: in England, Germany, Italy, Spain, Mexico, and needless
to say, in many parts of this country. There has been a great
deal of discussion as to what it all means. Perfectly clearly it
means something different in Mexico from what it does in France,
and something different in France from what it does in Tokyo, and
something different in Tokyo from what it does in this country.
Yet unless we are to assume that students have gone crazy all
over the world, or that they have just decided that it's the thing to
do, there must be some common meaning.

I am a teacher, and at Harvard, I have a class of about three
hundred fifty students — men and women — most of them fresh-
men and sophomores. Over these past few years I have felt increasingly that something is terribly wrong — and this year ever
so much more than last. Something has gone sour, in teaching
and in learning. It's almost as though there were a widespread
feeling that education has become irrelevant.

I think I know what's the matter. I think that this whole generation of students is beset with a profound uneasiness. I don't
think that they have yet quite defined its source. I think I understand the reasons for their uneasiness even better than they do.
What is more, I share their uneasiness.

What's bothering those students? Some of them tell you it's the
Vietnam war. I think the Vietnam war is the most shameful epi-
sode in the whole of American history. The concept of war crimes
is an American invention. We've committed many war crimes in
Vietnam; but I'll tell you something interesting about that. We
were committing war crimes in World War II, even before the
Nuremberg trials were held and the principle of war crimes
started. The saturation bombing of German cities was a war
crime and if we had lost the war, some of our leaders might have
had to answer for it. I've gone through all of that history lately,
and I find that there's a gimmick in it. It isn't written out, but I
think we established it by precedent. That gimmick is that if one
can allege that one is repelling or retaliating for an aggression —
after that everything goes. And, you see, we are living in a world
in which all wars are wars of defense. All War Departments are
now Defense Departments. This is all part of the double talk of
our time. The aggressor is always on the other side. And I suppose this is why our ex-Secretary of State, Dean Rusk — a man in
whom repetition takes the place of reason, and stubbornness takes
the place of character — went to such pains to insist, as he still
insists, that in Vietnam we are repelling an aggression.

I think we've lost that war, as a lot of other people think, too.
The Vietnamese have a secret weapon. It's their willingness to
die, beyond our willingness to kill. In effect they've been saying,
You can kill us, but you'll have to kill a lot of us, you may have to
kill all of us. And, thank heavens, we are not yet ready to do that.

Yet we have come a long way — far enough to sicken many
Americans, far enough even to sicken our fighting men. Far
enough so that our national symbols have gone sour. How many of
you can sing about "the rockets' red glare, bombs bursting in air"
without thinking, those are our bombs and our rockets bursting
over South Vietnamese villages? When those words were written,
we were a people struggling for freedom against oppression. Now
we are supporting real or thinly disguised military dictatorships
all over the world.

Part of my trouble with students is that almost all the students I teach were born since World War II. Just after World War II, a series of new and abnormal procedures came into American life. We regarded them at the time as temporary aberrations. We thought we would get back to normal American life some day. But those procedures have stayed with us now for more than twenty years, and those students of mine have never known anything else. They think those things are normal. They think we've always had a Pentagon, that we have always had a big army, and that we always had a draft. But those are all new things in American life; and I think that they are incompatible with what America meant before.

How many of you realize that just before World War II the entire American army including the Air Force numbered 139,000 men?

Now we have 3.5 million men under arms: about 600,000 in Vietnam, about 300,000 more in "support areas" elsewhere in the Pacific, about 250,000 in Germany. And there are a lot at home. Some months ago we were told that 300,000 National Guardsmen and 200,000 reservists had been specially trained for riot duty in the cities.

I say the Vietnam war is just an immediate incident, because so long as we keep the big army, it will always find things to do. If the Vietnam war stopped tomorrow, with that big a military establishment, the chances are that we would be in another such adventure abroad or at home before you knew it.

As for the draft: Don't reform the draft — get rid of it.

A peacetime draft is the most un-American thing I know.

A few months ago I received a letter from the Harvard Alumni Bulletin posing a series of questions that students might ask a professor involving what to do about the draft. I was asked to write what I would tell those students. All I had to say to those students was this: If any of them had decided to evade the draft and asked my help, I would help him in any way I could. I would feel as I suppose members of the underground railway felt in pre–Civil

War days, helping runaway slaves to get to Canada. It wasn't altogether a popular position then; but what do you think of it now?

A bill to stop the draft was recently introduced in the Senate (S. 503), sponsored by a group of senators that ran the gamut from McGovern and Hatfield to Barry Goldwater. I hope it goes through; but any time I find that Barry Goldwater and I are in agreement, that makes me take another look.

There is another thing being said closely connected with this: that to keep an adequate volunteer army, one would have to raise the pay considerably. That's said so positively and often that people believe it. I don't think it is true.

The great bulk of our present armed forces are genuine volunteers. Among first-term enlistments, 49 per cent are true volunteers. Another 30 per cent are so-called "reluctant volunteers," persons who volunteer under pressure of the draft. Only 21 per cent are draftees. All re-enlistments, of course, are true volunteers.

But there is something ever so much bigger and more important than the draft. The bigger thing, of course, is what ex-President Eisenhower warned us of, calling it the military-industrial complex. I am sad to say that we must begin to think of it now as the military–industrial–labor union complex. What happened under the plea of the Cold War was not only that we built up the first big peacetime army in our history, but we institutionalized it.

I don't think we can live with the present military establishment and its eighty- to a hundred-billion-dollar-a-year budget, and keep America anything like we have known it in the past. It is corrupting the life of the whole country. It is buying up everything in sight: industries, banks, investors, universities; and lately it seems also to have bought up the labor unions.

The Defense Department is always broke; but some of the things they do with that eighty billion dollars a year would make Buck Rogers envious. For example: the Rocky Mountain Arsenal on the outskirts of Denver was manufacturing a deadly nerve poison on such a scale that there was a problem of waste disposal. Nothing daunted, they dug a tunnel two miles deep under Denver, into which they have injected so much poisoned water that beginning a couple of years ago Denver began to experience a series of earth tremors of increasing severity. Now there is a grave fear of a major earthquake. An interesting debate is in progress as to whether Denver will be safer if that lake of poisoned water is removed or left in place.

Perhaps you have read also of those six thousand sheep that suddenly died in Skull Valley, Utah, killed by another nerve poison — a strange and, I believe, still unexplained accident, since the nearest testing seems to have been thirty miles away.

As for Vietnam, the expenditure of fire power has been frightening. Some of you may still remember Khe Sanh, a hamlet just south of the Demilitarized Zone, where a force of US Marines was beleaguered for a time. During that period we dropped on the perimeter of Khe Sanh more explosives than fell on Japan throughout World War II, and more than fell on the whole of Europe during the years 1942 and 1943.

One of the officers there was quoted as having said afterward, "It looks like the world caught smallpox and died."

The only point of government is to safeguard and foster life. Our government has become preoccupied with deaths, with the business of killing and being killed. So-called Defense now absorbs 60 per cent of the national budget, and about 12 per cent of the gross national product.

A lively debate is beginning again on whether or not we should deploy antiballistic missiles, the ABM. I don't have to talk about them; everyone else here is doing that. But I should like to mention a curious circumstance. In September, 1967, or about one and a half years ago, we had a meeting of M.I.T. and Harvard people, including experts on these matters, to talk about whether anything could be done to block the Sentinel system, the deployment of ABMs. Everyone present thought them undesirable; but a few of the most knowledgeable persons took what seemed to be the practical view: "Why fight about a dead issue? It has been decided; the funds have been appropriated. Let's go on from there."

Well, fortunately, it's not a dead issue.

An ABM is a nuclear weapon. It takes a nuclear weapon to stop a nuclear weapon. And our concern must be with the whole issue of nuclear weapons.

There is an entire semantics ready to deal with the sort of thing I am about to say. It involves such phrases as "Those are the facts of life." No — these are the facts of death. I don't accept them, and I advise you not to accept them. We are under repeated pressures to accept things that are presented to us as settled — decisions that have been made. Always there is the thought: Let's go on from there! But this time we don't see how to go on. We will have to stick with those issues.

We are told that the United States and Russia between them have by now stockpiles in nuclear weapons approximately the explosive power of fifteen tons of TNT for every man, woman, and child on earth. And now it is suggested that we must make more. All very regrettable, of course; but those are "the facts of life." We really would like to disarm; but our new Secretary of Defense has made the ingenious proposal that one must be practical. Now is that time to greatly increase our nuclear armaments so that we can disarm from a position of strength.

I think all of you know there is no adequate defense against massive nuclear attack. It is both easier and cheaper to circumvent any known nuclear defense system than to provide it. It's all pretty crazy. At the very moment we talk of deploying ABMs, we are also building the MIRV, the weapon to circumvent ABMs.

So far as I know, with everything working as well as can be hoped and all foreseeable precautions taken, the most conservative estimates of Americans killed in a major nuclear attack run to about fifty million. We have become callous to gruesome statistics, and this seems at first to be only another gruesome statistic. You think, Bang! — and next morning, if you're still there, you read in the newspapers that fifty million people were killed.

But that isn't the way it happens. When we killed close to two hundred thousand people with those first little, old-fashioned uranium bombs that we dropped on Hiroshima and Nagasaki, about the same number of persons were maimed, blinded, burned, poisoned, and otherwise doomed. A lot of them took a long time to die.

That's the way it would be. Not a bang, and a certain number of corpses to bury; but a nation filled with millions of helpless, maimed, tortured, and doomed survivors huddled with their families in shelters, with guns ready to fight off their neighbors, trying to get some uncontaminated food and water.

A few months ago Senator Richard Russell of Georgia ended a speech in the Senate with the words: "If we have to start over again with another Adam and Eve, I want them to be Americans; and I want them on this continent and not in Europe." That was a United States senator holding a patriotic speech. Well, here is a Nobel Laureate who thinks that those words are criminally insane.

How real is the threat of full-scale nuclear war? I have my own very inexpert idea, but realizing how little I know and fearful that I may be a little paranoid on this subject, I take every opportunity to ask reputed experts. I asked that question of a very distinguished professor of government at Harvard about a month ago. I asked him what sort of odds he would lay on the possibility of full-scale nuclear war within the foreseeable future. "Oh," he said comfortably, "I think I can give you a pretty good answer to that question. I estimate the probability of full-scale nuclear war, provided that the situation remains about as it is now, at 2 per cent per year. Anybody can do the simple calculation that shows that 2 per cent per year means that the chance of having that full-scale nuclear war by 1990 is about one in three, and by 2000 it is about fifty-fifty.

I think I know what is bothering the students. I think that what we are up against is a generation that is by no means sure that it has a future.

I am growing old, and my future so to speak is already behind me. But there are those students of mine who are in my mind always; there are my children, two of them now seven and nine, whose futures are infinitely more precious to me than my own. So it isn't just their generation; it's mine too. We're all in it together.

Are we to have a chance to live? We don't ask for prosperity, or security — only for a reasonable chance to live, to work out our destiny in peace and decency. Not to go down in history as the apocalyptic generation.

And it isn't only nuclear war. Another overwhelming threat is in the population explosion. That has not yet even begun to come under control. There is every indication that the world population will double before the year 2000; and there is a widespread expectation of famine on an unprecedented scale in many parts of the world. The experts tend to differ only in their estimates of when those famines will begin. Some think by 1980; others think they can be staved off until 1990; very few expect that they will not occur by the year 2000.

That is the problem. Unless we can be surer than we now are that this generation has a future, nothing else matters. It's not good enough to give it tender loving care, to supply it with breakfast foods, to buy it expensive educations. Those things don't mean anything unless this generation has a future. And we're not sure that it does.

I don't think that there are problems of youth, or student problems. All the real problems I know are grown-up problems.

Perhaps you will think me altogether absurd, or "academic," or hopelessly innocent — that is, until you think of the alternatives — if I say as I do to you now: we have to get rid of those nuclear weapons. There is nothing worth having that can be obtained by nuclear war — nothing material or ideological, no tradition that it can defend. It is utterly self-defeating. Those atom bombs represent an unusable weapon. The only use for an atom bomb is to keep somebody else from using it. It can give us no protection, but only the doubtful satisfaction of retaliation. Nuclear weapons offer us nothing but terror.

We have to get rid of those atomic weapons, here and everywhere. We cannot live with them.

I think we've reached a point of great decision, not just for our nation, not only for all humanity, but for life upon the Earth. I tell my students, with a feeling of pride that I hope they will share, that the carbon, nitrogen, and oxygen that make up 99 per cent of our living substance were cooked in the deep interiors of earlier generations of dying stars. Gathered up from the ends of the universe, over billions of years, eventually they came to form in part the substance of our sun, its planets, and ourselves. Three billion years ago life arose upon the Earth. It is the only life in the solar system. Many a star has since been born and died.

About two million years ago, man appeared. He has become the dominant species on the Earth. All other living things, animal and plant, live by his sufferance. He is the custodian of life on Earth, and in the solar system. It's a big responsibility. The thought that we're in competition with Russians or with Chinese is all a mistake, and trivial. We are one species, with a world to win. There's life all over this universe, but the only life in the solar system is on Earth; and in the whole universe, we are the only men.

Our business is with life, not death. Our challenge is to give what account we can of what becomes of life in the solar system, this corner of the universe that is our home and, most of all, what becomes of men — all men of all nations, colors, and creeds. It has become one world, a world for all men. It is only such a world that now can offer us life and the chance to go on.

The Open Truth
and Fiery Vehemence of Youth

This essay by Peter Marin, Director of Pacific High School, an experimental day school outside Palo Alto, California, is probably the single most important effort to understand young America at the turn of the decade of the 1970's. It was originally presented at the Center for Democratic Studies where Marin was a Visiting Fellow in 1969 and has since been reprinted widely. It is presented here in somewhat excerpted form.

IT IS MIDNIGHT and I am sitting here with my notes, enough of them to make two books and a half and a volume of posthumous fragments, trying to make some smaller sense of them than the grand maniacal design I have in my mind. I don't know where to begin. Once, traveling in summer across the country with a friend from Hollywood and my young son in a battered green Porsche, I stopped for lunch somewhere in Kansas on a Sunday morning. As we walked into the restaurant, bearded, wearing dark glasses and strange hats, and followed by my long-haired boy, one Kansas matron bent toward another and whispered: "I bet those two men have kidnaped that little girl." I took a deep breath and started to speak, but I did not know where to begin or how to explain just how many ways she was mistaken. Now, trying to write clearly about education and adolescence, I feel the same way.

For that reason I have chosen an eccentric method of composition, one that may seem fragmentary, jumpy, and broken. This article will be more like a letter, and the letter itself is an accumulation of impressions and ideas, a sampling of thoughts at once disconnected but related. There is a method to it that may disappear in its mild madness, but I do not know at this juncture how else to proceed.

An entire system is hiding behind this, just beginning to take form, and these notes are like a drawing, a preliminary sketch. I feel comfortable with that notion, more comfortable than with the idea of forcing them together, cutting and pasting to make a more conventional essay.

One theme, as you will see, runs through what I have written or thought: we must rethink our ideas of childhood and schooling. We must dismantle them and start again from scratch. Nothing else will do. Our visions of adolescence and education confine us to habit, rule perception out. We make do at the moment with a set of ideas inherited from the nineteenth century, from an industrial, relatively puritanical, repressive, and "localized" culture; we try to gum them like labels to new kinds of experience. But that won't do. Everything has changed. Adolescents are, each one of them, an arena in which the culture transforms itself or is torn between contrary impulses; they are the victims of a culture raging within itself like man and wife, a schizoid culture — and these children are the unfinished and grotesque products of that schism.

They are grotesque because we give them no help. They are forced to make among themselves adjustments to a tension that must be unbearable. They do the best they can, trying, in increasingly eccentric fashions, to make sense of things. But we adults seem to have withdrawn in defeat from that same struggle.

As for me, an adult, I think of myself as I write as an observer at a tribal war — an anthropologist, a combination of Gulliver and a correspondent sending home news by mule and boat. By the time you hear of it, things will have changed.

Adolescence: a few preliminary fragments . . .

(FROM MY STUDENT, V): *yr whole body moves in a trained way & you know that youve moved this way before & it contains all youve been taught its all rusty & slow something is pushing under that rusted mesh but* STILL YOU CANNOT MOVE *you are caught between 2 doors & the old one is much closer & you can grab it all the time but the other door it disappears that door you cant even scratch & kick (like the early settlers were stung by the new land) but this new land doesnt even touch you & you wonder if youre doing the right thing to get in.*

(FROM FRANZ KAFKA): *He feels imprisoned on this earth, he feels constricted; the melancholy, the impotence, the sicknesses, the feverish fancies of the captive afflict him; no comfort can comfort him, since it is merely comfort, gentle headsplitting comfort glazing the brutal fact of imprisonment. But if he is asked what he wants he cannot reply . . . He has no conception of freedom.*

(FROM TAPES RECORDED IN PACIFIC PALISADES, 1966, SEVERAL BOYS AND GIRLS AGED TWELVE TO FOURTEEN): — *Things are getting younger and younger. Girls twelve will do it now. One guy said I fuck a girl every Friday night. What sexual pleasure do you get out of this (he's very immature you know) and he would say, I don't know I'm just going to fuck.*

or

— How old are you? — *Twelve.* — Will you tell us your first experience with drugs, how you got into it? — *Well, the people I hung around with were big acid heads. So one day my friend asked me if I wanted to get stoned and I said yes. That was about five months ago and I've been getting on it ever since. Started taking LSD about one month ago. Took it eleven times in one month. I consider it a good thing. For getting high, smoking grass is better, or hashish — it's about six times stronger than marijuana.*

(FROM PAUL RADIN: Primitive Man As Philosopher): *It is conceivably demanding too much of a man to whom the pleasures of life are largely bound up with the life of contemplation and to whom analysis and introspection are the self-understood prerequisites for a proper understanding of the world, that he appreciate . . .*

expressions which are largely nonintellectual — where life seems, predominatingly, a discharge of physical vitality, a simple and naive release of emotions or an enjoyment of sensations for their own sake. Yet . . . it is just such an absorption in a life of sensations that is the outward characteristic of primitive peoples.

Can you see where my thought leads? It is precisely at this point, adolescence, when the rush of energies, that sea-sex, gravitation, the thrust of the ego up through layers of childhood, makes itself felt, that the person is once more like an infant, is swept once more by energies that are tidal, unfamiliar, and unyielding. He is in a sense born again, a fresh identity beset inside and out by the rush of new experience. It is at this point, too — when we seem compelled by a persistent lunacy to isolate him — that what is growing within the adolescent demands expression, requires it, and must, in addition, be received by the world and given form — or it will wither or turn to rage. Adolescence is a second infancy. It is then that a man desires solitude and at the same time contact with the vivid world.

In this condition, with these needs, the adolescent is like a primitive man, an apocalyptic primitive: he exists for the moment in that stage of single vision in which myth is still the raw stuff of being, he knows at first hand through his own energies the possibilities of life — but he knows these in muddled, sporadic, contradictory ways. The rush of his pubescent and raw energy seems at odds with public behavior, the *order* of things, the tenor of life around him, especially in a culture just emerging — as is ours — from a tradition of evasion, repression, and fear.

The contradictions within the culture itself intensify his individual confusion. We are at the moment torn between future and past: in the midst of a process of transformation we barely understand. The direction and depth of feeling responds accordingly; the adolescent tries — even as a form of self-defense against the pressure of his own energies — to move more freely, to change his styles of life, to "grow." But it is then that he finds he is locked into culture, trapped in a web of ideas, law, and rituals that keep him a child, deprive him of a chance to test and assimilate his newer self. It is now that the culture turns suddenly repressive.

Thus the young, in that vivid confrontation with the thrust of nature unfolding in themselves, are denied adult assistance. I once wrote that education through its limits denied the gods, and that they would return in the young in one form or another to haunt us. That is happening now. You can sense it as the students gather, with their simplistic moral certainty, at the gates of the universities. It is almost as if the young were once more possessed by Bacchanalian gods, were once again inhabited by divinities whose honor we have neglected. Those marvelous and threatening energies!

At times they seem almost shell-shocked, survivors of a holocaust in which the past has been destroyed and all the bridges to it bombed. I cannot describe with any certainty what occurs in their minds, but I do know that most adults must seem to the young like shrill critics speaking to them in an alien language about a Greek tragedy in which they may lose their lives. The words we use, our dress, our tones of voice, the styles of adult lives — all of these are so foreign to that dramatic crisis that as we approach them we seem to increase the distance we are trying to cross.

The inner events in an adolescent demand from what surrounds him life on a large scale, in a grand style. This is the impulse to apocalypse in the young, as if they were in exile from a nation that does not exist — and yet they can sense it, they know it is there — if only because their belief itself demands its presence.

Primitive cultures dealt with this problem, I think, through their initiation rites, the rites of passage; they legitimized and accepted these energies and turned them toward collective aims. In most initiation rites the participant is led through the mythical or sacred world (or a symbolic version) and is then returned, transformed, to the secular one as a new person, with a new role. He is introduced through the rites to a dramatic reality coexistent with the visible or social one and at its root. Occasionally the initiate is asked at some point to don the ritual mask himself — joining, as he does, one world with another and assuming the responsibility for their connection. This shift in status, in *relation*, is the heart of the rite; a liturgized merging of the individual with shared sources of power.

Do you see what I am driving at? The rites are in a sense a social contract, a binding up; one occurring specifically, profoundly, on a deep psychic level. The individual is redefined in the culture by his new relation to its mysteries, its gods, to one form or another of nature. These ritualized relationships of each man to the shared gods bind the group together; they form the substance of culture.

I hope that makes sense. That is the structure of the kaleidoscopic turning of culture that Blake makes in "The Crystal Cabinet," and it makes sense too, in America, in relation to adolescents. What fascinates me is that our public schools, designed for adolescents — who seem, as apocalyptic men, to demand this kind of drama, release, and support — educate and "socialize" their students by depriving them of everything the rites bestow.

We appear to have forgotten in our schools what every primitive tribe with its functional psychology knows: allegiance to the tribe can be forged only at the deepest levels of the psyche and in extreme circumstance demanding endurance, daring, and awe.

I believe that it is precisely this world that drugs replace; adolescents provide for themselves what we deny them: a confrontation with some kind of power within an unfamiliar landscape involving sensation and risk. It is there, I suppose, that they hope to find, by some hurried magic, a new way of seeing, a new relation to things, to discard one identity and assume another. They mean to find through their adventures the *ground* of reality, the resonance of life we deny them, as if they might come upon their

golden city and return still inside it: at home. You can see the real
veterans sometimes on the street in strange costumes they have
stolen from dreams.

When you begin to think about adolescence in this way, what
sense can you make of our schools? None of the proposed changes
makes sense to me. The changes suggested and debated don't go
deeply enough; they don't question or change enough.

In few other cultures have persons of fifteen or eighteen been so
uselessly isolated from participation in the community, or been
deemed so unnecessary (in their elders' eyes), or so limited by
law. Our ideas of responsibility, our parental feelings of anxiety,
blame, and guilt, all of these follow from our curious vision of the
young; in turn, they concretize it, legitimize it so that we are no
longer even conscious of the ways we see childhood or the strain
that our vision puts upon us. That is what needs changing: the
definitions we make socially and legally of the role of the young.

In general the school system we have inherited seems to me
based upon three particular things:

1. What Paul Goodman calls the idea of "natural depravity":
our puritanical vision of human nature in which children are perceived as sinners or "savages" and in which human impulse or desire is not to be trusted and must therefore be constrained or
"trained."

2. The necessity during the mid-nineteenth century of "Ameri-
canizing" great masses of immigrant children from diverse back-
grounds and creating, through the schools, a common experience
and character.

3. The need in an industrialized state for energy and labor to
run the machines: the state, needing workers, educates persons to
be technically capable but relatively dependent and responsive to
authority so that their energies will be available when needed.

These elements combine with others — the labor laws that
make childhood a "legal" state, and a population explosion that
makes it necessary now to keep adolescents off both the labor

market and the idle street — to "freeze" into a school system that resists change even as the culture itself and its needs shift radically. But teachers can't usually see that. Time and again, speaking to them, one hears the same questions and anguish:

"But what will happen to the students if they don't go to school?" "How will they learn?" "What will they do without adults?"

Most learning — especially the process of socialization or acculturation — has gone on outside schools, more naturally, in the fabric of the culture. In most cultures the passage from childhood to maturity occurs because of social necessity.

We seem to have lost all sense of that. The school is expected to do what the community cannot do and that is impossible. In the end, we will have to change far more than the schools if we expect to create a new coherence between the experiences of the child and the needs of the community. We will have to rethink the meaning of childhood; we will begin to grant greater freedom *and* responsibility to the young; we will drop the compulsory-schooling age to fourteen, perhaps less; we will take for granted the "independence" of adolescents and provide them with the chance to live alone, away from parents and with peers. At some point, perhaps, we will even find that the community itself — in return for a minimum of work or continued schooling — will provide a minimal income to young people that will allow them to assume the responsibility for their own lives at an earlier age, and learn the ways of the community outside the school; finally, having lowered the level of compulsory schooling, we will find it necessary to provide different *kinds* of schools, a wider choice, so that students will be willing voluntarily to continue the schooling that suits their needs and aims.

All these changes, of course, are aimed at two things: the restoration of the child's "natural" place in the community and lowering the age at which a person is considered an independent member of the community.

•

One problem, put simply, is that in every school I have visited, public or private, traditional or "innovational," the students have only these two choices: to drop out (either physically or mentally) or to make themselves smaller and smaller until they can act in ways their elders expect. One of my students picked up a phrase I once used, "the larger and smaller worlds." The schools we visit together, he says, are always the smaller world: smaller at least than his imagination, smaller than the potential of the young. The students are asked to put aside the best things about themselves — their own desires, impulses, and ideas — in order to "adjust" to an environment constructed for children who existed one hundred years ago, if at all.

I don't know. I know only that during the Middle Ages they sometimes "created" jesters by putting young children in boxes and force-feeding them so that, as they grew, their bones would warp in unusual shapes. That is often how the schools seem to me. Students are trapped in the boxes of pedagogic ideas, and I am tempted to say to teachers again and again: more, much more, you must go further, create more space in the schools, you must go deeper in thought, create more resonance, a different feeling, a different and more human, more daring style.

Even the best teachers, with the best intentions, seem to diminish their students as they work through the public-school system.

In one way or another our methods produce in the young a condition of pain that seems very close to a mass neurosis: a lack of faith in oneself, a vacuum of spirit into which authority or institutions can move, a dependency they feed on. Students are encouraged to relinquish their own wills, their freedom of volition; they are taught that value and culture reside outside oneself and must be acquired from the institution, and almost everything in their education is designed to discourage them from activity, from the wedding of idea and act.

The system breeds obedience, frustration, dependence, and fear: a kind of gentle violence that is usually turned against one-

self, one that is sorrowful and full of guilt, but a violence nonetheless, and one realizes that what is done in the schools to persons is
deeply connected to what we did to the blacks or are doing now in
Vietnam. That is: we don't teach hate in the schools, or murder,
but we do isolate the individual; we empty him of life by ignoring
or suppressing his impulse toward life; we breed in him a lack of
respect for it, a loss of love — and thus we produce gently "good"
but threatened men, men who will kill without passion, out of
duty and obedience, men who have in themselves little sense of
the vivid life being lost nor the moral strength to refuse.

From first to twelfth grade we acclimatize students to a fundamental deadness and teach them to restrain themselves for the
sake of "order." The net result is a kind of pervasive cultural in-
version in which they are asked to separate at the most profound
levels their own experience from institutional reality, self from society, objective from subjective, energy from order — though
these various polarities are precisely those which must be made
coherent during adolescence.

I remember a talk I had with a college student.

"You know what I love to do?" he said. "I love to go into the
woods and run among the trees."

"Very nice," I said.

"But it worries me. We shouldn't do it."

"Why not?" I asked.

"Because we get excited. It isn't *orderly*."

"Not orderly?"

"Not orderly."

"Do you run into the trees?" I asked.

"Of course not."

"Then it's orderly," I said.

In a small way this exchange indicates the kind of thinking we
encourage in the schools: the mistaking of rigidity and stillness
for order, of order as the absence of life.

The end of learning is wisdom and wisdom to me, falling back as I do on a Jewish tradition, is, in its simplest sense, "intelligent activity" or, more completely, the suffusion of activity with knowledge, a wedding of the two. For the Hassidic Jews every gesture was potentially holy, a form of prayer, when it was made with a reverence for God. In the same way a gesture is always a form of wisdom — an act is wisdom — when it is suffused with knowledge, made with a reverence for the truth.

Does that sound rhetorical? I suppose it does. But I mean it. The end of education is intelligent activity, *wisdom*, and that demands a merging of opposites, a sense of process. Instead we produce the opposite: immobility, insecurity, an inability to act without institutional blessing or direction, or, at the opposite pole, a headlong rush toward motion without balance or thought. We cut into the natural movement of learning and try to force upon the students the end product, abstraction, while eliminating experience and ignoring their perception. The beginning of thought is in the experience through one's self of a particular environment — school, community, culture. When this is ignored, as it is in schools, the natural relation of self and knowledge is broken, the parts of the process become polar opposites, antitheses, and the young are forced to choose between them: objectivity, order, and obedience as against subjectivity, chaos, and energy. It doesn't really matter which they choose; as long as the two sets seem irreconcilable their learning remains incomplete. Caught between the two, they suffer our intellectual schizophrenia until it occupies them, too. They wait. They sit. They listen. They learn to "behave" at the expense of themselves. Or else — and you can see it happening now — they turn against it with a vengeance and may shout, as they did at Columbia, "Kill all adults," for they have allied themselves with raw energy against reason and balance — our delicate, hard-won virtues — and we should not be surprised.

Students don't need the artificiality of schools; they respond more fully and more intelligently when they make direct contact with the community and are allowed to choose roles that have some utility for the community and themselves. What is at stake here, I suppose, is the freedom of volition.

Thus, it seems inescapably clear that our first obligation to the young is to create a place in the community for them to act with volition and freedom. They are ready for it, certainly, even if we aren't. Adolescents seem to need at least some sense of risk and gain "out there" in the world: an existential sense of themselves that is vivid to the extent that the dangers faced are "real." The students I have worked with seem strongest and most alive when they are in the mountains of Mexico or the Oakland ghetto or out in the desert or simply hitchhiking or riding freights to see what's happening. They thrive on distance and motion — and the right to solitude when they want it. Many of them want jobs; they themselves arrange to be teachers in day-care centers, political canvassers, tutors, poolroom attendants, actors, governesses, gardeners. They returned from these experiences immeasurably brightened and more sure of themselves, more willing, in that new assurance, to learn many of the abstract ideas we had been straining to teach them.

What we were after was a *feeling* to the place: a sense of intensity and space. We discarded the idea of the microcosm and replaced it with an increased openness and access to the larger community. The campus itself became a place to come back to for rest or discussion or thought. What students learned at the school was simply the feel of things; the sense of themselves as makers of value; the realization that the environment is at best an extension of men and that it can be transformed by them into what they vitally need.

What we tried to create was a flexible environment, what a designer I know has called permissive space. It was meant to be in a sense a model for the condition in which men find themselves, in which the responsibility of a man was to make connections, value, and sense. We eliminated from the school all preconceptions about what was proper, best, or useful; we gave up rules and penalties. What we were after was a "guilt-free" environment, one in which the students might become or discover what they were without having to worry about preconceived ideas of what they had to be.

What we found was that our students seemed to need, most of all, relief from their own "childhood" — what was expected of them. Some of them needed merely to rest, to withdraw from the strange grid of adult expectation and demand for lengthy periods of introspection in which they appeared to grow mysteriously, almost like plants. But an even greater number seemed to need independent commerce with the world outside the school: new sorts of social existence. Nothing could replace that.

We came to see that learning is natural, yes, but it results naturally from most things adolescents do. By associating learning with one particular form of intellection and insisting upon that in school we make a grave error.

Indeed, it is hard for them to do anything without some kind of learning, but that may be what we secretly fear — that those other forms of learning will make them less manageable or less like ourselves. That, after all, may be one reason we use all those books. Levi-Strauss insists on the relation of increased literacy and the power of the state over the individual. It may well be that dependence on print and abstraction is one of the devices we use to make students manipulable. When we permitted students the freedom of choice and gave them easy access to the community, we found that ideas acquired weight and value to the extent that students were allowed to try them out in action. We learned to take their risks with them — and to survive. In that sense we became equals, and that equality may in the end be more educational for students than anything else. That, in fact, may be the most important thing we learned.

In some ways it is compulsory schooling itself which is the problem, for without real choice students will remain locked in childhood and schools, away from whatever is vivid in life. But real choice, as we know, includes dominion over one's own time and energies, and the right to come and go on the basis of what has actual importance. And I wonder if we will ever get round, given all our fears, to granting that privilege to students.

.

One thing alone of all I have read has made recent sense to me concerning adolescents. That is the implicit suggestion in Erik Erikson's *Young Man Luther* that every sensitive man experiences in himself the conflicts and contradictions of his age. The great man, he suggests, is the man who articulates and resolves these conflicts in a way that has meaning for his time; that is, he is himself, as was Luther, a victim of his time and its vehicle and, finally, a kind of resolution.

If there is such a shared condition it seems to me a crucial point, for it means that there is never any real distance between a man and his culture, no real isolation or alienation from society. It means that adolescents are not in their untutored state cut off from culture nor outside it. It means instead that each adolescent is an arena in which the contradictions and currents sweeping through the culture must somehow be resolved.

Do you see where this leads? I am straining here to get past the idea of the adolescent as an isolate and deviant creature who must be joined — as if glued and clamped — to the culture. For we ordinarily think of schools, though not quite consciously, as the "culture" itself, little models of society.

The problem is a different one: What kind of setting will enable him to discover and accept what is already within him; to articulate it and perceive the extent to which it is shared with others; and, finally, to learn to change it within and outside himself? For that is what I mean when I call the adolescent a "maker of value." He is a trustee, a trustee of a world that already exists in some form within himself — and we must both learn, the adolescent and his teachers, to respect it.

In a sense, then, I am calling for a reversal of most educational thought. The individual is central; the individual, in the deepest sense, *is* the culture, not the institution. His culture resides in him, in experience and memory, and what is needed is an education that has at its base the sanctity of the individual's experience and leaves it intact.

What keeps running through my mind is a line I read twelve years ago in a friend's first published story: *The Idea in that idea is: there is no one over you.* I like that line: *There is no one over you.* Perhaps that signifies the gap between these children and their parents. For the children it is true, they sense it: there is no one over them; believable authority has disappeared; it has been replaced by experience. As Thomas Altizer says, God is dead; he is experienced now not as someone above or omnipotent or omniscient or "outside," but inwardly, as conscience or vision or even the unconscious or Tillich's "ground of being." This is all too familiar to bother with here, but this particular generation is a collective dividing point. The parents of these children, the fathers, still believe in "someone" over them, insist upon it; in fact, demand it for and from their children. The children themselves cannot believe it; the idea means nothing to them.

This is, then, a kind of Reformation. Arnold was wrong when he said that art would replace religion; education replaced it. Church became School, the principal vehicle for value, for "culture," and just as men once rebelled against the established Church as the mediator between God and man, students now rebel against the *public* school (and its version of things) as the intermediary between themselves and experience, between themselves and experience and the making of value.

I remember one moment in the streets of Oakland during the draft demonstrations. The students had sealed off the street with overturned cars and there were no police; the gutters were empty and the students moved into them from the sidewalks, first walking, then running, and finally almost dancing in the street. You could almost see the idea coalesce on their faces: The street is ours! It was as if a weight had been lifted from them, a fog; there was not at that moment any fury in them, any vengefulness or even politics; rather, a lightness, delight, an exhilaration at the sudden inexplicable sense of being free. George Orwell describes something similar in *Homage to Catalonia:* that brief period in Barcelona when the anarchists had apparently succeeded and men shared what power there was.

That sudden feeling is familiar to us all. We have all had it from time to time in our own lives, that sense of "being at home," that ease, that feeling of a Paradise which is neither behind us nor deferred but is around us, a natural household. It is the hint and beginning of Manhood: a promise, a clue. One's attention turns to the immediate landscape and to one's fellows: toward what is there, toward what can be felt as a part of oneself. I have seen the same thing as I watched Stokely Carmichael speaking to a black audience and telling them that they must stop begging the white man, like children, for their rights. They were, he said, neither children nor slaves, no, they were — and here they chanted, almost cried, in unison — a beautiful people: *yes our noses are broad and our lips are thick and our hair is kinky . . . but we are beautiful, we are beautiful, we are black and beautiful.*

But there is a kind of pain in being white and watching that, for there is no one to say the same things to white children; no "fathers" or brothers to give them that sense of manhood or pride. The adolescents I have seen — white, middle-class — are a long way from those words *we are beautiful, we are beautiful.* I cannot imagine how they will reach them, deprived as they are of all individual strength.

It is this feeling that pervades both high school and college, this Kafkaesque sense of faceless authority that drives one to rebellion or withdrawal, and we are all, for that reason, enchanted by the idea of the Trial, that ancient Socratic dream of confrontation and vindication or martyrdom. It is then, of course, that Authority shows its face. In the mid-fifties I once watched Jack Kerouac on a television show and when the interviewer asked him what he wanted he said: to see the face of God. How arrogant and childish and direct! And yet, I suppose, it is what we all want as children: to have the masks of authority, all its disguises, removed and to see it plain. That is what lies in large part behind the riots in the schools.

The schools seem to enforce the idea that there *is* someone over you; and the methods by which they do it are ritualized, pervasive. The intrusion of guilt, shame, alienation from oneself, dependence, insecurity — all these feelings are not the accidental results of schools; they are intentional, and they are used in an attempt to make children manipulable, obedient, "good citizens" we call it, and useful to the state.

But I must admit this troubles me, for there is little choice between mindless violence and mindless authority, and I am just enough of an academic, an intellectual, to want to preserve much of what will be lost in the kind of rebellion or apocalypse that is approaching. And yet, and yet . . . the rapidity of events leaves me with no clear idea, no solution, no sense of what will be an adequate change. It may be that all of this chaos is a way of breaking with the old world and that from it some kind of native American will emerge.

I believe that the young must have values, of course, be responsible, care, but I know too that most of the violence I have seen done to the young has been done in the name of value, and that the well-meaning people who have been so dead set on making things right have had a hand in bringing us to where we are now. The paradox is a deep and troubling one for me. I no longer know if change can be accomplished — for the young, for any of us, without the apocalyptic fury that seems almost upon us. The crisis of youth and education is symptomatic of some larger, deeper fault in our cities and minds, and perhaps nothing can be done consciously in those areas until the air itself is violently cleared one way or another.

So I have no easy conclusions, no startling synthesis with which to close. I have only a change in mood, a softening, a kind of sadness. It may be, given that, that the best thing is simply to close with an unfinished fragment in which I catch for myself the hint of an alternative:

. . . *I am trying to surround you, I see that, I am trying to make with these words a kind of city so natural, so familiar, that the other world, the one that appears to be, will look by comparison absurd and flat, limited, unnecessary. What I am after is liberation, not my own, which comes often enough these days in solitude or sex, but yours, and that is arrogant, isn't it, that is presumptuous, and yet that is the function of art: to set you free. It is that too which is the end of education: a liberation from childhood and what holds us there, a kind of midwifery, as if the nation itself were in labor and one wanted to save both the future and the past — for we are both, we are, we are the thin bridge swaying between them, and to tear one from the other means a tearing of ourselves, a partial death.*

And yet it may be that death is inevitable, useful. It may be. Perhaps, as in the myth, Aphrodite can rise only where Cronos's testicles have fallen into the sea. It may be that way with us. The death of the Father who is in us, the death of the old authority which is part of us, the death of the past which is also our death; it may all be necessary: a rending and purgation. And yet one still seeks another way, something less (or is it more) apocalyptic, a way in which the past becomes the future in ourselves, in which we become the bridges between: makers of culture.

Unless from us the future takes place, we are Death only, *said Lawrence, meaning what the Chassids do: that the world and time reside within, not outside, men; that there is no distance, no "alienation," only a perpetual wedding to the world. It is that — the presence in oneself of Time — that makes things interesting, is more gravid and interesting than guilt. I don't want to lose it, don't want to relinquish that sense in the body of another dimen-*

sion, a distance, the depth of the body as it extends backward into the past and forward, as it contains and extends and transforms.

What I am after is an alternative to separation and rage, some kind of connection to things to replace the system of dependence and submission — the loss of the self — that now holds sway, slanted toward violence. I am trying to articulate a way of seeing, of feeling, that will restore to the young a sense of manhood and potency without at the same time destroying the past. That same theme runs through whatever I write: the necessity for each man to experience himself as an extension and maker of culture, and to feel the whole force of the world within himself, not as an enemy — but as himself:

. . . An act of learning is a meeting, and every meeting is simply the discovery in the world of a part of oneself that had previously been unacknowledged by the self. It is the recovery of the extent of one's being. It is the embrace of an eternal but elusive companion, the shadowy "other" in which one truly resides and which blazes, when embraced, like the sun.

Our Beloved Sandy Is Gone Forever

Martin Scheuer, 269 Millcreek Drive, Boardman, Ohio, is the father of Sandy Scheuer, killed with Allison Krause, William Schroeder and Jeffrey Miller at Kent State on May 4, 1970.

SHE WAS THE MOST PRECIOUS JEWEL in our life, she was everything we lived for, and now our lives are an empty shell. Sandy represented everything good in this world. She was a gentle girl blessed with a fine sense of humor, a love for life tempered with compassionate concern for the misfortunes of others — qualities which made her warm personality so appealing to all who knew her. What greater anguish is there than the thought that Sandy's devotion to her studies, her desire to help people, and her ability to fulfill this desire in the field of speech therapy should lead her into the path of a bullet, shot through her lovely neck?

For those on this planet who enjoy American citizenship, their right to life and liberty is guaranteed by the most stirring and inspiring document ever penned by man. Sandy was an American, as were the three who perished with her. They were killed by a state militia without benefit of due process. Yet there is a reluctance to render justice, to uphold their constitutional rights, and this reluctance touches us all, because it damages our reputation as a nation of honorable people.

On May 3, 1970, Governor Rhodes of Ohio unleashed the kind of irresponsible and inflammatory rhetoric we associated with Hitler and his cohorts.

"We are going to employ every weapon possible," he said. "No one is safe in Portage County."

He categorized student demonstrators as the "worst type of people we harbor in America," and then, to his eternal shame, cried: "We are going to eradicate this problem in Ohio."

This calculated attempt by Governor Rhodes to salvage his waning chances of winning the Republican primary race for the US Senate no doubt left a deep impression on some of those tired and angry guardsmen. Prior to their arrival in Kent, they were subjected to injuries and abuse at the hands of tough strikers. But Kent State was somehow different. The antagonists were college kids, and Rhodes made it clear that when students get out of hand, they are to be crushed by whatever means necessary. The next day, his words still fresh in their minds, some of the guardsmen felt unsafe; some saw the students as enemies; some used their combat weapons, and one of them eradicated my daughter as she walked to class some 300 feet away. Nearby, Allison Krause lay dying; ROTC student William Schroeder lay prone, unable to comprehend what had happened to him, and why, and on a path 275 feet from the guardsmen Jeffrey Miller lay dead.

The cruel injustice in these deaths is self-evident in the actions of General Canterbury and university president Robert White. The general's pathetic inability to control his men was compounded by his contemptible effort to escape criticism by deliberately distorting the truth and arousing public animosity toward the students — particularly the four who died. The absence of White, enjoying lunch at a nearby restaurant for one and a half hours with the knowledge of the planned rally at noon, as well as Canterbury's determination to forcefully disperse any assembly, exhibited an inexcusable lack of judgment.

America's rush to judgment on Kent State shocked and embittered me. I believe in our sense of justice and the American people's fierce pride in our ability to distinguish right from wrong — the kind of morbid conscience that is democracy and in which Sandy believed so deeply. But now, having judged in the passions of last May, most Americans no longer care that the reasons given by the Ohio National Guard for the shooting have been rejected by the Justice Department as unsubstantiated by the facts. Who is listening when James Michener says, "No student did anything that day for which he deserved to be shot"?

Human beings were so important to Sandy, and although she believed it was senseless to send her brothers to die in Vietnam, she was not politically active. Instead she directed her energies to helping others through caring and love and making them laugh.

"She was just a happy kid," her roommate said after her death, "and we shall forever remember her beautiful laughter."

This terrible wrong cannot be ignored, if we are a nation of just and honorable people.

Our beloved Sandy is gone, but we cannot believe she has no kindred souls now willing to be her advocates in the halls of justice.

The Crime at Kent State

These are the conclusions (slightly excerpted) of the report by Peter Davies of the Board of Christian Social Concerns of the United Methodist Church in 1971 on the Kent State killings.

THE KILLING OF FOUR STUDENTS at Kent State now stands as a classic example of justice delayed, circumvented and mocked. Very few tragedies like this are so extensively photographed, and very few occur in conditions where so many witnesses are able to provide investigators with so much invaluable information. Unlike the inexcusable shootings at South Carolina State in 1968, and Jackson State in 1970, the killing at Kent State took place in broad daylight beneath a brilliant sun. Consequently, we have an almost step-by-step record of what happened on May 4, 1970, and this record suggests that the shooting began as the result of a planned and prearranged act involving a certain number of guardsmen. Nothing occurred at Kent State to compare with the assault upon these same units by strikers in Cleveland. At the time of the shooting no student was closer than sixty feet in the area into which the firing would be directed. At the moment of the supposed "grave threat" to the lives of the guardsmen they had their backs to this "threat" and, therefore, were incapable of evaluating its gravity. The sudden turn upon the sound of a shot, the incredible precision of that turn, the number of guardsmen involved in that sudden turn, the advance back toward the parking lot "led by a man with a forty-five," the deliberate aiming into the parking lot where certain students had harassed them five to ten minutes earlier, the pointed disinterest in so many students close by them along the terrace of Taylor Hall who could be considered a "threat." All of these facts strongly indicate the execution of a conspiracy.

Section 241 of the United States Code, Title 18, provides the Department of Justice the statute necessary to convene a federal grand jury for the purpose of investigating every aspect of the points raised in this appeal, an investigation the Ohio National Guard has so desperately sought to prevent by whatever means necessary. One judicial decision on Section 241 bears inclusion here:

> It is not necessary to find the conspiracy charged was formed against a particular individual, but it is sufficient if it appears that he was included in a class actually conspired against.

I submit the conduct of a number of Ohio National Guardsmen from the time they were on the practice field to the time they ceased shooting was such it "appears" that Allison Krause, Jeffrey Miller, Alan Canfora and several other Kent State students were "included" in the "class" conspired against, i.e., college dissenters, longhairs, college girls using obscenities, campus hippies and antiwar demonstrators.

To deny the existence of an element in our society whose hatred for student protesters is such they do not only approve of the killings, but genuinely wish more had been shot is to deny reality. To assume that a uniform, whether of the police or the National Guard, cleanses the wearer of his prejudices is to assume he is not a human being. Who can deny, without an investigation, that there might not have been a man in Troop G and Company A who had recently been incensed by the sight of campus disorders at Ohio State and elsewhere on his television screen and perchance expressed his belief that a good shooting would put an end to their nonsense only to suddenly find himself face to face with the object of his anger and an M-1 or .45 pistol in his hand?

Justice delayed is not only justice denied, it is the undermining of the very system of justice. But beyond that, by what law do we deny the parents of those killed and wounded the right to know exactly what their children did that day, exactly what the FBI investigation found concerning their children that day, and precisely why their children were shot, especially those who were shot to death when all of them were nowhere near the National Guard to pose any kind of threat at all? The parents, and the American people, have a right to know the answers to all these questions. This is not a police state where people are shot down by the militia and the nation compelled to accept without question the reasons given by those responsible for the shooting.

Four human lives were not only inexcusably destroyed; they may very well have been deliberately taken by a number of men using their uniform, anonymity and subsequent lies to satisfy their personal animosity toward a "class of persons" they had decided were long overdue for punishment. It was time they were taught a lesson. It was, as one guardsman said, "Time they got it like that." That this might be possible is deeply disturbing to the orderly routine of our lives because it raises the horror and the specter of another My Lai.

In this case, the victims are Americans, and the site of the massacre is an American campus. It is too much for the mind to contemplate let alone accept.

We would much prefer to let the dead rest in peace and the reasons why they are dead at nineteen and twenty remain buried with them. Unfortunately, however, we must also reconcile their deaths with our Constitution and our laws. We would rather forget about Kent State than face up to this challenge. Why? Because to do so would require our submitting every aspect of the events of May 4, 1970, to our judicial process, and we know that to do so could culminate in several convictions of Ohio National Guardsmen for first degree murder.

Is it possible that this administration does not want to expose itself to the public reaction which was unleashed by the conviction of Lieutenant Calley? Why else is the Department of Justice so reluctant to expose the Ohio National Guard to the scrutiny of a federal grand jury? Why else did the state of Ohio convene a grand jury for the sole purpose of exonerating the National Guard of any responsibility for the four deaths and nine injuries? Why else does the Attorney General of the United States suggest that the "intervening action" of the Ohio grand jury "affect" his department's deliberations without mentioning that their exoneration of the Guard has been declared unconstitutional by a federal court? Why else are the parents of the dead being denied the public judicial forum of a courtroom to compel Generals Del Corso and Canterbury to prove that the killing of their children was justified?

The answers to these questions, as recent American history has taught us, are painfully obvious. First, those primarily responsible for creating the atmosphere and conditions conducive to this kind of official act of violence have always been protected no matter how many lives were deliberately destroyed, particularly when the dead are seemingly as insignificant as blacks or students. Who are these human beings of such power in this instance? One is former Governor James Rhodes of Ohio. This is the man who authorized the sending of troops onto the Kent State campus with live ammunition and then, after the guardsmen were there, went to Kent and whipped up hatred and emotions in a speech obviously designed to enhance his chances of winning a primary for the United States Senate. Did he use Kent State for political profit? He uttered wild and irrational statements totally unsubstantiated factually and accused his opponent, Robert Taft, Jr., of being "soft" on campus disturbances. He obviously seized upon the situation at Kent State in the hope that it would salvage his waning chances of winning the primary. The minds of some National Guardsmen inferred free license to shoot at students. Why?

The governor categorized them [the students] as "the worst type of people we harbor in America today." The extent of his culpability in the killing of the four students will never be established as long as the courts protect him from having to answer for his conduct.

Another gentleman of such power is General Del Corso who, at the same news conference on May 3, when Rhodes fished so desperately for votes, stated publicly that every means under the Guard's authority would be utilized to crush the Kent State uprising, including "shooting" if necessary. To some guardsmen this could have been the seal of approval from their adjutant general to use the license they believed the governor had granted them.

The appalling façade of officialdom's integrity, loyalty and devotion to duty has plagued our society for far too long. At My Lai this nation squarely faced its responsibility as a democracy in a world torn between two diametrically opposed ideologies. That we did so can only enhance our stature in this conflict and command the respect of nations wavering on the brink between our concept of society and the totalitarian concept of domination and injustice.

At Kent State we are faced with the same responsibility in a domestic concept. We are a nation torn between two opposing attitudes on priorities with a great many Americans wavering on the brink between the two concepts of national urgency. The tragic deaths at Kent State provide us with the unhappy, but unique, opportunity to demonstrate to our children that the hypocrisy, the lies, the self-preservation at any price, the contemptible façade is not more important than human life when those lives might have been taken deliberately with malice of forethought, as were the lives of those old men, mothers, young women and children at My Lai. Kent State, whether we like it or not, is America's My Lai in Ohio. If we fail to do what the United States Army has already done, then we are subscribing to the very philosophy we, as a people, have abhorred and sacrificed our lives to oppose — the philosophy that the state can do no wrong.

On November 5 last year the Akron *Beacon Journal* editorially took note of the fact the Justice Department has reason to believe some Ohio guardsmen were lying when they claimed they fired in "self-defense." This conclusion by the Department, the editorial said, "merits a full presentation of all relevant evidence to a federal grand jury." The *Beacon Journal* expressed the belief that "many persons will lose confidence in our judicial system unless the facts go to a federal grand jury." Many Americans, however, feel there have been more than enough investigations of Kent State and that nothing can be gained from rehashing the tragedy before a federal grand jury. The truth of the matter is that there has been but one investigation of any consequence, and that one ended up being consigned to the incinerator by a federal judge. Why should there be a federal grand jury inquiry? The *Beacon Journal* says: "Because of the involvement of the National Guard, which is an arm of the federal defense establishment, and because of the possibility that an infringement of federal civil rights laws may be involved, presentation of evidence to a federal grand jury becomes necessary." Those reasons alone warrant the convening of such an investigation. The President's Commission was powerless to explore any possible criminal acts on the part of guardsmen or students and steered clear of any questioning which could possibly be construed as touching upon criminal responsibility for the four deaths. Consequently, the Kent State tragedy has yet to be investigated in accordance with the provisions of federal laws applicable to this case in which four Americans were shot to death. In both the Orangeburg and Jackson State tragedies, the Department of Justice convened federal grand juries despite the intervening action of local grand juries, and neither of the local findings were ruled unconstitutional by a federal court.

In view of these known facts, it appears that the principal reason the Justice Department has not yet fulfilled its obligation imposed by our Constitution is a reluctance to submit to a grand jury the ballistics, photographic and physical evidence now available for such an investigation. This evidence indicates that murder was committed at Kent State, as Vice President Agnew asserted over a year ago, and as others have intimated recently. The Ohio National Guard claims the shooting was justified and, therefore, the killings were justified. The Guard has yet to be called upon to produce any evidence to substantiate their claim. Why are we so reluctant to make this demand of the Ohio National Guard?

The President of the United States, in a letter to William Scranton, chairman of his Commission on Campus Unrest, said, "Law enforcement officers should use only the minimum force necessary in dealing with disorders when they arise. A human life," said the President, "the life of a student, soldier or police officer, is a precious thing, and the taking of a life can be justified only as a necessary and last resort." Two young women and two young men were shot to death at Kent State. Was the taking of those four precious lives a necessary and last resort?

No Room for Slobs

Dr. K. Ross Toole, professor of history at the University of Montana at Missoula, originally wrote this as a letter to his brother at the end of the school year 1969–70.

I AM FORTY-NINE YEARS OLD. It took me many years and considerable anguish to get where I am — which isn't much of any place except exurbia. I was nurtured in depression; I lost four years to war; I am invested with sweat; I have had one coronary; I am a "liberal," square, and I am a professor. I am sick of the "younger generation," hippies, Yippies, militants and nonsense.

I am a professor of history at the University of Montana, and I am supposed to have "liaison" with the young. Worse still, I am father of seven children. They range in age from seven to twenty-three — and I am fed up with nonsense. I am tired of being blamed, maimed and contrite; I am tired of tolerance and the reaching out (which is always my function) for understanding. I am sick of the total irrationality of the campus "rebel," whose bearded visage, dirty hair, body odor and "tactics" are childish but brutal, naive but dangerous, and the essence of arrogant tyranny — the tyranny of spoiled brats.

I am terribly disturbed that I may be incubating more of the same. Our household is permissive, our approach to discipline is an apology and a retreat from standards — usually accompanied by a gift in cash or kind.

It's time to call a halt, time to live in an adult world where we belong and time to put these people in their places. We owe the

"younger generation" what all "older generations" have owed
younger generations — love, protection to a point and respect
when they deserve it. We do not owe them our souls, our privacy,
our whole lives, and above all, we do not owe them immunity
from our mistakes, or their own.

Every generation makes mistakes, always has and always will.
We have made our share. But my generation has made America
the most affluent country on earth; it has tackled, head-on, a racial
problem which no nation on earth in the history of mankind had
dared to do. It has publicly declared war on poverty and it has
gone to the moon; it has desegregated schools and abolished polio;
it has presided over the beginning of what is probably the greatest
social and economic revolution in man's history. It has begun
these things, not finished them. It has declared itself, and com-
mited itself, and taxed itself, and damn near run itself into the
ground in the cause of social justice and reform.

Its mistakes are fewer than my father's generation — or his father's, or his. Its greatest mistake is not Vietnam; it is the abdication of its first responsibility, its pusillanimous capitulation to its
youth, and its sick preoccupation with the problems, the mind,
the psyche, the raison d'être of the young.

Since when have children ruled this country? By virtue of what
right, by what accomplishments should thousands of teen-agers,
wet behind the ears and utterly without the benefit of having
lived long enough to have either judgment or wisdom, become the
sages of our time?

The psychologists, the educators and preachers say the young
are rebelling against our archaic mores and morals, our materialis-
tic approaches to life, our failures in diplomacy, our terrible inep-
titude in racial matters, our narrowness as parents, our blindness
to the root ills of society. Balderdash!

Society hangs together by the stitching of many threads. No
eighteen-year-old is simply the product of his eighteen years: he is
the product of three thousand years of the development of man-

kind — and throughout those years, injustice has existed and been fought; rules have grown outmoded and been changed; doom has hung over men and been avoided; unjust wars have occurred; pain has been the cost of progress — and man has persevered.

As a professor and the father of seven, I have watched this new generation and concluded that most of them are fine. A minority are not — and the trouble is that minority threatens to tyrannize the majority and take over. I dislike that minority; I am aghast that the majority "takes" it and allows itself to be used. And I address myself to both the minority and the majority. I speak partly as a historian, partly as a father and partly as one fed-up, middle-aged and angry member of the so-called "Establishment" — which, by the way, is nothing but a euphemism for "society."

Common courtesy and a regard for the opinions of others are not merely decorations on the piecrust of society; they are the heart of the pie. Too many "youngsters" are egocentric boors. They will not listen, they will only shout down. They will not discuss but, like four-year-olds, they throw rocks and shout.

Arrogance is obnoxious; it is also destructive. Society has classically ostracized arrogance without the backing of demonstrable accomplishment. Why, then, do we tolerate arrogant slobs who occupy our homes, our administration buildings, our streets and parks, urinating on our beliefs and defiling our premises? It is not the police we need (our generation and theirs); it is an expression of our disgust and disdain. Yet we do more than permit it; we dignify it with introspective flagellation. Somehow it is our fault. Balderdash again!

Sensitivity is not the property of the young, nor was it invented in 1950. The young of any generation have felt the same impulse to grow, to reach out, to touch stars, to live freely and to let their minds loose along unexplored corridors. Young men and young women have always stood on the same hill and felt the same vague sense of restraint that separated them from the ultimate experience — the sudden and complete expansion of the mind, the final fulfillment. It is one of the oldest, sweetest and most bitter experiences of mankind.

Today's young people did not invent it; they do not own it. And what they seek to attain, all mankind has sought to attain throughout the ages. Shall we, therefore, approve the presumed attainment of it through heroin, speed, LSD and other drugs? And shall we, permissively, let them poison themselves simply because, as in most other respects, we feel vaguely guilty because we brought them into this world? Again, it is not police raids and tougher laws that we need; it is merely strength — the strength to explain, in our potty, middle-aged way, that what they seek, we sought; that it is somewhere but not here and sure as hell not in drugs; that, in the meanwhile, they will cease and desist the poison game. And this we must explain early and hard — and then police it ourselves.

Society, "the Establishment," is not a foreign thing we seek to impose on the young. We know it is far from perfect. We did not make it; we have only sought to change it. The fact that we have only been minimally successful is the story of all generations — as it will be the story of the generation coming up. Yet we have worked a number of wonders. We have changed it. We are deeply concerned about our failures; we have not solved the racial problem but we have faced it; we are terribly worried about the degradation of our environment, about injustices, inequities, the military-industrial complex and bureaucracy. But we have attacked these things. We have, all our lives, taken arms against our sea of troubles — and fought effectively. But we also have fought with a rational knowledge of the strength of our adversary; and, above all, knowing that the war is one of attrition in which the "unconditional surrender" of the forces of evil is not about to occur. We win, if we win at all, slowly and painfully. That is the kind of war society has always fought — because man is what he is.

Knowing this, why do we listen subserviently to the violent tacticians of the new generation? Either they have total victory by Wednesday next or burn down our carefully built barricades in adolescent pique; either they win now or flee off to a commune and quit; either they solve all problems this week or join a wrecking crew of paranoids.

Youth has always been characterized by impatient idealism. If it were not, there would be *no* change. But impatient idealism does not extend to guns, fire bombs, riots, vicious arrogance, and instant gratification. That is not idealism; it is childish tyranny. The worst of it is that we (professors and faculties in particular) in a paroxysm of self-abnegation and apology, go along, abdicate, apologize as if we had personally created the ills of the world — and thus lend ourselves to chaos. We are the led, not the leaders. And we are fools.

As a professor I meet the activists and revolutionaries every day. They are inexcusably ignorant. If you want to make a revolution, do you not study the ways to do it? Of course not! Che Guevara becomes their hero. He failed; he died in the jungles of Bolivia with an army of six. His every move was a miscalculation and a mistake. Mao Tse Tung and Ho Chi Minh led revolutions based on a peasantry and an overwhelmingly ancient rural economy. They are the pattern-makers for the SDS and the student militants. I have yet to talk to an "activist" who has read Crane Brinton's *The Anatomy of Revolution,* or who is familiar with the works of Jefferson, Washington, Paine, Adams or even Marx or Engels. And I have yet to talk to a student militant who has read about racism elsewhere and/or who understands, even primitively, the long and wondrous struggle of the NAACP and the genius of Martin Luther King — whose name they invariably take in vain.

An old and scarred member of the wars of organized labor in the US in the 1930's recently remarked to me: "These 'radicals' couldn't organize well enough to produce a sensible platform let alone revolt their way out of a paper bag." But they can, because we let them destroy our universities, make our parks untenable, make a shambles of our streets and insult our flag.

I assert that we are in trouble with this younger generation not because we have failed our country, not because of affluence or stupidity, not because we are antedeluvian, not because we are middle-class materialists — but simply because we have failed to keep that generation in its place and we have failed to put them back there when they got out of it. We have the power; we do not have the will. We have the right; we have not exercised it.

To the extent that we now rely on the police, mace, the National Guard, tear gas, steel fences and a wringing of hands, we will fail.

What we need is a reappraisal of our own middle-class selves, our worth and our hard-won progress. We need to use disdain, not mace; we need to reassess a weapon we came by the hard way, by travail and labor, firm authority as parents, teachers, businessmen, workers and politicians.

The vast majority of our children from one to twenty are fine kids. We need to back this majority with authority, and with the firm conviction that we owe it to them and to ourselves. Enough of apology, enough of analysis, enough of our abdication of responsibility, enough of the denial of our maturity and good sense.

The best place to start is at home. But, the most practical and effective place, right now, is our campuses. This does not mean a flood of angry edicts, a sudden clamp-down, a "new" policy. It simply means that faculties should stop playing chicken, that demonstrators should be met not with police but with expulsions. The power to expel (strangely unused) has been the legitimate recourse of universities since 1209.

More importantly it means that at freshman orientation, whatever form it takes, the administration should set forth the ground rules — not belligerently but forthrightly.

A university is the microcosm of society itself. It cannot function without rules for conduct. It cannot, as society cannot, legislate morals. It is dealing with young men and women, eighteen to twenty-two. But it can, and must, promulgate rules. It cannot function without order — and, therefore, who disrupts order must leave. It cannot permit students to determine when, what and where they shall be taught; it cannot permit the occupation of its premises, in violation both of the law and its regulations, by "militants."

There is room within the university complex for basic student participation but there is no room for slobs, disruption and violence. The first obligation of the administration is to lay down the rules early, clearly and positively, and to attach to this statement the penalty for violation. It is profoundly simple, and the failure to state it — in advance — is the salient failure of university administrators in this age.

Expulsion is a dreaded verdict. The administration merely needs to make it clear, quite dispassionately, that expulsion is the inevitable consequence of violation of the rules. Among the rules, even though it seems gratuitous, should be these:

1. Violence, armed or otherwise, the forceful occupation of buildings, the intimidation by covert or overt act of any student or faculty member or administrative personnel, the occupation of any university property, field, park, building, lot or other place shall be a cause for expulsion.

2. The disruption of any class, directly or indirectly, by voice or presence or the destruction of any university property, shall be cause for expulsion.

This is neither new nor revolutionary. It is merely the reassertion of an old, accepted and necessary right of the administration of any such institution. And the faculty should be informed, firmly, of this reassertion, before trouble starts. This does not constitute provocation. It is one of the oldest rights and necessities of the university community. The failure of university administrators to use it is one of the mysteries of our permissive age — and the blame must fall largely on faculties because they have consistently pressured administrators not to act.

Suppose the students refuse to recognize expulsions, suppose they march, riot, strike. The police? No. The matter, by prearrangement, publicly stated, should then pass to the courts. If buildings are occupied, the court enjoins the participating students. It has the awful power to declare them in contempt. If violence ensues, it is in violation of the court's order. Courts are not subject to fears, not part of the action. And what militant will shout obscenities in court with contempt hanging over his head?

Too simple? Not at all. Merely an old process which we seem to have forgotten. It is too direct for those who seek to employ Freudian analysis, too positive for "academic senates" who long for philosophical debate and too prosaic for those who seek orgastic self-condemnation.

This is a country full of decent, worried people like myself. It is also a country full of people fed up with nonsense. We need (those of us over thirty — tax-ridden, harried, confused, weary and beat-up) to reassert our hard-won prerogatives. It is our country too. We have fought for it, bled for it, dreamed for it, and we love it. It is time to reclaim it.

The Agony of the Counterculture

Kenneth Keniston of Yale Medical School delivered this commencement address at Notre Dame University on May 23, 1971. It has been somewhat excerpted.

THIS HAS BEEN a bad year for Consciousness III. The expressive exuberance, the romantic optimism and the political radicalism of May 1970 have been replaced by what the president of Yale, Kingman Brewster, has aptly termed an "eerie tranquillity." The students who were working toward major changes in national priorities, toward massive reordering of our goals and purposes, have fallen silent. They have turned inward — to meditation, to studying the *I Ching*, to communes in the mountains, to macrobiotic diets, to reliving the television programs of their childhoods, or even to doing their homework. *Time* magazine has announced the "cooling of America."

Has youthful alienation indeed become a thing of the past?

I suspect that I express more than my own personal views when I doubt that sanity, firmness, or adroitness on the part of Mr. Nixon explains the relative tranquillity on campus. Unresponsiveness to the expressed wishes of the American people hardly seems to me evidence of sanity. A policy of widespread wiretapping, harassment of dissenters, and illegal confinement of demonstrators hardly seems consistent for an administration that has pledged itself to preserve law and order.

A second explanation for the silence comes closer to the truth. In May 1970, following the invasion of Cambodia and the killings

at Kent State and Jackson State, at least a million and a half
students were mobilized in largely peaceful demonstrations of
concern and grief: almost half of America's twenty-five hundred
campuses were affected. Especially at the most selective and visible colleges, there was a massive outpouring of revulsion against
the war, against the policies that led to its continuation, and
against the administration. But that outpouring of feeling and
energy led to no visible results. Despite the withdrawal of American land forces, American aerial bombardment of Southeast Asia
actually increased, as did the civilian and military casualties of all
groups except Americans. The many evils in American society
against which dissenting students have protested continued.
Students hoped that they could help change our society, reorder
our national priorities, convince others with moral suasion. But
many believe that events proved them wrong. As a result they are
both exhausted and depressed. Far from being won over, I think
students have if anything become even more discouraged about
affecting the political process.

But discouragement alone is not, I believe, an adequate explanation of the silence. If you talk at any length with students, you
quickly detect an undercurrent of embarrassment and even
shame. Many students nourished the secret fantasy that their un-
aided efforts might produce a "total change" in American politics,
an apocalyptic or revolutionary reordering of our society. But
when autumn came, a more sober reappraisal of the possibilities
of basic social change was inevitable. For example, students who
had believed that the Black Panther Party constituted a "revolutionary vanguard" realized that the Panthers neither expressed
the aspirations of most American blacks, nor were they themselves
above deceit, exploitation, and racism. Radical students painfully
realized that a great many young people, especially those who do
not attend college, are primarily motivated by a desire to take
part in the American system, rather than to change it. The understandable result was a justified sense of embarrassment at their

own previous naiveté, shame that they had allowed themselves to entertain apocalyptic fantasies of revolution.

But even discouragement and shame are not enough, I believe, to explain the relative tranquillity. Underlying these feelings is what I will term a genuine agony of the student movement. This agony springs from a new awareness that violence lies not only within the rest of American society, but within the student movement itself.

In emphasizing the secret flaws and vices of the student movement, I do not want to draw attention away from the real evils of American society, evils which the student movement has helped pinpoint. I am well aware that if we tally deaths, cracked skulls, or even minor injuries, the members of the counterculture have suffered far more violence than they have perpetrated.

The agony of the student movement ultimately revolves around the issue of violence, which I believe to be the central issue of our national existence today. As a nation, we possess the most terrible weapons of world destruction owned by any nation in the history of mankind. Domestically, we are one of the most violent nations of the world. And in a distant war in a far-off land, our country has been implicated so far in the deaths of two million men, women, and children, of whom less than 2 percent are Americans. From the start of the student movement in the early 1960's, violence has been its unwanted companion. The civil rights movement was committed to nonviolence, but it constantly brought upon itself the violence of those who opposed it. Throughout the 1960's, there have been killings of student activists: students shot at Orangeburg; at Isla Vista; at the People's Park in Berkeley; in Lawrence, Kansas; at Kent State; at Jackson State. Members of the student movement have come to expect harassment, to fear brutality and even death from their adversaries, including the very public forces pledged to maintain law and order in the community. Yet if there is any one goal that has traditionally been central to the student movement, that goal has been the abolition of violence

— whether it be the violence inflicted upon blacks by American racism, or the violence which we, the most powerful nation in the world, have inflicted upon the people of a third-rate military power in Southeast Asia.

This commitment of the student movement to nonviolence corresponded very well with the particular psychology of its white members, most of whom are children of fairly prosperous, educated, humanitarian, and idealistic middle-class parents. If we study the childhood experiences of such middle-class students, we find that physical violence was almost completely absent during their earlier years. Even death was eliminated from the public landscape, isolated in distant hospitals and antiseptic funeral homes. If we ask white college students how often they were involved as children in major physical fights, the answer is generally once or twice if ever. Furthermore, the parents of these middle-class children rarely expressed anger physically: verbal attacks took the place of physical assault. In other words, we have taught our children to express their rage and destructiveness in largely indirect ways. As a group, middle-class Americans take out their anger on themselves by becoming depressed, or express it verbally by making cutting remarks. And even if anger finally overflows, it overflows in the form of words, of obscenity. But physical violence — hitting, striking, hurting other people — has been almost completely taboo.

This upbringing, coupled with the real violence inflicted by others upon student activists, made it very easy for members of the student movement to see violence and destructiveness as existing only "out there" — only in their adversaries, only in American racism, only in American foreign policy. An obscenity shouted at a policeman did not seem violent, but the policeman's billy club in response to that obscenity was seen as a shocking form of violence.

What has happened with increasing speed in the last year is that the denial of rage, anger, and destructiveness by members of the student movement has been undercut. This confrontation with inner violence is symbolized by two events: the murder of an innocent onlooker by Hell's Angels at the rock festival at Altamont; the killing of an innocent graduate student in the terrorist bombing of the mathematics building at the University of Wisconsin in Madison. These events are dreadful, criminal, and inexcusable in their own right; but they also have a special symbolic importance. They symbolize the fact that from *within* the youth movement, there were emerging groups who were prepared to use violence in a systematic way in order to attain their ends.

In light of Altamont and Madison, the inner significance of earlier events became clearer. Recall, for example, the positions adopted by the Weathermen and expressed in their Days of Rage in Chicago in the fall of 1969, when they marched virtually unarmed into battle against a much larger force of armed police. Recall, too, the explosion in the townhouse in Greenwich Village, which ended by killing three of the Weathermen who were making bombs. Or recall the rapidity with which some of the peace-loving flower children of the hippie movement became embroiled in the sordid exploitativeness and destructiveness of the hard-drug culture.

In retrospect, the uglier side of these events has become more clear. Nominally opposing violence and suffering violence from others, some fringes of the counterculture became infected by the very violence it opposed. The shouted obscenity calculated to offend the policeman was all along a form of violence; so, too, was the categorization of the opponents of the student movement as subhuman — as pigs. And above all, that ideological argument which led a few members of the youth movement to consider their fear for violence a "bourgeois hang-up" to be overcome by the practice of terrorism — this was no less a symptom of the pathological violence in American life than were the police riots at the Democratic Convention in Chicago in 1968 or our indiscriminate bombing in Southeast Asia.

The murders at Altamont and Madison symbolized the end of an era for the student movement. During that earlier era, it was possible for student activists to blind themselves to their own rage, to see themselves as happy exceptions to that morbid fascination with violence which affects our nation as a whole. The violent rhetoric that came to pervade the student movement could be passed off as mere talk. But when that rhetoric culminated in murder, then the members of the student movement had to face for the first time their own complicity with the very violence against which they struggled. Woodstock was transformed into Altamont; Berkeley and Columbia were transformed into Madison.

The agony of the counterculture, then, involves above all its confrontation, at an individual and a collective level, with its own destructiveness. Underlying the turn inward, the turn away from politics, has been the realization that some people in a movement dedicated to peace, justice, democracy and equality were moving toward the systematic betrayal of these very principles. The members of the student movement gradually came to realize that if they allowed themselves to be led by a rigid and destructive minority, dogmatism and murder lay at the end of their own road. The silence this year springs from a recoil from violence.

In a peculiar way then, the introspectiveness, the self-criticism and self-examination that has characterized most American campuses testify to the ultimate sanity of most student activists. Confronted with dogmatism and murder at the end of the road, most student activists have pulled back, have turned inward, have spent the year "trying to get their heads together." This process of self-confrontation can aptly be termed an agony, for it has involved depression and anguish, inner uncertainty, struggle, and self-reevaluation.

I am a psychologist, and I see an analogy between the agony of the counterculture and the agony of the individual patient. In the course of psychotherapy, the patient may eventually come to the point where he must confront his own complicity in his misery, his own involvement in the very motives which he criticizes in others. The result is a stage of inner agony, a period of withdrawal, gloom, and depression. The evils that were seen as largely outside of the patient are now acknowledged as existing inside him as well.

But an agony is also a contest, a crisis, a potential turning point. In psychotherapy, the recognition of one's own dark motives can lead to either one of two outcomes. It *can* lead to the termination of treatment, to flight, and to regression. The patient who is unable to look at himself in a clear mirror flees from his truthful image in order to preserve his illusions about himself and, with them, his neurosis. But there is also a second, more hopeful outcome. It involves accepting the awareness of one's own destructiveness, one's own covetousness, one's own dark side. As the acknowledgment of inner evil is extended, and *only then,* a more creative and integrative process may begin. Without ceasing to oppose evil in himself or others, a man may nonetheless come to acknowledge that he too shares in complicity with evil, and that, in this respect as in others, he is his fellows' brother. It becomes more difficult for him to polarize mankind neatly into good and evil, for he recognizes that in himself both coexist. He sees the world in a more complex, less black-and-white, more realistic way. And he becomes more effective in his deeds, for he is less prone to an unconscious complicity with the very forces which he consciously seeks to overcome. From this agony of self-confrontation, then, there can come a more mature, more integrated, more effective person.

A social movement is very different from an individual patient. Yet the analogy suggests two possibilities. One is a dark one. The agony of the counterculture could mark its imminent death. The youth movement which gave so much to America in the 1960's, which helped redefine our national priorities, which helped expose the persistent wrongs of American society, which began to define new life-styles, new values, and new institutions could continue to fragment, splinter, go underground, be suppressed, and eventually disappear. Members of the movement would then become cynical and despairing, alienated from the existing society yet utterly convinced of inability to change that society. Or, unable to confront the potential for evil that lies within the student movement, some might continue the disastrous process of externalization that leads to dogmatism and violence, to the denial of the humanity of one's adversaries, or to withdrawal into hedonistic concerns. Were this to occur, the generation would indeed lapse into silence. It would not be a silence that springs from satisfaction, but a silence of despair. Human idealism is immensely fragile: it can easily be corroded into the destructive cynicism of the ex-idealist. For this to happen would be, I believe, the worst thing that could befall our country — we would lose the idealism of the young, morality would become soured to cynicism, and those who were once impatient and hopeful would be overwhelmed by a sense of their own impotence.

The second scenario is a more optimistic one. Just as the individual patient may confront his own dark side, and through this painful insight gain in compassion, maturity, and strength, so the recognition of violence within the student movement could ultimately strengthen and renew that movement. The result could be a generation and a movement more inoculated against self-righteousness, dogmatism, moralism, and a secret collusion with violence, a movement that did not need to view the world as consisting simply in the struggle of good men against evil men, a counterculture that could recognize the enormous difficulties in resolving the problems of our society, but without losing its determination to resolve them.

I do not believe we can predict which of these two outcomes will occur. Much of what happens to the members of any generation happens because of events which are beyond their control. The future of the student movement will partly be determined by what happens in Washington, Moscow, Peking, Hanoi, South Bend, and Indianapolis. A speedy end to the war in Southeast Asia, a vigorous effort to uproot racism in all of its virulent forms from American society, a concern with the quality of life and the environment that went beyond electioneering rhetoric, and above all a desperately needed renewal of tolerance for dissent in American society — these changes could well make the difference between the two alternatives.

I have made clear my conviction that the greatest danger which confronts those who struggle against violence is the danger that they themselves will become secretly contaminated by the violence they oppose, and unconsciously collude in creating more violence than they prevent. I have made clear that I consider the eerie tranquillity a recoil from the violence that was beginning to appear in naked form within the student movement itself. But I see this recoil from violence as a mark not of the perversity of your generation, but of your honesty, your insight, and the reality of your idealism. And finally, I have made clear that this confrontation with violence need not mark the end of the youth culture that has defined your generation, but *could* mark the beginning of a new, more powerful, more compassionate and more comprehensive movement that extended far beyond youth and the universities.

This is the challenge that lies ahead. The student movement and the counterculture have so far spoken largely to the young, the affluent, and the educated. What is now needed is an extension and translation of the values and ideals of the student culture into a broader social, cultural, and political context. Your education provides you with skills, competence, knowledge, and understanding that could enable you to continue and transform the youth culture in which you have directly or vicariously participated. That culture has been so far too much of a *counter*culture, too much defined by opposition to the evils which you correctly perceived in American society, too much an outcry against our culture's failure to fulfill its promises or to build upon its achieve-ments. The student movement, for understandable reasons, has so far largely been a movement of opposition.

It is now time that it become a movement of affirmation. To transform the student movement will require not merely the en-thusiasm of Consciousness III, but the professionalism and skill of Consciousness II. It will require not only the celebration of life and the expansion of consciousness advocated by the new culture, but the hard work, the persistence, and the dedication that has characterized the old culture. It will require an alliance not merely of the young, the privileged, and educated, but of those who are not young, or privileged, or educated, and of that vast majority of Americans who refuse to ally themselves with either camp.

On one issue virtually all Americans are agreed: if we are in a period of national crisis, it is because, in a dozen ways, our society is going out of control. The technology we created to serve us has come to dominate us, and now threatens to destroy us. The insti-tutions we founded to serve the public interest too often have come to manipulate public opinion and exploit public anxieties. I doubt that anyone has a precise, detailed, and sure-fire prescrip-tion for reversing these trends. But it is clear that to reverse them will not be the work of one apocalyptic moment, one revolution-ary spasm, or one outcry of opposition and despair. It will be the work of a lifetime, of a generation of competent and skilled men and women who are dedicated to the hard work of making the best ideals of the youth culture real throughout society, and who are willing to continue in that struggle long after they themselves cease to be students. I hope you will undertake that struggle, for if you do, you will find many allies among the rest of us, and to-gether we may be able to realize the extraordinary — and still un-realized — potentials of our American society.

The Dream Is Over

No phenomenon of youth culture has more complex connotations or is more troubling to straight culture than the Manson cult, which arose in the wake of Woodstock and Altamont and was even (if briefly) embraced by some members of the Weather Underground. J. Marks, author of Rock and Other Four Letter Words, *examines the problem in this article first published in* The Last Supplement to the Whole Earth Catalogue.

CHARLES MANSON ANNOUNCED the new decade: *"Death is psychosomatic,"* he said. "I am just a mirror. If God is One, what is bad?" he asked. His message is terrifying and inscrutable. It promised the marriage of two outlaw cultures: the hood and the head. Clearing space for the complex metaphysical gangster film *Performance.* Decreeing the ruthless realism of the new John Lennon and the grizzly *cinéma verité* of Altamont.

It also resounds of the romantic vision of death which haunted Poe and Swinburne and the whole romantic movement:

> *But the decadence of history is looking for a pawn*
> *To a nightmare of knowledge he opens up the gate*
> *A blinding revelation is served upon his plate*
> *That beneath the greatest love is a hurricane of hate*
> — from *Crucifixion* by Phil Ochs

And so death walks among us like a painted groupie, dusty with old embellishments and faded myths and mysteries. Like the fragile princess who was destined to prick her finger on the needle of a spinning wheel and fall into eternal sleep, our generation has been marked for death almost since its birth. A strange and great impending shadow has fallen over the profile of our generation.

But death has always been part of our mystique. After all, weren't both Dylan and McCartney "wished" dead? And isn't the acute awareness of death the prime motive for our nervous sensualism? And hasn't every summer ended with the Red Spectre himself walking into our rooms and changing his face fourteen times before he covered us, like a cocoon, with the saliva of demise?

Ceremonies such as the 1968 funeral procession down Haight Street have been an integral part of the theatrical rituals of the children of the bomb. One trip or one earthquake does more in sixty seconds to shake our belief in the stability of all things than two centuries of philosophical reflection. And therefore it is true that we are highly idealistic at the same time that we believe in nothing.

And we are realistic. Realistic enough to recognize that the evolution of our life-style into fashion and show biz is a burial in plastic if not exactly a matter of death itself. The hip ideal has been buried alive! Isn't that also a kind of idealized death?

Contrasting with such morbid insights into the eventual and inevitable demise of that pure, innocent and total belief in the inherent goodness of mankind were our celebrations of such heightened optimism and sensual affirmation that they almost succeeded in momentarily obscuring the pessimism which is intrinsic to a finite animal. Monterey and Woodstock, the be-ins and love-ins and the private festivities of living rooms and dorms were so involved in the facts of life that they almost obscured the simple fact of death.

Then came the heartless assassination of Linda and Groovy in New York's derelict Lower East Side. Irrefutably demonstrating the innocent stupidity of our belief that you could build a good life in society's dead cities: the slums.

If you couple that small but devastating atrocity with the brutality of the minority attacks on Diggers' free stores and clinics and the slow rage of blacks for weirdos and hippies who were corrupting all the symbols of middle-class affluence which they sought — if you couple these things with the indifference of longhair proprietors of head shops and the meanness of Fillmore East ushers (called the Fillmore Gestapo by the rock fans of 1969) and the inhumanity of superstars which has been gradually revealed in their views of women (groupies) and money (capitalism) and politics (liberals) — then it becomes clear that something has been happening not only to Mr. Jones but also to his street-talking, long-haired, fashion-following kid: and *neither* of them know exactly what it is!

In fact, not just one world — the Establishment — but two worlds were crumbling. The world of the young, with all its fervent belief in man and myth, was also heading rapidly toward extinction.

Nothing made these unhappy facts quite as clear as the financial politics of the Beatles — who started out wanting to hold our hand and ended up after a couple of pills taking love equal to the love they gave — or the Biblical saga of Charlie Manson or the thoroughly bad vibes of the Maysles brothers' excellent documentary *Gimme Shelter.*

For some of this film was a chronicle of the sexual strategy of the greatest performer and prefabrication of this century's theater: Mick Jagger. For others who know Jagger better, it was an unheard of chink in the fine decorative veneer of his transvestite characterization of himself.

In the awesome presence of the Hell's Angels we gleaned something of that deep, silent terror we had of brutes when we were kids on the playground. And in the scuffles and glares of anger we began to recognize the sheer helplessness of our great pop super-fathers and prick-deities who could not turn back the sea with a single command so that we might safely stride uninterrupted toward the magic milieu of their music as we had at Woodstock and Monterey.

The brutalized crowd, cowering from the erratic blasts of

motorcycle bravado, reminded us of old movies about juvenile delinquents with beards and leather jackets, about gang wars and drag races and street rumbles: antiques from our elder brothers' nightmares. Monsters arising like rubber models in some Jap sci-fi flick: *dinosaurs!*

And when finally the pool cues began to beat back some enormously fat, nude, crazy and other demented foundlings who had joined the multitude of hippies, we knew it was all over. We were dying again. Dying of our own massive appetite for humanity: the act of faith which had directed us not only to imbibe mysterious potions which changed our heads, but also directed us to engulf and to absorb huge, fatal doses of derelict humanity.

The huge ranks of alienated, antisocial psychopaths were being naively absorbed into the generation's main flank where they were then turning into mad dogs and destroying those who had welcomed them.

We were not mad. "But if you were not mad," said the Mad Hatter, "you would not be here!" We were the product of education and middle-class morality. But we were certain, until recently, that we were not mad. We had simply broken out of the psychological enclosure of our parents' social order and we had found a new premise for being both politically critical and creatively sane. We were not outcasts — we had cast the past out of our lives. That was sanity.

But the crazies recognized us by our isolation, our contempt for authority, our self-description as *freaks*. We had dropped a couple of caps of this or that, and we were the symptoms of the dementia of which they were the disease. None of us could tell the difference. Not the press, which had been searching for four years for the ultimate embodiment of the young maniac, long-haired freak Devil. Not the hippies, who had sought the stranger willing to step over the edge.

So it was inevitable that the Charles Mansons would appear in our image and enact their insane rituals in our name. It is even inevitable that we would then embrace them, defend them and care about them since it is our prime virtue and prime weakness to love and to protect the foundlings of our parents' cruel society.

The confusion of dreams and realities have become song in John Lennon's first solo album. We have never tried to separate our individual fate from the fate of our generation, so for John it appears that everything has been a compromise and a record company hoax — that everybody in the world has been playing the role of sideman to somebody's gigantically destructive ego. "The dream is over," John sings. We blew it! We have become media turds.

Behind him John leaves all of our heroes, our sojourn in the confusing and beguiling mysteries of orientalism, our belief in absolute evil (Hitler) as clearly opposed to absolute good (Kennedy), and even our music (Elvis, Dylan, the Beatles).

He leaves everything behind. Except of course our sense of wonder. And that fragile debris ultimately saves us and our most primal ideal. Like Lennon we are fashioning from our disillusionment the bright structure of some kind of new reality. And nothing is lost . . . nothing is lost! Like a freaked-out friend said to me when I was lamenting Altamont: "Ah, yes, it's true, there were some really terrible things that went down in 1970. But just think of it — just think what a bright, strong light it took to cast such a dark shadow!"

A Few Parting Words

Henry F. Ottinger delivered these remarks at his final meeting with the English class which he instructed in 1970–71 at the University of Missouri.

AND NOW, LIKE IT or not, I'd like to say a few parting words.

As you know, I began the semester in a way that departed from the manner in which I had taught composition classes in the past. Much of my attitude at that time was influenced by Farber's book, *The Student As Nigger.* On the first day of class, I read to you the following:

> *School is where you let the dying society put its trip on you. Our schools may seem useful: to make children into doctors, sociologists, engineers — to discover things. But they're poisonous as well. They exploit and enslave students; they petrify society; they make democracy unlikely. And it's not what you're taught that does the harm but how you're taught. Our schools teach you by pushing you around, by stealing your will and your sense of power, by making timid, apathetic slaves of you — authority addicts.*

That sounded like a breath of fresh air back in February — and I suggested that we try to break the mold, that we could write papers on any subject we wanted, that we could spend class time discussing things, either "the burning issues of the day" or otherwise. You seemed to agree, and we spent time agreeing together that indeed Farber had *the* word, and we would do what we could to break the mold.

As you know, things went from initial ecstasy to final catastrophe. And recently I fell back — no, you forced me back — into assigning general topics. As a result of that action, and a lot of other factors, this semester has been the worst I have ever taught. In fact, I even debated with myself whether or not to go on teaching next year. But in some ways, the semester was valuable because I learned something, if you didn't.

Let me share with you some of the things I learned. Keep in mind that this does not apply to all of you, but it does apply to the majority.

I learned that all this bull about "getting it together" or "working together" (be it for peace or a grade) is just that — bull. The 1950's were labeled by pop sociologists as "the silent generation." I assure you that they had nothing on you. Ten years ago, the people around the fountains wore saddle shoes, chinos and long hair. Now they're barefoot, wear army fatigues and have long hair. Big revelation: it's the same bunch of people.

Generally, this class has been the most silent, reticent, paranoid bunch of people in a group I have ever encountered.

You had an opportunity to exchange ideas (which, it often turned out, "you have not got"), and you were too embarrassed to do so.

You had an opportunity to find out something about yourselves. This, by the way, is the crux of education. And as far as I can see, you found out very little.

You had an opportunity to explore ideas — on your own — and didn't. Most of the papers hashed over the usual cliché-ridden topics. One person went so far as to churn out a masterpiece on the pros and cons of fraternities, a topic that was really hot back in 1956.

Most of all, you had the opportunity to be free — free from the usual absurdities of a composition class where topics are assigned, thesis statements are submitted, and so on. You also had freedom of thought, as long as it was confined to the standards of formal

English. You had the opportunity to be free — to be responsible to yourselves — and you succeeded in proving to me and to yourselves that freedom is slavery, a line from *1984* which I hope, for the sake of all of us, isn't prophetic.

But you protest (Oh, how I have wished you would): "We're incapable of handling all this freedom at once. You see, Mr. Ottinger, we've been conditioned; we're not used to all of this."

Well, I read that in Farber, too, and it's bull. Rats and dogs are conditioned, and are usually incapable of breaking that conditioning. Human beings can break conditioning, if it's to their advantage. But here it's too good an excuse to say, "I'm conditioned." Obviously, then, it's to your advantage not to break out of the mold.

Why is it to your advantage? In short, why did the class fail?

It failed because thinking causes pain. And, like good little utilitarians, you want to avoid pain. It's so much easier to come up with instant esthetics, instant solutions, instant salvation, instant thoughts. After all, instant things, like breakfasts and TV dinners, are easily digestible — and easily regurgitated — and not terribly nourishing.

One of the most nauseating remarks I have heard this semester is, "Gosh, college is no fun," or, when an idea is presented, "It doesn't turn me on."

If you don't believe that knowledge for its own sake is a valid and valuable goal, then you're in the wrong place, and you'd do much better in a vocational school, studying how to be a plumber or a beautician.

Granted, there are problems within the university itself — serious problems — that, despite what you may think, show some sign of possible solution. One step they could take (but probably won't) is to limit enrollment, and keep the 45 per cent of you out who don't belong here, because it's no fun.

Well, it's time, I suppose, to bring this to a halt, and let you go over to the Commons or wherever. As to the next-to-last comment, I invite you to listen to the lyrics of the Beatles' "Nowhere Man" and, if it fits, take it to heart.

Last, I will bid a good-bye (until the final) and say that if at any time some sly hint, or clue, or (God forbid) a half-truth slipped out of my unconscious and out of the corner of my mouth and (pardon the expression) "turned one of you on," then we have not failed, you and I.

And to all of you this: I love you for what you might be; I'm deeply disturbed by what you are.

Race

Race

THE CONTEMPORARY STRUGGLE for racial equality in the United States began in 1954 with the US Supreme Court decision thrusting down the hoary doctrine of "separate but equal" public schools for black and whites. Its course has been marked by passion, violence and eloquence. A dozen anthologies would not encompass the declarations which marked the sit-in movement, the Birmingham campaign, the march on Selma, the march on Washington, the SNCC campaigns, the tidal surges which swept blacks forward in fifteen years further toward the goal of equality than in the ninety previous years since Lincoln's Emancipation Proclamation.

With the years the temper of the eloquence has shifted away from the simple oratory of Martin Luther King's "I have a dream" or his Letter from a Birmingham Jail to the brutal obscenities of the Northern ghetto, and with this has come a spreading realization that Black is merely a symbol for oppression and inequality visited on the many who differ in some respect from the majority. That is, the realization that nigger is a synonym for Indian and Wop and student and woman. Student as nigger. Woman as nigger. Priest as nigger. Nigger becomes a synonym for oppressed. For the disinherited.

Here we have the new voices of race as they spoke on the threshold of the 1970's. The reversal of roles from the 1950's and the 1960's is notable. The fire and the intensity is in the North. From the South comes the wise and compassionate wisdom of Mary Mebane looking out onto the black world of North Carolina or P. D. East, a white veteran of all the wars over race, speaking philosophically from Mississippi and Alabama.

The question can be raised as to whether Attica belongs in a section devoted to Race. I believe it does. True, there were whites involved in Attica. But it was, essentially, a confrontation of black versus white just as George Jackson and Angela Davis represent the same fateful division. Attica was black against white within a steel and cement cage of hate. The ultimate, the almost primal struggle. It was guard against convict, law against criminal. Oh, yes. But that was merely a brutal mask for race, for white against black. Whites stood with blacks in the prison yard at Attica. That is true. But only whites stood against the "inmates," only white guns fired on the inmates. This was race in its raw bloodiness, just as Hampton was race, dying as Deborah Johnson records while ". . . the Pigs are vampin' . . . the mattress was just . . . goin' . . The Pigs run around laughing — they was really happy, ya know . . . talkin' about Chairman Fred is dead . . ."

This is the way race entered the 1970's. The spirit of nonviolence, of passive resistance, of the long marches on the highways in the southern sun were over. No longer the nervous youngsters crowding into the lunch-counter stools of Woolworth's in Nashville or Roanoke. No longer "Mississippi summer" with the youngsters from Sarah Lawrence and Amherst and Chicago and Berkeley joining the pilgrimage to help their black peers in miserable Mississippi. In the 1970's all of that has a faintly nostalgic, old-fashioned air. The spirit of the 1970's is coarse and brutal and dangerous. It is guns, guns, guns and hasty eloquence, phrases snatched from the mouths of the dying or hastily scrawled by those like Jackson who have come to believe that they are bound to die. It is in this segment that tragedy is anthologized.

The Jesus People

Mary E. Mebane (Liza) teaches English at South Carolina State College, Orangeburg, South Carolina. She adds "Liza" to her writing signature because that was her father's nickname for her.

THOUGH IT IS NOW FASHIONABLE in some quarters to put religion down — James Baldwin writes a letter to his nephew disparaging religion and two black psychiatrists are not too happy about blacks in the Jesus bag — their views are not necessarily those of the black folk.

Such views are symptomatic of the split between the world of a great many black folk and the black intelligentsia. For the black folk have developed a strong institution in their churches, and, though it may cause some to smile or sneer, it is well to remember that during the 1960's the church was the headquarters out of which the activists went forth to the sit-ins; and where the plans for the registration drive and the boycott were made. The dark-suited deacons gave protection to visitors from afar and the good sisters cooked the tons of fried chicken and made the mountains of potato salad that the Freedom Army marched on during the thirteen-year trek from Montgomery to Memphis.

The original Jesus People were the black folk of the South. If they've heard about the other Jesus Freaks, which I doubt, they are glad that some disillusioned flower children have decided to join them. They themselves were never dropouts.

Most of the Jesus People I knew as a child were Baptists. It was understood that they were the best. I had never heard of some-

thing called an Episcopalian and nobody could pronounce Pres-
byterian. Even my Aunt Joe was suspect; she was a Methodist.
Methodists believed in sprinkling. Baptists believed in immersion, that is, coming up out of the water soaking wet, gasping for
breath. But my aunt had never been dipped. After she died, I
worried about her soul.

Immersion was a very colorful ceremony. Those to be baptized
dressed in white and everyone else stood on the banks of the river
or pond and prayed and sang. I'm afraid that most children who
were baptized, though, missed much of the pageantry; they were
concerned about being dropped, and about water snakes.

In the Mill Grove community, my home in northern Durham
County, North Carolina, there are four churches, two Holiness
and two Baptist. When I was a child the Baptists held service
once a month; the Holiness every night if possible.

One Baptist church was hardside. The hardsides believed in
washing feet and long sermons. Once a year there was a great
preaching. Four or five preachers would take turns preaching and
I can still remember the pain I felt when my mother made me sit
still on the straight-backed slated benches through long sermon
after long sermon. Lucky for me this event occurred only once a
year. Across from the hardsides was one of the holy churches.
Their main speaker, a venerable lady, used to take her text in
Adam.

Right in the middle of the community was another Holiness
church which provided a great deal of glamour and color in our
community. Though the good Baptists looked down on the cym-
bals, tambourines and shouting of the holy people, we children
loved it. It was in that church that I first heard an electric guitar,
long before the advent of the shaggy rock musicians. It was
played by a traveling evangelist who could sing and dance with
his guitar better than Chuck Berry or Jimi Hendrix.

The holy folks got even with the Baptists by repeatedly declaring that everybody who wasn't holy and sanctified was going to

hell. Since that included a number of sinners and all of the Baptists, the Baptists were not amused. Sometimes the leading sister would pray by banging with closed fists on the church bench in a rhythmic patter, prompting the elder to remonstrate with her that "God is not deaf." Once they held a march to drive the devil out of Mill Grove. He was supposed to flee at midnight in front of the singing, tambourine-playing group. Those without tambourines were advised to beat cake pans. They did. The Baptists, again, were not amused.

At the farthest boundary of our community was the establishment church. It was the strait-laced, decorous, prim Baptist church, much given to singing Old Hundreds, and was a foe of all worldly music and instruments. They frowned on the acquisition of a piano and absolutely refused to let a quartet with a guitar accompaniment in the church. But it encouraged Sunday school. I first served an apprenticeship as a secretary and a pianist there; it encouraged scouting and took the community children to the park on vacations, to the U.S.S. *North Carolina*, the beach and other places of interest and amusement. And when the community organizers in Durham decided that they needed the help of the people in the county in order to run a selective buying campaign, they came to the churches to make their appeal. The church is a strong institution in black communities in the South. It may well survive its critics.

The Petal Paper

P. D. East for many years published The Petal Paper, *first in Petal, Mississippi, and more lately in Fairhope, Alabama. He is the author of* The Magnolia Jungle.

THERE'S A DREAM QUALITY about the past for most who choose to look back. The past seems to consist of about 5 per cent fact and the balance is imagination. Would that I were so lucky.

I, too, have occasion to look back. There isn't too much pleasure; I look back in pain.

At eight o'clock on the morning of November 26, 1921, I was born in the small town of Columbia, Mississippi. In less than a week my mother had let me for adoption.

I grew up an only child, with a kind of gentle old man for a father and a real, honest-to-God witch for a mother. She dragged me to Methodist revival meetings and pumped me so full on hellfire and brimstone that I would often cry myself to sleep at night.

Not only was I Jim and Birdie's little red-headed, freckle-faced, adopted boy, but, what with moving from sawmill camp to sawmill camp in south Mississippi, I always found myself an outsider.

One of my earliest fistfights was with a local farm lad who, because I was "a sawmill kid," decided to take my place in a school line.

When the lumber barons had succeeded in raping the giant pine forests in south Mississippi in 1934, we moved to a village called Brooklyn. My father took a job as night watchman. I entered high school and, five years later, I graduated.

As far back as I can remember I wanted to study medicine, but in 1939 a night watchman's son was hardly in a position to do so. I enrolled that September at Pearl River Junior College with the sum of fourteen dollars, which I had borrowed. The only job I could find was working all night at a service station café. I managed to live; I would sometimes fall asleep in class. I lasted only a year there.

Having absolutely no training, I found a job with Greyhound Bus Lines, hustling baggage in Hattiesburg, Mississippi. I left Greyhound for a better-paying job with the Southern Railway System, where I started as a clerk. Ten years and one war later I was still a clerk. One day I reached a decision. If I had to spend another hour in the place I would go raving mad. I tendered my resignation at noon one day.

So at my thirtieth year of life I was unemployed, in debt, and completely happy about it. An acquaintance told me about a chemical plant union which wanted to start a house organ. I talked with the fellow who, almost literally, owned the union. We agreed on terms and responsibilities.

I worked with eagerness, but I was slowly becoming disenchanted. I had less than three thousand dollars. What could I do? I decided I would like to own a small-town weekly newspaper. I could be my own boss, all profits would be mine, and I'd be completely independent.

So I rented an office in Petal, Mississippi, a village about three miles from Hattiesburg, and contracted with a large weekly in Pascagoula to do the printing. I was in business.

Now, the operation of a weekly newspaper is simple. The best thing is to adopt an editorial policy of loving American motherhood and hating sin. The next best thing is to have no policy at all.

But something was wrong. I simply wasn't happy. Oh, sure, I covered all the local events, taking pictures, putting local names in the paper. The sole aim of *The Petal Paper* was to make money, just that, nothing more.

On Monday, the 17th of May, 1954 [the day the Supreme

Court decided *Brown* v. *Board of Education of Topeka*], I was busy all day calling on advertisers, talking with people, and I finished off the day by photographing a large egg some farmer brought to my office. It was a big egg, I must admit. I was totally unaware of the most important court decision in the history of this nation.

The following weeks I began to hear some questions and comment. It dawned on me that perhaps I'd be wise to find out what the decision was. I did, and thought it was a good decision; I was becoming more and more aware, however, that my fellow citizens didn't think much of it. I decided to let the matter rest, to make no comment. After all, there wasn't any profit in it — I could figure out that much. Yet, somehow, I sincerely believed that if I so chose I could write anything I wished. I'd read about freedom of speech and I knew I had that right.

The months that followed were agonizing. I took a number of trips during those months, visiting Negro schools and homes, and talking with Negro citizens, friends and strangers. My God! It dawned on me finally, these people are human beings, no different from me, except for the color of their skins.

I wondered how to keep what I had and, at the same time, live with myself. I had some help from a Petal merchant. The legislature proposed an amendment whereby the schools would close if integration were required. This merchant told me that if anyone opposed the amendment, that meant he was for integration; furthermore, he got specific, saying that if I opposed the amendment he would cancel his advertising. Well, at last, thank God, I didn't have to deliberate anymore. I had an editorial on my desk at that moment. I ran the copy and he canceled his advertising.

Having been pushed off the fence, I went into several counties and photographed schools, Negro and white, and ran the photographs in my paper, generally with the caption: SEPARATE BUT EQUAL.

I found I couldn't sit by and do nothing.

In less than five years I managed to lose every single subscriber in Petal. As to advertising, that, with rare exception, had long since gone. I picked up a little money from lecturing dates. In 1959 a group in New York formed a "P. D. East Committee," and a number of persons supported it.

What I wrote was what I thought and what I felt. I woke up one morning with an ulcer, and I still have the damned thing.

I found myself in a trap, and it's common to whites who think and feel as I do. I was critical of behavior by whites, but I hesitated, and was often unable to criticize the Negro. This, of course, is stupid. If one is honest and truly without prejudice, he must be critical of any and everyone who acts an ass. Finally, realizing that, I arrived at an editorial policy. It was simply this: FAIRNESS. And that remains the policy of my paper and, I hope, of my life. I must admit it is often damned hard to follow such a policy.

Hostility was on the increase. In the course of one week, three persons came to me (two of them on the same day), assuring me over and over, and with considerable emotion, that I was going to be killed. Such threats had been made before, several times, as a matter of fact, but three in one week was a bit much, I can assure you.

With such knowledge, I never entered my car without first searching it thoroughly — the trunk, under the seats, under the hood. This kind of thing — and other minor aggravations, like not being served in restaurants — went on and on.

I drove into Dallas for a weekend with friends; that was the Sunday of the bombing in Birmingham where four children were killed. After that tragic and horrible incident, my friends said to me: "It's no longer a question of whether you want to leave Mississippi. Your only question is where do you want to move."

I began to get worried, to tell the truth, I got a large number of letters from all over the nation, each of them urging me to leave.

So that's exactly what I did. I now live in a small village on

Mobile Bay. People have left me alone, and I try to do the same for them.

I continue my paper, now on a monthly basis, and the policy remains as fairness. The word has more meaning to me than a policy; it has become a part of my way of living. I am aware of falling short quite often, but I am also aware of trying every day of my life.

"I Believe I'm Going to Die"

These are excerpts from The Murder of Fred Hampton, *a documentary film on the life and death of the Black Panther leader in Illinois. Mr. Hampton and an associate, Mark Clark, were shot to death in a police raid in Chicago on December 4, 1969. The first excerpt is by Mr. Hampton, the second by Deborah Johnson, who was a survivor of the raid.*

I WAS BORN in a so-called bourgeois community and had some of the better things you could say of life. And I found that even some of the better things of life for black people wasn't too cool. And I found that there was more people starvin' than there was people eatin'. And I found there was more people didn't have clothes than did have clothes. And I found that I just happened to be one of the few. And I made a commitment to myself that I wouldn't stop doin' what I'm doin' until all those people were free.

We talkin' about we goin' ta make some changes in this system. We know they have our pictures. We know they lookin' for us. We know they want us. But we're still sayin' that even though we could be — in a sense — as far as this system goes — "on the mountaintop" — we in the Black Panther party — because of our dedication and understanding what's in the valley — knowing that the people are in the valley — knowing that we originally came from the valley — knowing that our plight is the same plight as the people in the valley — knowing that our enemy is on the mountaintop — our freedom's in the valley . . . we say even though it's nice to be on the mountaintop — we're goin' back to the valley!

I want you to know that I want you to think. If you ever think about me and if you think about me Niggers and if you ain't gonna do no revolutionary act, forget about me. I don't want myself on your mind if you're not going to work for the people. Like we always said, if you're asked to make a commitment at the age of twenty and you say, I don't want to make a commitment only because of the simple reason that I'm too young to die, I want to live a little bit longer, what you did is, you're dead already.

You have to understand that people have to pay the price for peace. If you dare to struggle, you dare to win. If you dare not struggle then damn it — you don't deserve to win. Let me say peace to you if you're willing to fight for it.

I've been gone for a little while. At least my body's been gone for a little while. But I'm back now and I believe that I'm back to stay. I believe that I'm going to do my job and I believe that I was born not to die in a car wreck; I don't believe that I'm going to die in a car wreck. I don't believe I'm going to die slipping on a piece of ice; I don't believe I'm going to die because I got a bad heart; I don't believe I'm going to die because of lung cancer. I believe that I'm going to be able to die doing the things I was born for. I believe that I'm going to be able to die high off the people. I believe that I will be able to die as a revolutionary in the international revolutionary proletarian struggle. And I hope that each one of you will be able to die in the international proletarian revolutionary struggle or you'll be able to live in it. And I think that struggle's going to come. Why don't you live for the people? Why don't you struggle for the people? Why don't you die for the people?

.

SOMEONE CAME INTO THE ROOM . . . started shakin' the chairman. Said "Chairman, chairman, wake up — the Pigs are vampin'." Still half-asleep I looked up and I saw bullets comin' from it looked like the front of the apartment — from the kitchen area — they were . . . the Pigs were just shootin'. And about this time I jumped on top of the chairman. He looked up . . . looked like all the Pigs just converged at the entranceway to the bedroom area — the back bedroom area. The mattress was just . . . goin'. You could feel the bullets goin' into it. I just knew we'd be dead, everybody in there.

When he looked up, he just looked up — he didn't say a word and he didn't move 'cept for movin' his head up. He laid his head back down . . . to the side like that. He never said a word and he never got up off the bed . . . a person who was in the room — they kept hollerin' out "stop shootin' — stop shootin' we have a pregnant woman or a pregnant sister in here." At that time I was eight and a half to nine months pregnant. My baby was to be delivered in two weeks. The Pigs kept on shootin' so I kept on hollerin' out. Finally they stopped. They pushed me and the other brother by the kitchen door and told us to face the wall. I heard a Pig say, "He's barely alive, he'll barely make it." I assumed they were talkin' about Chairman Fred. So then . . . they started shootin' — the Pigs started shootin' — shootin' again. I heard a sister scream. They stopped shootin'. The Pig said, "He's good and dead now." The Pigs run around laughing — they was really happy, ya know . . . talkin' about Chairman Fred is dead. I never saw Chairman Fred again . . .

A Black Panther Speaks

Richard Moore was one of thirteen Black Panthers being tried on a bomb conspiracy charge in New York City. He and Michael Tabor, another defendant, disappeared February 8, 1971, and later were reported to be in Algiers. His explanation was published a few days before his associates in the trial were acquitted and not long before he himself was arrested in New York in connection with the murder of a policeman.

FIRST, LET IT BE UNDERSTOOD that the only reason that I undertook to explain why it was necessary for I and Cetewayo (Michael Tabor) to leave the fascist farce of a trial presided over by the evil likes of John Murtagh is because it has come to my attention that there is confusion as to why we did it.

Because it is beyond the *New York Times*, as the organ of the ruling class, to present the necessary information to the masses of misinformed people in such a manner that will truly help them understand and differentiate between the revisionist clique of West Coast pimps headed by Huey P. Newton, and those who have cast their fate in the making of the American Revolution, I think it appropriate to also explain why we split, even if such as the *New York Times* will print this only in their quest for the sensational.

The reason that impelled us to leave the country was sheer necessity. The situation that existed at the time of our departure was one of desperation. Desperation in the court, in the streets, and in the objective conditions of our people's liberation struggle.

Truly, we found ourselves between the devil and the deep blue sea. On the one hand Judge Murtagh, in cahoots with Assistant District Attorney Joseph Phillips, was plotting to put us in jail under the guise of "American justice." Needless to say this did not, and does not appeal to us. Being old hands of the American penal system and its systematic dehumanization, we could not tolerate this prospect. As revolutionaries, we are dedicated to the eradication of these institutional tools of class rule. Therefore we are outlaws. On the other hand we were aware of the plots emanating from the co-opted fearful minds of Huey Newton and the arch revisionist, David Hilliard [another Black Panther leader]. We knew of their desires to destroy, with their fear-oriented plans and bourgeois dreams, the only truly revolutionary organ of social change that black people possessed. Of course we guessed correctly that they would cop out on us once Murtagh made his scurvy move in the courts. Because we are outlaws we could not allow the destruction of our people's just struggle and the machinery we so painstaking put together for our liberation.

So we therefore discarded the cloak of overt struggle. Indeed the time had come to wear the mantle of outlaws. We therefore took up completely the war against our people's oppressor — to either win or die.

.

Now, concerning the split in the party. Historically we have seen how those revolutionary struggles of an oppressed people who allowed themselves to be confined to parliamentary procedure, whether out of fear of repression or ignorance of the dynamics of class rule, have failed. It became clear almost a year ago that David Hilliard was destroying the desire in comrades to wage resolute struggle by confining the party to mass rallies and "fund-raising benefits." Of course mass mobilization is important and money is necessary to function, but the effects that these restrictions have upon the mentality of a brother or sister are horrifying.

One's perspective is not allowed to blossom beyond the rally mentality and all that accompanies it. Thus efficiency is strictly hampered. Also, obsession with fund raising leads to dependency upon the very class enemies of our people. To appeal to the conscience of the bourgeoisie is neither revolutionary in nature nor practical in our people's struggle. The misappropriation of this money, its squandering on clothes, pads and other irrelevancies and whims of Huey Newton and David Hilliard is the logical result of distorted perceptions brought on by their restricted commitment.

To the front line troops there is no progress — only their squalor and poverty confront them as fruits of their efforts. Newton's harping on survival programs is not in the interest of the people. Just as the reform programs instituted in the Philippines by ex-Huk leaders were geared to remove the mass base of the Revolutionary Huks, Huey's programs are geared to remove revolutionary mass action that could jeopardize his new-found material freedom, and position.

These internal contradictions have naturally developed to the point where those within the party found themselves in an organization fastly approaching the likes of the NAACP — dedicated to modified slavery instead of putting an end to all forms of slavery. Outlaws cannot enjoy penthouses and imported furniture. It is this type of leadership that saw the slogan substituted for the action.

Huey P. Newton and his Peralta Street Gang betrayed their people. If they were on a college campus and did this they might have gotten away unnoticed. But they betrayed young black men and women who came out of the depths of despair that are the ghetto streets and who transformed themselves for an idea that gave new meaning to their existence. These young men and women for the most part remain true to that idea of freedom and those that betrayed it can command neither their devotion nor respect.

ALL POWER TO THE PEOPLE

Dearest Angela

George Jackson, shot to death at San Quentin prison in August 1971, carried on an extensive correspondence with Angela Davis in 1970 before Miss Davis herself was arrested and imprisoned.

May 29, 1970

Dearest Angela,

I'm thinking about you. I've done nothing else all day. This photograph that I have of you is not adequate. Do you recall what Eldridge said regarding pictures for the cell? Give Frances several color enlargements for me. This is the cruelest aspect of the prison experience. You can never understand how much I hate them for this, no one could, I haven't been able to gauge it myself.

Over this ten years I've never left my cell in the morning looking for trouble, never once have I initiated any violence. In each case where it was alleged, it was defense/attack response to some aggression, verbal or physical. Perhaps a psychiatrist, a Western psychiatrist that is, could make a case against me for anticipating attacks. But I wasn't born this way. Perhaps this same psychiatrist would diagnose from the overreactions that I am not a very nice person. But again I refer you to the fact that I was born innocent and trusting. The instinct to survive and all that springs from it developed in me as it is today out of necessity.

I am not a very nice person, I confess. I don't believe in such things as free speech when it's used to rob and defame me. I don't believe in mercy or forgiveness or restraint. I've gone to great lengths to learn every dirty trick devised and have improvised some new ones of my own. I don't play fair, don't fight fair. As I think of this present situation, the things that happen all day, the case they've saddled me with, in retrospection of the aggregate injury — all now drawn against the background of this picture you've given me — no one will profit from this, sister. No one will ever again profit from our pain. This is the last treadmill I'll run. They created this situation. All that flows from it is their responsibility. They've created in me one irate, resentful nigger — and it's building — to what climax? The nation's undertakers have grown wealthy on black examples, but I want you to believe in me, Angela. I'm going to make a very poor example, no one will profit from my immolation. When that day comes they'll have to bury ten thousand of their own with full military honors. They'll have earned it.

Do you sense how drunk this photograph has made me?

You've got it all, African woman. I'm very pleased, if you don't ask me for my left arm, my right eye, both eyes, I'll be very disappointed. You're the most powerful stimulus I could have.

From now on when you have books for me to read in preparing my motions and jury selection questions, send them through John Thorne, people's lawyer, he is less pressed. And I do want Lenin, Marx, Mao, Che, Giap, Uncle Ho, Nkrumah, and any black Marxists. Mama has a list. Tell Robert to provide money for them, and always look for the pocket editions, all right? My father — you'll have to try to understand him. He'll be with me in the last days in spite of whatever he says and thinks now. I've told him that I love you, and I told him that if he respects me at all, and wants me to spare his neck at Armageddon, he must be kind to you.

I got a letter from him this evening wherein he called the pigs by their very accurate moniker — pigs — he'll be all right. I see your influence already. But back to the books. With each load of heavy stuff throw in a reference book dealing with pure fact, figures, statistics, graphs for my further education. Also books on the personnel and structure of today's political, military, and economic front. I am doing some serious theory work for you concerning the case, dedicated to Huey and Angela. If you understand what I want, let me know. Sister, it's been like being held incommunicado these last ten years. No one understood what I was attempting to do and to say. We belong among the righteous of the world. We are the most powerful. We are in the best position to do the people's work. To win will involve taking a chance, crawling on the belly, naming, numbering, infiltrating, giving up meaningless small comforts, readjusting some values. My life means absolutely nothing without positive control over the factors that determine its quality. If you understand, rush to send all that I've asked for. A load should come in each day. I've read it all, once anyway, but I need it now . . . and time has become very important. I want you to believe in me. I love you like a man, like a brother, and like a father. Every time I've opened my mouth, assumed my battle stance, I was trying in effect to say I love you, African — African woman. My protest has been a small one, something much more effective is hidden in my mind — believe in me, Angela. This is one nigger who's got some sense and is not afraid to use it. If my enemies, your enemies, prove stronger, at least I want them to know that they made one righteous African man extremely angry. And that they've strained the patience of a righteous and loving people to the utmost.

I've stopped several times in this writing to exercise, to eat, and it has grown late. I want to get this off tonight. I must know as soon as you get this and the others. Are you sure about your mail? I can imagine that the CIA is reading all your mail before you get it and deciding what you should and shouldn't have. Big Brother. He is rather transparent. I don't care about him. I have his number. I know he's a punk, he can't stop me.

Should we make a lovers' vow? It's silly, with all my tomorrows accounted for, but you can humor me.

Power to the People!

GEORGE

My Brother, George

Roger Wilkins, Assistant Attorney General under Ramsey Clark, wrote this essay immediately after the killing of George Jackson in San Quentin prison, August 1971.

AUGUST IN EAST HAMPTON is a lovely time. Gusts from the ocean hint fall, and the late summer sun casts a soft light over brown meadows, green potato fields and deep blue ponds. People fret over communal picnics, speculate over names included or left off weekend guest lists, and compare notes on the household help available in the local talent pool. In serious moments, a disgruntled intellectual may talk of emigrating to Ireland, or the alienation of modern man and his ceaseless search for identity.

Then comes the news from California. George Jackson couldn't get to Ireland. He couldn't even reach the San Quentin wall. The paper said that in the yard at his prison Jackson received a rifle bullet "on top of the head . . . that went through the base of his skull, down his back alongside the spine, fracturing a rib and leaving from his lower back."

Talk on the beaches and at backyard cocktail parties turned to the inconsistencies in the official reports and to speculation about prison authorities having set him up to die. Jackson, the general judgment goes, though for perhaps good reason — imprisoned for up to life for a seventy-dollar robbery — was a desperate man and alienated from our society.

Jackson was certainly alienated from East Hampton's late summer ennui and that strain of American life that encourages people to fritter their lives away heedless of casual and calculated cruelties inflicted on people who do not belong, but he was not alienated from himself. He was the ultimate nigger and he knew it. A man of intelligence and dignity, George Jackson was one of those against whom American law contorts, degrades and mocks itself. For a crime for which a white youth might have received probation for two years, Jackson served eleven years — most of them in stench-filled solitary cells — at the mercy of officials who had some need to break his will. He told Angela Davis in a letter: "They created the situation. All that flows from it is their responsibility. They've created in me one irate, resentful nigger — and it's building — to what climax?"

George Jackson never really had a chance to live the life of the empty spirit, worrying about status, his next promotion or the right place to live. He suffered the final American degradation — he was poor and black and smart and a prisoner.

Jackson knew the value of seventy dollars and a black life in the California prisons. He wrote often that he never expected to be given back his freedom — to leave prison alive. But he also made clear that his soul was his own. He refused to cede his spirit to coarse prison authority in return for the mean favors of a system that could pen men for years in cramped "adjustment center" cells smaller than a family bathroom, behind solid metal doors with two-inch by five-inch slits to see the "free" corridor area outside. To preserve his mind, Jackson read everything from Stendhal to Engels. To preserve his body, he did exercises in his cell for six hours a day. To preserve his soul he resisted prison brutality and evolved a philosophy of rebellion which he preached to all who would listen. He saved his soul and lost his life following the precepts of the prisoner Sologdin in Solzhenitsyn's *The First Circle:*

> *The most rewarding past . . . is the greatest external resistance in the presence of the least internal resistance. Failures must be considered the cue for further applications of efforts and concentration of willpower. And if substantial ef-*

forts have already been made, the failures are all the more joyous. It means our crowbar has struck the iron box containing the treasure. Overcoming the increased difficulties is all the more valuable because in failure, the growth of the person performing the task takes place in proportion to the difficulty encountered!

No matter how hard they pressed George Jackson's face in the slime, he always thrust his hand toward the sun.

The state says George Jackson was a murderer and perhaps he killed a man or more but if he did, he did it inside an iron circle of hell where the agents of a careless people have almost unlimited sovereignty over the bones and spirits of the men they keep. Death of prisoner and keeper alike are the natural consequences of state-sponsored savagery. If some men kill to prevent the theft of the goods of their store or their family jewels, might others not also kill to prevent the theft of their lives and their spirits?

In East Hampton and other places — where iron boxes are rarely struck — people will speculate briefly on the nature of Jackson's life and the reasons for his death and go on to the next headline. Whatever the details of his last day — whether or not he had a gun in his hair — the brothers, not Soledad, but mainly black — George Jackson helped define for all time our iron boxes and some of the ways to approach them.

In his time and in his place, he built a powerful life and suffused our spirits with the nigger suffering and the steel force of the Black Everyman he had come to be. In California they could snatch his life for seventy dollars, but the bullet that split his skull and creased his spine could not kill what he had become.

And now, as August wanes, waves lap quietly on the sandy Hampton shores.

The Animals at Attica

Tom Wicker was one of the observers called in by the Attica convicts to try to help settle the strike. He wrote these impressions after the slaughter.

AFTER THE MASSACRE at Attica, Governor Rockefeller issued a statement that began with this sentence: "Our hearts go out to the families of the hostages who died at Attica."

Much of what went wrong at Attica — and of what is wrong at most other American prisons and "correction facilities" — can be found in the simple fact that neither in that sentence nor in any other did the governor or any official extend a word of sympathy to the families of the dead prisoners.

True, at that time, it was thought that the deaths of the hostages had been caused by the prisoners, rather than — as is now known — by the bullets and buckshot of those ordered by the state authorities to go over the walls shooting.

But even had the prisoners, instead of the police, been the killers of the hostages, they still would have been human beings; certainly their mothers and wives and children still would have been human beings. But the official heart of the State of New York did not go out to any of them.

That is the root of the matter; prisoners, particularly black prisoners, in all too many cases are neither considered nor treated as human beings. And since they are not, neither are their families. Yesterday, the families of sixteen Attica inmates, gathered outside the medical examiner's office in Rochester, could not find out whether their husbands and sons were dead or alive; since last Thursday night they had not even been able to find out whether the men were involved in the prison rebellion, because the state would not trouble to tell them.

Dead hostages, for another example, were sent to the morgue tagged with their names; dead prisoners went tagged "P-1," "P-2," and so on. That is an almost unbearable fact to those who heard an eloquent prisoner shouting in the yard of D-Block last Friday night: "We no longer wish to be treated as statistics, as numbers. We want to be treated as human beings, we *will* be treated as human beings!" But even in death, they were still just numbers.

Time and again, members of the special observers' group that tried to negotiate a settlement at Attica heard the prisoners plead that they, too, were human beings and wanted above all to be treated as such. Once, in a negotiating session through a steel-barred gate that divided prisoner-held and state-held territory, Assistant Correction Commissioner Walter Dunbar told the prisoner leader, Richard Clark, "In thirty years, I've never lied to an inmate."

"But how about to a man?" Clark said quietly.

The physical aspect of a place like Attica — the grim walls, the bare yards, the clanging steel — bespeaks the attitude that prisoners are wild animals to be caged. Entering a tier in Cellblock C, where prisoners were under control, the observers were struck by the pathetic sight of shaving mirrors popping instantly from the window of each steel door; the windows are too small for the cells' occupants to see anywhere but straight ahead, and only the mirrors can show the prisoners what is happening in their "home."

Attica — like most prisons — is not a "correctional facility" at all; the phrase is a gruesome euphemism. No "correctional officer" there has any real training in correcting or teaching or counseling men; rather, they are armed guards set to herd animals. Senselessly, every guard at Attica is white, save one reported Puerto Rican no observer ever saw; but the prisoners are 75 per cent, or maybe 85 per cent — no one seems to know for sure — black and

Puerto Rican. There is no Spanish-speaking doctor. All work for thirty cents a day, and one of their grievances claimed that they often were bilked of that.

The emphasis on guns and clubs during the crisis was incredible; it had to be seen to be believed. Once, standing alone and unarmed at the steel gate, Richard Clark refused to negotiate any further because the room beyond was packed with so many men bearing clubs, rifles, pistols, shotguns and tear-gas launchers. Three or four blocks from the prison, tourists were stopped at roadblocks by as many as four uniformed men, each carrying a club, a pistol, a rifle. So much weaponry was bound to be used sooner or later, and indiscriminately. And it was.

These guns, moreover, were in the hands of men who left no doubt they wanted to use them. Correction Commissioner Oswald's long delay of the assault and his efforts to negotiate were met with impatience and anger by the prison staff; the observers who were trying to prevent bloodshed saw hostility at every turn. A guard bringing them a box of food said as he put it down, "If I'd known it was for you people, I wouldn't have brought it."

The observers, after all, were standing between the men with the guns and the prisoners, who had none. Even the strong belief that an assault on the stronghold in Block D would cause the prisoners to kill their thirty-eight hostages seemed to make little difference to those who had the guns; they wanted to go in.

The observers knew that. They said so to Commissioner Oswald and Governor Rockefeller, forcefully and in every way they could. They predicted a massacre. They said that waiting, while it might not ultimately prevent the slaughter, could hardly cause it; while attacking could result in nothing else.

But time is for men, not for prisoners and animals. Now the dead lie tagged in the morgue, and the men with the guns are counting their kill. They may even be looking forward to the same highly practical form of amnesty American society has already granted to the killers at Kent State and Orangeburg and Jackson State.

The Root Causes of Attica

Vice President Agnew offered his impressions of Attica after it had been revealed that the hostages as well as the convicts had been slain by the bullets of the "liberating" force.

WHEN EVEN A LIBERAL with the doughty credentials of David Susskind is impelled to react against what he called "rancid liberal rhetoric," it is obvious that the polemics of the doctrine of societal guilt have gone too far. Yet, that is exactly what has occurred in the aftermath of the riot and ensuing bloodshed at Attica state prison.

What happened at Attica could not have been foreseen, unless one is willing to accept the radiclib ideological premise of original sin which holds every outbreak of violence in our society to be further evidence of the intrinsic evil of the system. However, what has happened since — the litany of recrimination against "the authorities," the naive equating of antisocial with social goals, the call for examination of "root causes" — all of this could have been foreheard in the rhetorical excesses which followed previous confrontations between society's authority and antisocial force.

Very well, then, let us examine some of the "root causes" of Attica — though not in the sense of attributing indiscriminate blame of American institutions. This is not to say that all is perfect within our system, or that penological theory and practice in the United States is beyond criticism. We all know that improvement is needed. But perspective constitutes the first requisite of wisdom. Little credit is due otherwise responsible public spokesmen whose desire to placate a far Left constituency has caused them to overlook the fact that, for all its shortcomings, the theory of American criminology and our penal system remain among the most humane and advanced in the world. Thus, to assert that the question raised at Attica was "Why men would rather die than live another day in America" is the purest political fatuity.

To position the "demands" of convicted felons in a place of equal dignity with legitimate aspirations of law-abiding American citizens — or to compare the loss of life by those who violate the society's law with a loss of life of those whose job it is to uphold it — represents not simply an assault on human sensibility, but an insult to reason. Worst of all, it gives status and seeming respectability to the extremists in our society whose purpose it is to exacerbate rather than ameliorate the problems of race relations — the very problems to which the spokesmen, in this instance, allude.

In my opinion, then, it is the approbation given extremists by some responsible leaders of both races that has nurtured the roots of violence such as occurred at Attica and, not long before, at San Quentin.

To be sure, when law-abiding citizens of both the white and black races are daily subjected to the editorial elevation of convicted felons into "revolutionary leaders," the effect of such near apotheosis is to blur lines of rational, democratic discussion, not simply of penological but of all the broad social problems which concern our society. As for the effect of such exaltation of criminality on lawbreakers both within and outside prison walls, who can doubt that violence is encouraged when the violent-prone are provided a civilized rationale for their psychopathic proclivities?

"Let's not try to compromise the demands," said the Black Panther leader sent to Attica to help "negotiate" a settlement. The roots of such reckless intransigence, which contributed to the need to use force to break the strike, do not lie in "social injustice" or "revolutionary" fervor. Rather, what we heard there was the voice of criminal arrogance fed by the long-time accommodation of moderate spokesmen, white and black alike, to the extremism of word and deed practiced by black power militants.

Again, when a Panther leader vows to "chop off the head" of a United States senator, and another threatens to "slit every throat that threatens our freedom," the seeds of violence are sown and flourish. The situation is not helped by the words of a heretofore responsible Negro leader who said that, although he "may not agree all down the line" with the Panthers, he is "on the same side" because "they complain of things the average Negro knows are true"; or by the Atlanta-based black leader who, though committed to the doctrine of nonviolence, lost no time in gratuitously endorsing the Panthers when they recently announced an intention to move their headquarters to that community.

What happened at Attica proves once again that when the responsible voices of society remain mute, the forces of violence and crime grow arrogant. One need only recall the era of Hitler's storm troopers to realize what can happen to the most civilized of societies when such a cloak of respectability is provided thugs and criminals.

In taking the necessary steps to end the confrontation at Attica, Governor Rockefeller acted courageously. Those who would have had him act otherwise have yet to learn the paramount lesson of our century; that acquiescence to the demands of the criminal element of any society only begets greater violence.

War

HERE IS WAR — the catalyst of our times. What can be said of war that we have not said long since? It is war which sharpens the blade of our conscience and heats the rebellion of the young, which melts the divisions between the races and erases the artificial barriers of national frontiers.

In this handful of selections all of us confront war as the children of this particular decade — historically and literarily with Iceland's Nobelist, Laxness, and in the terror technology which Robert Bly knows so well. We hear the simple voice of a woman's conscience and the cynical sadness of Russell Baker, who has seen men come and go in Washington for a generation without any remission of the hypocrisy count. A fine young man writes his obituary and goes off to war, almost certain of his death and certain that if it comes it is only a fair price for what country and life have given him. An honest young officer challenges his President, accusing him, I guess it must be said, of moral failure. Another soldier puts the case for ending the war more eloquently than any of the civilians and statesmen.

War. It is *the* moral issue of our time and it is an American issue paramount. This is not simply because it is the United States which has fought so long in Southeast Asia (and in so many other parts of the world). There is no real reason why an Englishman or an Egyptian should not feel moral outrage at American war-making. But the fact is that the issue is perceived in the United States with a clarity and purity which does not come through in the statements and feelings of those who are not directly involved. Not even the victims of America, not even the Vietnamese themselves, feel the moral outrage which possesses so many Americans.

It takes an American to understand that war is the horror of our day. (The Russians, who suffered more than any other people in World War II, still fear and abhor war; but they do not possess the moral imperatives of Americans. The Japanese, who renounced war after Hiroshima and MacArthur, now see war more in philosophical and even mystical terms. Only Americans suffer the agony of the damned.) The struggle against war centers in America. Here is where men of conscience fight to end the power of the state to compel men to kill, and this is what impels Louise Bruyn and thousands of other Americans to individual acts of conscience to end war.

These selections testify to war and America — the testimony of Americans on the tragedy of their times, their petitions, their acts, their invocations in the effort to halt war.

Yet, year after year it has gone on. Not, however, because of the ancient runic glory invoked by Halldor Laxness. This is no game in which Man is Hunter and Hunted with Death the winner, the "consummate glory of man" and the "mass of swords" celebrated by the Nordic scalds of whom Laxness writes. No joy in this war, not even to the hungry raven, the eagle or the swift wolves which moved among the carrion of the Nordic battlefield. This is electronic, dehumanized, computerized war conducted by men who have never seen the country they are fighting let alone its inhabitants. This is the war of Robert Bly's Teeth Mother. Why does it go on? Bly answers for the Teeth Mother:

> It is because we have so few women sobbing in back rooms,
> because we have so few children's heads torn apart by high-
> velocity bullets,
> because we have so few tears falling on our own hands
> that the Super Sabre turns and screams down toward the
> earth . . .

The Marines use cigarette lighters to light the thatched roofs
   of huts
because so many Americans own their own homes.

So. War goes on, choking some with profits, choking some with
shame.

The Teeth Mother Naked at Last

These are excerpts from the poem by Robert Bly published in 1971.

I

Massive engines lift beautifully from the deck.
Wings appear over the trees, wings with eight hundred rivets.

Engines burning a thousand gallons of gasoline a minute
  sweep over the huts with dirt floors.

The chickens feel the new fear deep in the pits of their beaks.
Buddha with Padma Sambhava.
Slate ships float on the China Sea,
gray bodies born in Roanoke,
the ocean to both sides expanding, "buoyed on the dense
  marine."

Helicopters flutter overhead. The death-
bee is coming. Supersabres
like knots of neurotic energy sweep
around and return.
This is Hamilton's triumph.
This is the advantage of a centralized bank.
B-52's come from Guam. All the teachers
die in flames. The hopes of Tolstoy fall asleep in the ant-heap.
Do not ask for mercy.

Now the time comes to look into the past-tunnels,
the hours given and taken in school,

the scuffles in coatrooms,
foam leaps from his nostrils,
now we come to the scum you take from the mouths of the
dead,

now we sit beside the dying, and hold their hands, there
is hardly time for goodbye,
the staff sergeant from North Carolina is dying — you hold
his hand,
he knows the mansions of the dead are empty, he has an
empty place
inside him, created one night when his parents came home
drunk,
he uses half his skin to cover it,
as you try to protect a balloon from sharp objects . . .

Artillery shells explode. Napalm canisters roll end over end.
800 steel pellets fly through the vegetable walls.
The six-hour infant puts his fists instinctively to his eyes to
keep out the light.
But the room explodes,
the children explode.
Blood leaps on the vegetable walls.

Yes, I know, blood leaps on the walls —
No need to cry at that —
Do you cry at the wind pouring out of Canada?
Do you cry at the reeds shaken at the edges of the sloughs?
The Marine battalion enters.
This happens when the seasons change,
This happens when the leaves begin to drop from the trees
too early
"Kill them: I don't want to see anything moving."
That happens when the ice begins to show its teeth in the
ponds

that happens when the heavy layers of lake water press down
on the fish's head, and sends him deeper, where his tail
swirls slowly, and his brain passes him pictures of heavy
reeds, of vegetation fallen on vegetation . . .

Hamilton saw all this in detail:
*"Every banana tree slashed, every cooking utensil smashed,
every mattress cut."*

Now the Marine knives sweep around like sharp-edged jets;
how easily they slash open the rice bags,
the mattresses . . .
ducks are killed with $150 shotguns.

Old women watch the soldiers.

II

Excellent Roman knives slip along the ribs.

A stronger man starts to jerk up the strips of flesh.

*Let's hear it again, you believe in the Father, the Son, and
the Holy Ghost?*

A long scream unrolls.

More.

*From the political point of view, democratic institutions are
being built in Vietnam, wouldn't you agree?*

A green parrot shudders under the fingernails.
Blood jumps in the pocket.
The scream lashes like a tail.

"Let us not be deterred from our task by the voices of
dissent . . ."

The whines of jets
pierce like a long needle.

As soon as the President finishes his press conference,
     black wings carry off the words,
bits of flesh still clinging to them.

*   *   *

The ministers lie, the professors lie, the television lies, the
     priests lie . . .
These lies mean that the country wants to die.
Lie after lie starts out into the prairie grass,
like enormous trains of Conestoga wagons . . .

And a long desire for death flows out, guiding
the enormous caravans from beneath,
stringing together the vague and foolish words.

It is a desire to eat death,
to gobble it down,
to rush on it like a cobra with mouth open,

It's a desire to take death inside,
to feel it burning inside, pushing out velvety hairs,
like a clothes brush in the intestines

This is the thrill that leads the President on to lie

*   *   *

The Chief Executive enters; the Press Conference begins:
First the President lies about the date the Appalachian
     Mountains rose

Then he lies about the population of Chicago, then about the
     weight of the adult eagle, next about the acreage of the
     Everglades

He lies about the number of fish taken every year in the
Arctic, he has private information about which city *is* the
capital of Wyoming, he lies about the birthplace of Attila
the Hun

He lies about the composition of the amniotic fluid, he insists
that Luther was never a German, and insists that only
the Protestants sold indulgences,
That Pope Leo X *wanted* to reform the church, but the
"liberal elements" prevented him,

That the Peasants' War was fomented by Italians from the
North.
And the Attorney General lies about the time the sun sets.

❋   ❋   ❋

This is only the deep longing for death.
It is the longing for someone to come and take us by the
hand to where they all are sleeping:
where the Egyptian Pharoahs are asleep, and your own
mother,
and all those disappeared children, who used to go around
with you in a swing at grade school . . .

Do not be angry at the President — he is longing to take in
his hand
the locks of death hair —
to meet his own children sleeping, or unborn . . .
He is drifting sideways toward the dusty places

III

That's what it's like for a rich country to make war,
That's what it's like to bomb huts (afterwards described as
"structures")

That's what it's like to kill marginal farmers (afterwards described as "Communists")

This is what it's like to watch the altimeter needle going mad

Baron 25, this is 81. Are there any friendlies in the area? 81 from 25, negative on the friendlies. I'd like you to take out as many structures as possible located in those trees within 200 meters east and west of my smoke mark.

diving, the green earth swinging, cheeks hanging back, red pins blossoming ahead of us, 20 millimeter cannon fire, leveling off, rice fields shooting by like telephone poles, smoke rising, hut roofs loom up huge as landing fields, slugs going in, half the huts on fire, figures running, palm trees burning, shooting past, up again; blue sky, cloud mountains

That is what it's like to have a gross national product

It's because a hospital room in the average American city now costs $60 a day that we bombed hospitals in the North

It's because the aluminum window-shade business is doing so well in the United States that we roll fire over entire villages

It's because the milk trains coming into New Jersey hit the right switches every day that the best Vietnamese men are cut in two by American bullets that follow each other like freight cars

This is what it's like to send firebombs down in 110° heat from air-conditioned cockpits,

This is what it's like to be told to fire into a reed hut with an automatic weapon,

It's because we have new packaging for smoked oysters that
bomb holes appear in the rice paddies

It is because we have so few women sobbing in back rooms,
because we have so few children's heads torn apart by high-
velocity bullets,
because we have so few tears falling on our own hands
that the Super Sabre turns and screams down toward the
earth

It's because tax-payers move to the suburbs that we transfer
populations.
The Marines use cigarette lighters to light the thatched roofs
of huts
because so many Americans own their own homes.

Letters to Our Friends

On February 17, 1971, Louise Bruyn of Newton Centre, Massachusetts, began a walk to Washington, D.C., in protest against the war. She, her husband and daughter wrote letters telling of her decision.

14 February 1971

Dear Friends and Relatives —

I feel I must write each of you to tell you my plans.

This Wednesday, February 17, I am leaving our house in Newton, Massachusetts, and walking to Washington, D.C. It should take about forty-five days to get there. I may arrive around April 2, providing I make it.

I am moved to do this because I can no longer sit in the comfort of our beautiful home, knowing the death and destruction we are causing in another land. I cannot separate myself from this though heaven knows I am well insulated. But I know it is my money supporting the war machine, my senators and representatives in Congress approving war measures. People feel so trapped. I felt that I must break my own routine in order to make my protest heard. For me, this is what my action means. I am speaking as strongly as I know how. It is my deep hope that others will be moved to take some action which for *them* is right — as strongly as they know how — to end the war.

None of you needs to have the horrors of the war described. I know of no one who feels the war should continue. Many of you are already engaged in a total commitment to work toward peace. I am trying to reach those who have become anaesthetized and feel there is nothing one person can do. I am asking them to look for alternatives, to actively say *no* to the death machine which is war, in *their own way*.

In hope,
LOUISE

•

14 February 1971

To Whom It May Concern:

My wife, Louise, has decided to walk from Newton, Massachusetts, to Washington, D.C., as a protest against the spiraling effects of the war in Vietnam and against the war itself. She is a housewife, a dance instructor at the All Newton Music School, a mother of teen-age children, a person whose home means a great deal to her. I believe her protest is noteworthy because she is willing to give up the comforts of her home, her family, her artistic involvements, in order to make an action statement against the war; furthermore, her protest is one which should be communicated to those who have felt it impossible to be articulate about the developing holocaust in Southeast Asia.

Her reasons are simple. They augur a change in the temper of protest. The war has developed into a system of such devastating proportions that there is no longer time to debate its morality. The time has come for a fundamental kind of action which will bring it to a halt. It is the kind of action in which ordinary people who lead ordinary lives — housewives, businessmen, teachers, mailmen, bus drivers — can stop their routines and say that the war has become a seven-year massacre. It can no longer be tolerated by any measure of humanity. Debate has ended. This must be the year of citizen action.

If nonviolent means of protest are not exercised quietly and firmly across the nation to end the war — by halting work, by ceasing to perform housely duties, in order to engage full time in

protest — then surely action as violent as that which the administration is perpetrating on the people of Vietnam will take place.
Ordinary, conscientious people must begin to take the leadership
to bring this war to a forceful halt.

Soldiers have been in our home telling us about the many My
Lais not open to public view. They have told us about the established practice of cutting ears and heads off Vietnamese by our
own soldiers. The war is brutalizing American youth. Six million
people have been forcibly relocated and close to a million people
have been killed — according to our own Defense Department
statistics. The massive air attacks on Laos, Cambodia, and Vietnam, the vast destruction of foliage and natural life with its hor-
rendous radiation effects on the people and the genetic consequences to their children are morally indefensible.

If China were moving troops into Canada in support of the
Quebec Liberation Front, we would take extreme measures to
protect this hemisphere from foreign invasion and ideology. Can
China be expected to remain silent much longer? The American
war in Southeast Asia must come to an end before extreme measures — a Chinese nuclear bomb with delivery power — enter into
the framework of war or into negotiations.

The German people did not do anything collectively and openly
to resist their war and the atrocities perpetrated against the Jewish people. This inaction was condemned by the Nuremburg
trials. In the United States, many people have debated and talked
against the war but little direct action to stop the war has occurred except for the bombings of a radical few. These bombings
have been called outrageous by the public when they are directed
against buildings and the offenders are hunted down and sentenced. What a twist of morality!

The amount of bombings over Vietnam released by American
airborne to kill, burn, and ravage the land of a foreign people av-
erages two and one-half Hiroshima bombs per month! The fact
that the public should condemn rock throwing in store windows

and at the same time support the administrative policy which brings massive human destruction is almost beyond belief! People then wonder why, after the futile attempts to change such morally outrageous war policies, youth turn to a rock or a bomb, or finally, violence against themselves with drugs. Where has the leadership of this nation gone?

My wife expects to leave next Wednesday, February 17. We will miss her — but she goes with our full support and all our love. She will have the support of her friends in the area. She hopes that her walk will signal others to act nonviolently on a scale that will bring this monstrous policy of killing people in Southeast Asia to an end.

SEVERYN T. BRUYN

·

14 February 1971

Life
Rockefeller Center
New York, New York

DEAR SIRS:

I write this letter to inform you that my mother, protesting the war in Indochina, is walking to Washington, D.C., from Newton, Massachusetts. The distance is 450 miles and she is going alone. I have often asked myself how I deserved a mother like this. She is a beautiful woman, strong in her beliefs, and full of love and understanding. Yet, this war, she cannot understand.

Thousands of people have died without knowing why and yet we continue to further the massacres and self-destruction to "save" the South Vietnamese. All we have been able to accomplish is to destroy a good portion of that same population which we are trying to "save." To decrease casualties, you pull out or never enter the war, instead of finding new borders to invade.

Thousands of beautiful Vietnamese children have suffered so incredibly because their skin has melted into grotesque distortions from American napalm. They could have lived normal lives.

We have protested, leafleted, signed petitions, and gathered in rallies. We cry for recognition — not for us, but for our country's mistakes. We are thrown in jails for getting exasperated enough to throw rocks, yet at the same time a soldier in Vietnam is being awarded a medal for killing innocent women and children. What has our country come to? Are we looking for a nuclear war with China? We must stop now in order to save the lives of husbands and sons who would have died in vain.

For these reasons my mother walks. What does she think it will accomplish? Perhaps nothing. But she wants people to realize that the war will not stop by itself.

My mother will leave February 17 from Newton and hopes to arrive in Washington, D.C., on April 2. She needs support. My love and prayers walk with her. I ask for your support to help her through this difficult journey.

Thank you.

SUSAN BRUYN

This Old War

Tom Wicker excerpted these remarks from his talk at the teach-in February 22, 1971, at Sanders Theater, Harvard University.

THIS OLD WAR, from beginning to end, has been rooted and grounded in misapprehension. I recall being in Vietnam in early 1966 with Hubert Humphrey, who was then Vice President. At the conclusion of that trip, we were taken around to the ambassador's house. The ambassador was then Henry Cabot Lodge — I'm sure most of you remember Henry Cabot Lodge. And Mr. Lodge sat at one side of the portico there, and the Vice President of the United States sat at the other side, and they lined up the television cameras back here, and in between they sat six hapless, helpless American advisers to local district officials, and they said, "Fellas, how's it going?" They told them how it was going. It was going pretty good. And I was a rookie at that game and was taking notes pretty madly there, and a friend of mine who had spent about two years in Vietnam came up to me and said, "This sounds good, doesn't it? You ought to have heard what that fellow told me the other night when I was talking with him in his tent. What he said did not go anywhere near what he said on the television cameras."

So I think that, in many ways, is the story of this war. We've been fooling ourselves. We've been fooling ourselves time and time again. I would take issue to some extent with some of the things that have been said here tonight, because the impression, I think, has been left that evil politicians and evil administrators have fooled the American people into doing something that they did not want to do. I would not for one moment want to imply, you understand, that they haven't been trying to fool them. We were being fooled with talk about counterinsurgency back in 1961. What were we going to do in the jungle? President Kennedy was reading the handbook of the Irish Republican Army, and that's not a joke. And the White House press group at the time went down to Fort Bragg with President Kennedy, and we saw the Blue Berets at practice, or the Green Berets — well, one of those Berets — and they even had one of those ridiculous things where a fellow with something like a rocket on his back went up and over and down on the other side of a creek. He then was free to attack the enemy. They were more vulnerable than our helicopters in the Panhandle. While this show was going on, a reporter from Agence France-Presse came over to me and whispered in my ear and said — he had been in Indochina as far back as 1951 — "All this looks great. But none of it worked when we tried it in 1951." And it didn't.

But we fooled ourselves with counterinsurgency. We fooled ourselves with the bombing campaign. I remember when the planes went north from Danang and Pleiku. We all heard glorious stories of how we were going to pulverize them up there and within eighteen months they were going to come to the conference table and bring peace. There was one story in the *New York Times* that deserves honor — at least one on that occasion. It was written by a man named Charley Mohr, who was then and is now our premier war correspondent — it's getting to be a profession — and Charley brought out an important point. He said that the problem at Pleiku — Those of you who have read the history may remember that that was the place where there were some American airplanes and some American troops before they officially had a combat role, and that base was guarded by a perimeter of South Vietnamese troops. The perimeter was pierced, and the Vietcong came through and destroyed our planes at that base and killed a number of Americans. The next day, President Johnson ordered the beginning of the bombing attacks on the North. Charley Mohr pointed out in his article what has been true of this war from the start: that if the South Vietnamese can't hold the perimeter against the Vietcong in the South, then you can't do anything by bombing the North. But we fooled ourselves at that time into thinking we could do something with bombing in the North.

We fooled ourselves that we were pursuing the lesson of Munich. We fooled ourselves that somewhere in Peking, or in Hanoi, perhaps, but somewhere over there, there was a Hitler and we were holding the line against aggression. We fooled ourselves that a half million ground troops put in there with all their firepower could take care of a few little brown men.

Well, we've found since then that in the efforts to go in there — if there was ever any validity to the effort of going in to try and protect people, if that's what we thought we were doing — we found that in the long run to protect those people we were having to destroy them. And that was fooling ourselves with a vengeance.

We fooled ourselves in the progress we were making. I was at a dinner party in Washington along about that time — the fall of 1966, I believe. A very high administration official came up to me and assaulted me, verbally, in front of a lot of people that I didn't like to be assaulted brutally in front of. He said to me, "Why does your paper print lies?" And I said, "Well, I can't defend that case. Which lie are you talking about?" And he said that when "the Buddhists took Hue last month" or "attacked Hue last month," or whenever it was at that time — he said, "You printed a story in your paper that said they captured the radio station and held it for two hours and broadcast antigovernment propaganda." And he said, "I didn't believe that." And he said, "I picked up the phone and called our man in Hue. And he said they didn't take that radio station over there to broadcast their propaganda. Now, why do you print lies like that?" I said, "Mr. Secretary, there isn't very much I can do about that. I don't know." A few months later, I was in Vietnam, and I went to Hue and I found the secretary's man in Hue, and I found that he was only too eager to tell me that the Buddhists had indeed taken that radio station and broadcast propaganda. But you didn't expect him to tell that to the secretary of state in a long-distance telephone call.

Well, we've fooled ourselves. The American people are still fooling themselves. We are fooling ourselves on the Vietnamization program. We are told Vietnamization will bring a generation of peace. And not just peace but peace with honor, which is going to prevent the establishment of a Communist government or something less than a non-Communist government in South Vietnam. Vietnamization isn't going to do any one of those things. And, furthermore, even to the extent that Vietnamization will remove our troops from Vietnam, whether or not it brings a generation of peace, whether or not that peace has honor, Vietnamization has required the invasion of two countries and the bombing of three to evacuate one, and that is a policy that seems to me to have very little future to it and very little profit.

Worst of all, we are fooling ourselves that this war is winding down. This war is not winding down. It's not winding down for six million refugees. It's not winding down for the people on whom the bombs drop, for the children on whom the napalm drops, for those one million people who are going to be moved out of the northern provinces into the southern provinces. You know that in ancient times the southern provinces were a different country. They are moving them into a different country down there. The war is not winding down for those people. It's not winding down for the nearly one million refugees created in Cambodia after the incursion there. It's not winding down on the Plaine des Jarres, where we have dropped more bombs than we did throughout World War II. It's not even winding down for the Thais, because the Chinese have resumed building a road through the northern part of Laos up to Thailand. With our incursion into Laos, the Thais are going to become vulnerable.

So this war is not winding down. It is another case in which we are fooling ourselves. The American people have been fooling themselves over there for ten long years that their aim is selfless and their cause is just. Yet the truth of the matter is that it has always been a war for American objectives, however dubious and illusory they may be. It has become in recent years a war to conceal original American folly, if not original American sin. It has become a war to preserve American vanity, a war to preserve American self-regard and to preserve American delusions of grandeur. It's become a war of war crimes for those purposes.

We are creating — and I use the word advisedly, and with consciousness of its meanings to many people — we are creating a holocaust in Indochina. I went, a year ago, to Auschwitz. But there will never be in Indochina a glass case full of the eyeglasses of those who have been butchered, and there will never be there a glass case full of little children's shoes and the hair from women's heads. There will never be any such glass cases there, because we are incinerating the people without saving the booty.

We are fooling ourselves when we think that the war is winding down, and, above all, when we think that through any means whatsoever there can be honor in the end in a war which had no honor in the beginning and has even less in the process.

And, in the great tradition of this war, many of us, and many of us here in this hall tonight, are still fooling ourselves. There are some who are fooling themselves that nothing can be done. Well, something has been done. I wouldn't want to characterize it as much or little, but something has been done.

We stopped the bombing once; we suggest that it could be stopped again.

We got negotiations going once, and perhaps we can do it again.

We got one President out, and perhaps we can do that again.

We got one party turned by the hunger of being out of office from a war party to a peace party, and perhaps we can do that again.

But there are many things that we can do. We have done some things, and I say we can do more things. We can work more. Or, in my case, I can perhaps write more. But there are those who would not advocate that course. We can speak more, although there are those, I'm sure — there are those in this hall tonight — who wouldn't endorse that proposition.

We can vote when the time comes.

We can protest any time.

There are many things that we can do.

There are others in this hall, however, who are fooling themselves into thinking that we can do it overnight. They are fooling themselves when they say that. The history of this war is not merely a history of misapprehension — it is a history of the search for a quick fix. Something that would get it over with quickly — invasions of Laos and Cambodia. And, among those who want to end the war out of peaceful motives and who want to restore the character of America, those who think that they can do it with a quick fix are just as wrong, and, in the long run, are going to do just as much damage. This is true because the American people have not simply been duped and misled into a disaster. I think we must face up to the fact — and I know many who do face up to the fact — that there is something deeply wrong in our country. Something has gone wrong in our country, and it is not merely the war in Vietnam. The war is the sickest fruit of what is wrong in our country — it is not the only thing wrong. And until we begin to contemplate what is wrong with our country, then we are not going to be able to do much about the wrong things our country does. This is what we have got to face up to. I needn't enumerate those many things in our society that need to be dealt with. They all stem from the same basic problems in our society, which are the distorted values by which we have sought personal affluence and physical power and military power in the world as against human values and things that improve the human quality of life.

I say, also, that we are all fooling ourselves or will be fooling ourselves if we think that in this effort that lies before us only success matters. I believe that we can stop this war and I believe that we can deal with the problems that face the United States of America. I believe that we can redeem the soul of our country — I believe in redemption, and I believe that we can do it. But suppose, ladies and gentlemen, suppose we cannot. Just in case we can't, I will tell you what I think. Suppose we cannot redeem our country. I believe with the poet that a man's reach should exceed his grasp. I believe with William Faulkner that the basest of all things is to be afraid. And I hold with Cavafy: Honor to those who guard their Thermopylae, even if in the end Ephialtes will appear and the Medes will go through. If we're going to think that only success matters in the effort to redeem America, then we shall fail before we begin.

Sleep

Russell Baker wrote these words for the New York Times *March 6, 1971.*

GAZE DEEPLY INTO MY PUPILS as I spin this glittering antenna in my hand. Round and round it goes. It is one of Secretary Rusk's antennas that he used in the old days to detect signals from Hanoi. Secretary Rusk's antennas were very sensitive, remember. Very sensitive. "The secretary has very sensitive antennas," they used to say at the State Department. Do not fight me now. Lie back and breathe deeply.

You are no longer going to think of Secretary Rusk's antennas. You are going to sleep, and you are going to clear your mind of all thoughts of falling dominoes. You are not going to think of the paper tiger anymore. You are going to forget the hawks and the doves, and sleep.

I want you to clear your mind of the fishhook. You are no longer going to think of the parrot's beak. You are going to forget all about the tiger cages. You are no longer going to remember the coonskin. You are going to forget all the dragon ladies. You are going to sleep, sleep.

You are going to forget about the body count, the bombing pauses, free-fire zones and Tet.

Do you remember pacification? If so, I want you to put it out of your mind, and sleep. Do you remember strategic hamlets? If so, erase the memory and sleep, for you are very, very old if you remember pacification and strategic hamlets, and you want to sleep very, very much.

You want to forget all about captured documents. Close your eyes and let COSVN dissipate from memory, as though it had never existed. Sleep and make the tunnel go away forever, as well as the light at the end of it. Forget the reports of captured enemy rice supplies and sleep.

I want you to stop thinking of all the occasions on which the corner was turned, and sleep. Sleep, and in sleep let the iron triangle cease to be even a memory. Let there be no such place as the Michelin rubber plantation, and let there never have been. Sleep.

Your mind is drifting free now because great weights have been lifted from it. Sleep deeply, and away will go all memory of the weighty bawlings of "no wider war" and "honor our commitment." In sweet sleep, let search-and-destroy cease ever to have existed. I want your sleep to help you forget that those American casualties, which were always light to moderate no matter how heavy they were, were ever casualties at all. In sleep, dream fifty thousand men back into life and restore the bodies of the hurt. Sleep.

Sleep profoundly, for in the profoundest sleep there is blessed forgetfulness of privileged sanctuaries, interdiction and incursion.

You will keep your eyes tightly closed and dive deeply, deeply into the sweet springs of sleep's oblivion, there to be washed clean of the memory of Bao Dai, Big Minh, General Khanh, Madame Nhu and Hamburger Hill. Watch this glittering antenna spin and let fierce Meo tribesmen vanish in sleep.

In sleep purge your mind of thoughts of Thich Tri Quang, Ngo Dinh Diem, Nguyen Cao Ky. The Pathet Lao cannot survive if you sleep. Sleep and let Lon Nol and Souvanna Phouma be gone forever.

Gone with Ellsworth Bunker and Henry Cabot Lodge and Ambassador David Bruce and Xuan Thuy, coming and going, going and coming, coming nowhere, going nowhere, endlessly, endlessly, except to be gently forgotten in glorious sleep.

In your sleep, forget Vietnamization, another fruitless session of the Paris peace talks today, bombing halt, Senator Fulbright's Foreign Relations Committee, Gulf of Tonkin resolution, Melvin Laird, air force briefers, Ho Chi Minh Trail, no ground troops, Cooper-Church amendment. Sleep with a profoundity you have never slept with before.

Sleep away all thought of Professors Henry Kissinger and Walt W. Rostow and of the deans — Bundy, Acheson and Rusk. In such an all-obliterating sleep as you have never known, cease remembering proposals to bomb 'em back to the Stone Age. In sleep, cast off all remembrance of protective reaction and protective encirclement.

Sleep. Sleep. Sleep, until ditches filled with bodies may lose their existence, and the dread of becoming a pitiful helpless giant can never again haunt your sun-filled afternoons. In sleep, forget.

See my antenna spin. See how it glitters in the light, even through the deepest darkness of unutterably restful sleep, with the bone-eating brightness of liquid fire in the night. Sleep warm in its brightness. When you awake you shall think of sports or flowers, or of bills and of nice fun things to do after work.

The Liberty of Conscience

Chief Judge Charles Wyzanski, Jr., of the U.S. District Court of Massachusetts, on April 1, 1969, wrote this decision in exempting John Heffron Sisson, Jr., from the draft act. It is presented in slightly excerpted form.

EVERY MAN, not least the conscientious objector, has an interest in the security of the nation. Dissent is possible only in a society strong enough to repel attack. The conscientious will to resist springs from moral principles. It is likely to seek a new order in the same society, not anarchy or submission to a hostile power. Thus conscience rarely wholly disassociates itself from the defense of the ordered society within which it functions and which it seeks to reform, not to reduce to rubble.

In parallel fashion, every man shares and society as a whole shares an interest in the liberty of the conscientious objector, religious or not. The freedom of all depends on the freedom of each. Free men exist only in free societies. Society's own stability and growth, its physical and spiritual prosperity are responsive to the liberties of its citizens, to their deepest insights — to their free choices — "That which opposes, also fits."

Those rival categories of claims cannot be mathematically graded. There is no table of weights and measures. Yet there is no insuperable difficulty in distinguishing orders of magnitude.

The sincerely conscientious man, whose principles flow from reflection, education, practice, sensitivity to competing claims, and a search for a meaningful life, always brings impressive credentials. When he honestly believes that he will act wrongly if he kills, his claim obviously has great magnitude. That magnitude is not appreciably lessened if his belief relates not to war in general, but to a particular war or to a particular type of war. Indeed a selective conscientious objector might reflect a more discriminating study of the problem, a more sensitive conscience, and a deeper spiritual understanding.

It is equally plain that when a nation is fighting for its very existence there are public and private interests of great magnitude in conscripting for the common defense all available resources, including manpower for combat.

But a campaign fought with limited forces for limited objects with no likelihood of a battlefront within this country and without a declaration of war is not a claim of comparable magnitude.

Nor is there any suggestion that in present circumstances there is a national need for combat service from Sisson [the defendant] as distinguished from other forms of service by him. The want of magnitude in the national demand for combat service is reflected in the nation's lack of calls for sacrifice in any serious way by civilians.

Before adding up the accounts and striking a balance there are other items deserving notice.

Sisson is not in a formal sense a religious conscientious objector. His claim may seem less weighty than that of one who embraces a creed which recognizes a Supreme Being, and which has as part of its training and discipline opposition to war in any form. It may even seem that the Constitution itself marks a difference, because in the First Amendment reference is made to the "free exercise of religion," not to the free exercise of conscience. Moreover, Sisson does not meet the 1967 congressional definition of religion. Nor does he meet the dictionary definition of religion.

But that is not the end of the matter. The opinions in *U.S. v. Seeger* disclosed wide vistas. The court purported to look only at a particular statute. It piously disclaimed any intent to interpret the Constitution or to examine the limitations which the First and Fifth Amendments place upon Congress. But commentators have not forgotten the Latin tag *pari passu.*

The rationale by which Seeger and his companions on appeal were exempted from combat service under the statute is quite sufficient for Sisson to lay valid claim to be constitutionally exempted from combat service in the Vietnam type of situation.

Duty once commonly appeared as the "stern daughter of the voice of God." Today to many she appears as the stern daughter of the voice of conscience. It is not the ancestry but the authenticity of the sense of duty which creates constitutional legitimacy.

Some suppose that the only reliable conscience is one responsive to a formal religious community of memory and hope. But in *Religion in the Making,* Alfred North Whitehead taught us that "religion is what the individual does with his own solitariness."

Others fear that recognition of individual conscience will make it too easy for the individual to perpetrate a fraud. His own word will so often enable him to sustain his burden of proof. Cross-examination will not easily discover his insincerity.

Seeger cut the ground from under that argument. So does experience. Often it is harder to detect a fraudulent adherent to a religious creed than to recognize a sincere moral protestant. We all can discern Thoreau's integrity more quickly than we might detect some churchman's hypocrisy.

The suggestion that courts cannot tell a sincere from an insincere conscientious objector underestimates what the judicial process performs every day.

There have been suggestions that to read the Constitution as granting an exemption from combat duty in a foreign campaign will immunize from public regulation all acts or refusals to act dictated by religious or conscientious scruple. Such suggestions fail to note that there is no need to treat, and this court does not treat, religious liberty as an absolute. The most sincere religious or conscientious believer may be validly punished even if in strict pursuance of his creed or principles, he fanatically assassinates an opponent, or practices polygamy, or employs child labor. Religious liberty and liberty of conscience have limits in the face of social demands of a community of fellow citizens. There are, for example, important rival claims of safety, order, health, and decency.

Nor is it true that to recognize liberty of conscience and religious liberty will set up some magic line between nonfeasance and misfeasance. A religiously motivated failure to discharge public obligation may be as serious a crime as a religiously motivated action in violation of law. We may, argumentatively, assume that one who out of religious or conscientious scruple refuses to pay a general income or property tax, assessed without reference to any particular kind of contemplated expenditure, is civilly and criminally liable, regardless of his sincere belief that he is responding to a divine command not to support the government.

Most important, it does not follow from a judicial decision that Sisson cannot be conscripted to kill in Vietnam that he cannot be conscripted for non-combat service there or elsewhere.

It would be a poor court indeed that could not discern the small constitutional magnitude of the interest that a person has in avoiding all helpful service whatsoever or in avoiding paying all general taxes whatsoever. His objections, of course, may be sincere. But some sincere objections have greater constitutional magnitude than others.

There are many tasks, technologically or economically related to the prosecution of a war, to which a religious or conscientious objector might be constitutionally assigned. As Justice Cardozo wrote, "Never in our history has the notion been accepted, or even, it is believed, advanced, that acts thus indirectly related to service in the camp or field are so tied to the practice of religion as to be exempt, in law or in morals, from regulation by the state."

Sisson's case being limited to a claim of conscientious objection to combat service in a foreign campaign, this court holds that the free exercise of religion clause in the First Amendment and the due process clause of the Fifth Amendment prohibit the application of the 1967 draft act to Sisson to require him to render combat service in Vietnam.

The chief reason for reaching this conclusion after examining the competing interests is the magnitude of Sisson's interest in not killing in the Vietnam conflict as against the want of magnitude in the country's present need for him to be so employed.

The statute as here applied creates a clash between law and morality for which no exigency exists, and before, in Justice Sutherland's words, "the last extremity" or anything close to that dire predicament has been glimpsed, or even predicted, or reasonably feared.

When the state through its laws seeks to override reasonable moral commitments it makes a dangerously uncharacteristic choice. The law grows from the deposits of morality. Law and morality are, in turn, debtors and creditors of each other. The law cannot be adequately enforced by the courts alone, or by courts supported merely by the police and the military. The true secret of legal might lies in the habits of conscientious men disciplining themselves to obey the law they respect without the necessity of judicial and administrative orders. When the law treats a reasonable, conscientious act as a crime it subverts its own power. It invites civil disobedience. It impairs the very habits which nourish and preserve the law.

A Soldier's Obituary

John Alexander Hottell graduated from West Point in 1964, tenth in a class of 564. He earned two Silver Stars and served as commander, Company B, First Battalion, Eighth Cavalry, First Cavalry Division (Airmobile) before being killed in a helicopter crash July 7, 1970, at the age of twenty-seven. About a year earlier he had written this self-obituary.

I AM WRITING my own obituary for several reasons, and I hope none of them are too trite. First, I would like to spare my friends, who may happen to read this, the usual clichés about being a good soldier. They were all kind enough to me, and I not enough to them. Second, I would not want to be a party to perpetuation of an image that is harmful and inaccurate: "glory" is the most meaningless of concepts, and I feel that in some cases it is doubly damaging. And thirdly, I am quite simply the last authority on my own death.

I loved the Army: it reared me, it nurtured me, and it gave me the most satisfying years of my life. Thanks to it I have lived an entire lifetime in twenty-six years. It is only fitting that I should die in its service. We all have but one death to spend, and insofar as it can have any meaning it finds it in the service of comrades in arms.

And yet, I deny that I died FOR anything — not my country, not my Army, not my fellow man, none of these things. I LIVED for these things, and the manner in which I chose to do it involved the very real chance that I would die in the execution of my duties. I knew this, and accepted it, but my love for West Point and the Army was great enough — and the promise that I would some day be able to serve all the ideals that meant anything to me through it was great enough — for me to accept this possibility as a part of a price which must be paid for all things of great value. If there is nothing worth dying for — in this sense — there is nothing worth living for.

The Army let me live in Japan, Germany, and England with experiences in all of these places that others only dream about. I have skied in the Alps, killed a scorpion in my tent camping in Turkey, climbed Mount Fuji, visited the ruins of Athens, Ephesus, and Rome, seen the town of Gordium where another Alexander challenged his destiny, gone to the opera in Munich, plays in the West End of London, seen the Oxford-Cambridge rugby match, gone for pub crawls through the Cotswolds, seen the night life in Hamburg, danced to the Rolling Stones, and earned a master's degree in a foreign university.

I have known what it is like to be married to a fine and wonderful woman and to love her beyond bearing with the sure knowledge that she loves me; I have commanded a company and been a father, priest, income-tax adviser, confessor, and judge for two hundred men at one time; I have played college football and rugby, won the British national diving championship two years in a row, boxed for Oxford against Cambridge only to be knocked out in the first round, and played handball to distraction — and all of these sports I loved, I learned at West Point. They gave me hours of intense happiness.

I have been an exchange student at the German Military Academy, and gone to the German Jumpmaster school. I have made thirty parachute jumps from everything from a balloon in England to a jet at Fort Bragg. I have written an article that was published in an Army magazine, and I have studied philosophy.

I have experienced all these things because I was in the Army and because I was an Army brat. The Army is my life; it is such a part of what I was that what happened is the logical outcome of the life I loved. I never knew what it is to fail, I never knew what it is to be too old or too tired to do anything. I lived a full life in the Army, and it has exacted the price. It is only just.

A Decisive Moment

Jonathan Schell wrote this Talk of the Town in The New Yorker *April 10, 1970, after the Calley decision.*

NOTES AND COMMENT

The nation has reached a decisive moment. Regardless of what strategists may say about options and game plans in Indochina, and regardless, even, of whatever ends are being pursued in this war, the nation's response to the massacre of hundreds of villagers at My Lai may determine whether the nation lives or dies. With the conviction of Lieutenant Calley, the moral anguish that some Americans have been experiencing for years has touched nearly all of us: to judge by the latest Gallup Poll and an invaluable *New York Times* survey, the questions that have long occupied the minds of a few people have become for multitudes the stuff of daily conversation and concern. These powerful new currents of feeling have divided old allies and made unlikely new ones. The reactions range across the full gamut of opinion, from Representative John R. Rarick (who sees Lieutenant Calley as "a great American") and Governor George Wallace (who visited Calley in order to pay his respects) to those who have for the first time turned against the war in revulsion, and it is not yet possible to judge what shape this new mood will finally take or how it will affect our government's policy. It appears that the conviction of Lieutenant Calley has forced every American, whatever his position on the war, to face what war itself is, what the nature of war in Indochina in particular is, and what his own responsibility is. Everyone has had to ask himself, in effect, whether the crimes committed at My Lai were isolated atrocities in a just war or whether they represented the essential nature of what we were and are doing in and to Indochina. Each of us has had to ask himself just how deeply implicated he himself is, by his actions or his inaction, in murder. If Calley is guilty, who is *not* guilty?

Yet a democratic nation, even if it finds itself mired in crime, can redeem itself. Even if its crimes are unforgivable, it has — because it *is* a democracy — a chance to retrieve its honor. It can acknowledge what it has done, admit responsibility, and set itself on a different course. Democracy exists so that people may make choices such as this. This is what it means to be free. However, if a nation denies the truth and refuses responsibility, then brutality enters its bloodstream and threatens the survival of democracy. We in America are still a free people, and we can choose what this nation will become. But first we must choose to remain free.

The issue of freedom is not like other issues. In a sense, it is larger than any other issue, because without it there are no issues, there are only orders. Freedom must be defended as soon as the earliest signs of a threat to it appear, because while other losses can be recovered, the loss of freedom is usually irrevocable. And recently we have found around us much, much more than early signs of a threat. On every hand, the late signs have been out. It is not only in Indochina that boundaries have been overrun and familiar restraints ignored. Throughout our political life at home we have been finding disintegration and acts of usurpation. And, for the first time, elements that could one day form the basis of an American form of totalitarianism have come into clear view.

The first unmistakable indications that our trouble was deeply rooted at the dead center of our political life came in the summer of 1968, at the Democratic Convention, in Chicago. For a few days, we were given an intimate glimpse of a new, frightening America. On the streets of Mayor Daley's city, police were wantonly attacking demonstrators, newsmen, and bystanders. At the Convention itself, delegates were being subjected to open manipulation by a majority that had control of the public-address system, and delegates and newsmen were roughed up by "security" agents, who were suddenly ubiquitous. One newsman was knocked to the floor, and one delegate was thrown in jail. At a downtown hotel, the police raided the headquarters of one of the candidates and clubbed several of his workers. In effect, this was how, in 1968, we as a people were responding to the war. Some of us were dissenting, and some of us were seizing control of the microphones and clubbing the dissenters. A temporary, local police state had emerged.

The aftermath of the Convention was as important and as revealing as the Convention itself. When power is abused in a body politic, two courses of action are open. The body politic can admit the abuse and take measures to correct it, or it can deny the abuse and institutionalize it. America institutionalized the abuses of the Chicago Convention. The victims of the brutality were convicted, the police perpetrators went free, and the press was condemned by prominent members of both parties for having covered the Convention "unfairly." A new way of dealing with official abuses of power had been found: Suppress the truth and punish the victims. All this was in plain view on television. But a number of things were happening in 1968 that were not visible to the public at all. The public didn't yet know that Lieutenant Calley and other men in his company had extinguished the hamlet of My Lai, and there were a lot of other things about the war in Indochina that it didn't know. Nor did it know that in the FBI, in all branches of the military, in the CIA, and in many other arms of the government, thousands of secret agents were being sent out to spy on people who were not suspected of any crimes but were simply deemed politically suspect by the government, or just by J. Edgar Hoover or some other ideologue who happened to be in a position of control in the spying apparatus.

A dangerous pattern had been established in our national life. Vast bureaucratic machines in the government, in the military, and in industry — sometimes under orders and sometimes on their own initiative — were becoming involved in many brutal or sense-

less, or sometimes merely foolish, activities, which they disguised
with propaganda that tended eventually to fool the propagand-
izers as much as it fooled the public. In the case of the government, the elected officials who nominally control and oversee
these bureaucracies on behalf of the public — men who might
never have dreamed of advocating massacres, massive-reprisal
bombings, invasions, the killing of demonstrators, or secret surveillance of civilians — had shown themselves willing to defend
these things *once they had happened* and had been renamed
"pacification," "protective reaction," "protecting American lives,"
"overreacting," or "guarding national security." And not only
were the officials ready to defend these things but they were
ready to vote their support for them again and again, and to continue them and expand them. Outrages committed in the public's
name began to be presented as *faits accomplis*. We have consistently underestimated the importance — the nearly decisive
weight — of the accomplished fact in recent events. The accomplished fact deadens the spirit of public action, which is at the
heart of political freedom, and it teaches people not to think or
feel. Of Vietnam, people began to say glumly, "We're there," as
though this were the beginning and the end of the argument. The
choice presented to the people was not whether or not their sons
would fight in Indochina but whether or not they were willing to
give their assent to what their sons had already been made to do
in Indochina. Once the question was put this way, the people, on
the whole, seemed to accept the war; at any rate, the men who
were elected to public office accepted it. With regard to the war,
the country faced — and still faces — the same choice it faced
after the Chicago Convention: whether to correct the abuse or to
institutionalize it. The year 1968 is remembered as a year of opposition, but it should be remembered as a year of collapse. It
wasn't enough for the antiwar movement simply to stir things up
and attract notice; it had to prevail — to end the war. But it
failed. Public belief in the war was shaken, but calm — an acceptance of the war — was restored. And the war continued to

expand. Now, with Lieutenant Calley's conviction, the public's acceptance has once again been shaken, and the outcome is again in the balance.

Nobody can be sure whether the war in Indochina is a cause or a symptom of the spiritual crisis in our nation; it is doubtless both. But it seems clear that already a nearly intolerable strain has been placed on our system of government. The delicate relationships defined by the Constitution between the three branches of government, between the government and the press, and between the government and the people are out of kilter. The threat to the rights of the people has been building up for several years. Freedom of speech has been imperiled by a bullying campaign against the press on the part of the administration — a campaign that has had a severely damaging effect on the news. A heavy fog has moved in over the news. What investigative reporting we have been getting out of Vietnam — such as the story of corruption in the PX system, the story on "refugees" from the Cambodian invasion, and the story of the My Lai massacre itself — has reached us through the investigations of a few congressmen or through the efforts of self-employed reporters. As soon as any men of the press have taken a look at things themselves and given their own accounts of what was going on — as they tried to do during the Laos invasion, despite stringent administration-imposed handicaps — the administration has stepped up its pressure. Now the discrepancy between events and the administration's version of them is too great to continue. According to the polls, the public no longer trusts the administration's statements on the war. This means that we have reached a point beyond which the administration will no longer be able to win support for its war policies unless it changes its policies or actively manages the news. Recently, the Vice President demanded the right to edit a taped interview he had given which was about to appear on television. He was refused, but if he ever gets his way in a matter like this, the free press will be in the most serious peril. The right of assembly has also been endangered. The constitutionality of a provision of the 1968 Civil Rights Act which makes it a crime to cross state lines with "intent" to participate in or incite a riot has been challenged but has not yet been ruled on, and meanwhile that provision has been encroaching on the right of assembly. This right was further endangered by the shootings at Kent State and by the county grand jury's decision not to indict the National Guardsmen but — once again — to indict the victims, or at least those who were still alive. The "no-knock" and "preventive-detention" provisions of the District of Columbia Crime Control Act have violated, respectively, the public's right to be secure against unreasonable searches and seizures and the traditional presumption of innocence.

The very shape of the government has been badly warped by assaults on the principle of the separation of powers. The lines defining that separation have grown indistinct. The President has taken over Congress's prerogative of declaring war and, in general, its powers in the field of foreign policy. He has stated that he "alone" has responsibility for the recent invasions of countries in Indochina. Having invaded two more countries, he has refused to "rule out" an invasion of a third — North Vietnam. If he did order this invasion, we could find ourselves at war with China, though Congress would not have given a word of assent. Congress, for its part, while abdicating its foreign-policy duties, has meddled in affairs that are properly within the jurisdiction of the courts, by passing laws, such as the crime bills, that override rulings made by the Supreme Court. On paper, the three branches of government have powers that can be described as roughly equal. In times when the branches respect the limits of their authority set forth in the Constitution, their powers are roughly equal in reality, too. But when this respect dissolves, as it has done lately, a hierarchy of powers never mentioned in the Constitution begins to take shape, and the executive branch is found to be the most powerful, the Congress to be the second most powerful, and the Supreme Court to be the least powerful. Thus, it is not surprising that at the moment, as the system shows signs of breaking down, the executive branch has flouted Congress, and Congress has flouted the Court. This is merely one of the signs that the rule of law, unless we are watchful, may be replaced by the rule of force. Nor is it surprising that organizations for which there is no provision at all in the Constitution have begun to crop up — institutions like the domestic-surveillance branches of the military. The shadow of Big Brother looms higher behind our backs. The other day, at a Senate hearing on secret surveillance by the government, an Assistant Attorney General told Senator Sam Ervin that the federal government had the right to put Senator Ervin himself under surveillance, although it might be "a waste of the taxpayers' money." This was not the remark of a man who understands our system of government. In the context of a hearing on the propriety of secret surveillance, it was a threat.

However, it would be a mistake to believe that our trouble has been due primarily to usurpers who were trampling over indignant, loudly protesting, but helpless defenders of liberty. Our trouble has been due equally to the acquiescence, and even the cooperation, of those from whom one might have expected resistance. Each move of usurpation has been accompanied by a submissive giving way somewhere else, as in a ballroom dance. Congress had handed over its war-making powers to the President with hardly a murmur of protest long before Mr. Nixon began to formulate his doctrine of executive supremacy in decisions of war and peace. The passage of repressive crime legislation was not forced on Congress; it was Congress's own idea. The press had failed in Vietnam long before this administration launched its open attacks on the press: the wholesale killing of civilians has been going on in Vietnam at least since 1965, but although American reporters there were for the most part free to report what they wanted to, it took years for the fact even to begin to be widely known. (Now, with the Calley court-martial, this news has invaded everyone's life, and the accumulated horror is shaking the nation.)

New exigencies began to take precedence over freedom. In

each case, the principle of freedom — the very cornerstone of our system of government — was reduced to a question of simple efficiency. Consideration for the rights of criminal suspects was said to be slowing down the rate of convictions. Congress's duty of passing judgment on questions of war and peace was said to be encumbering the speed and flexibility of executive and military decision-making. The freedom of assembly was said to be weakening the war effort. The freedom of the press was leading to revelations that were getting in the way of the government's propaganda about the war. And this logic was accepted not only by Presidents and generals but by congressmen, newsmen, and ordinary citizens as well. People began to act as though they were in tacit agreement that freedom had had its day in America, that it was an anachronism left over from "simpler times." Even some members of the antiwar movement began to lose their grasp of the distinction between freedom and tyranny, but in a different way. They began shouting, "Totalitarianism is here!" But to call what we had — or what we have today — in America totalitarianism is to have a dreamer's notion of what the evils of real totalitarianism are, as anyone who is at all acquainted with the history of Nazi Germany or Stalinist Russia well knows. Now, having used up their strongest words, these people have no words left to name the darkness looming ahead of us that we must struggle to escape. In this atmosphere, the final loss of freedom might be experienced as some kind of minor adjustment. There is a lot of talk about the abstract notion of "the free world," but real freedom cannot exist apart from specific rights and specific structures of government. When they are lost, freedom is lost.

Our system of government is an instrument of great intricacy and ingenuity — even of some beauty — but in itself it does not promise the good life; it promises only that the people will get what they deserve. We have always cherished our system because we have believed that it offers the best chance to preserve and to develop human qualities. But there is evidence that the ten years of war have brutalized us, and have soured our vision of the things we want to preserve and develop. When the news of the massacre at My Lai reached the headlines, many people said that, in the light of what we had just learned, the war would surely have to end. Instead, we appeared to grow accustomed to the massacre — and to the war. (And last week, inconceivable as it may seem, voices in some of the highest places in the land were still being raised in defense of what happened at My Lai.) Over the years, as the war dragged on, we lost all sense of proportion. Finally, a bloody war took second billing in our press to an issue like revenue-sharing, or to a prizefight. Three years ago, a call to end the bombing of North Vietnam had the country in an uproar for months. A few weeks ago, the resumption of this bombing hardly made the front page.

As long as the war continues, each one of us faces the choice that the nation faces: whether to repudiate the war and call for its ending or to accept it and make it — and its massacres — part of us. Something worse than the beginnings of a collapse of our system emerged in the last three or four years. The standards with which to measure the collapse themselves collapsed. The vision we needed in order to spot the infection was itself infected. The minds we needed in order to perceive the derangement were themselves becoming deranged. It appeared that we had lost the sounding boards of mind and conscience against which a free nation tests its policies and actions. It is one thing to be at war, but it is another thing to be at war without knowing that you are at war. The men who were leading us were losing track of the difference between war and peace. The men who were voting for crime bills were losing track of what justice is. The men who were threatening our freedom were losing track of what freedom is. Now the conviction of Lieutenant Calley seems to have shocked the country in some new way and awakened it out of a long sleep. We seem to have been given another chance — possibly our last chance — to regain our soul.

A Letter to the President

Captain Aubrey M. Daniel, the prosecutor of Calley, directed this letter to President Nixon April 7, 1971, after the President's intervention in the case. It has been slightly excerpted.

SIR:

It is very difficult for me to know where to begin this letter as I am not accustomed to writing letters of protest. I only hope that I can find the words to convey to you my feelings as a United States citizen and as an attorney who believes that respect for law is one of the fundamental bases upon which this nation is founded.

On November 26, 1969, you issued the following statement through your press secretary, Mr. Ronald Ziegler, in referring to the My Lai incident:

> *An incident such as that alleged in this case is in direct violation not only of United States military policy but is also abhorrent to the conscience of all the American people.*
>
> *The Secretary of the Army is continuing his investigation. Appropriate action is and will be taken to assure that illegal and immoral conduct as alleged be dealt with in accordance with the strict rules of military justice.*
>
> *This incident should not be allowed to reflect on the some million and a quarter young Americans who have now returned to the United States after having served in Vietnam with great courage and distinction.*

At the time you issued this statement, a general court-martial had been directed for a resolution of the charges which have been brought against Lieutenant William L. Calley, Jr., for his involvement at My Lai.

On December 8, 1970, you were personally asked to comment on the My Lai incident at a press conference. At that time you made the following statement:

> *What appears was certainly a massacre, and under no circumstances was it justified.*
> *One of the goals we are fighting for in Vietnam is to keep the people from South Vietnam from having imposed upon them a government which has atrocity against civilians as one of it policies.*
> *We cannot ever condone or use atrocities against civilians in order to accomplish that goal.*

These expressions of what I believed to be your sentiment were truly reflective of my own feelings when I was given the assignment of prosecuting the charges which had been preferred against Lieutenant Calley.

My feelings were generated not by emotionalism or self-indignation but by my knowledge of the evidence in the case, the laws of this nation in which I strongly believe, and my own conscience. I knew that I had been given a great responsibility and I only hoped that I would be able to discharge my duties and represent the United States in a manner which would be a credit to the legal profession and our system of justice.

I undertook the prosecution of the case without any ulterior motives for personal gain, either financial or political.

Throughout the proceedings there was criticism of the prosecution but I lived with the abiding conviction that once the facts and the law had been presented there would be no doubt in the mind of any reasonable person about the necessity for the prosecution of this case and the ultimate verdict. I was mistaken

The trial of Lieutenant Calley was conducted in the finest tradition of our legal system. It was in every respect a fair trial in which every legal right of Lieutenant Calley was fully protected. It clearly demonstrated that the military justice system which has previously been the subject of much criticism was a fair system.

I do not believe that there has ever been a trial in which the accused's rights were more fully protected, the conduct of the defense given greater latitude, and the prosecution held to stricter standards. The burden of proof which the government had to meet in this case was not beyond a reasonable doubt, but beyond possibility. The very fact that Lieutenant Calley was an American officer being tried for the deaths of Vietnamese during a combat operation by fellow officers compels this conclusion.

The jury selection, in which customary procedure was altered by providing both the defense and the prosecution with three peremptory challenges instead of the usual one, was carefully conducted to insure the impartiality of those men who were selected. Six officers, all combat veterans, five having served in Vietnam, were selected.

From the time they took their oaths until they rendered their decision, they performed their duties in the very finest tradition of the American legal system. If ever a jury followed the letter of the law in applying it to the evidence presented, they did.

When the verdict was rendered, I was totally shocked and dismayed at the reaction of many people across the nation. Much of the adverse public reaction I can attribute to people who have acted emotionally and without being aware of the evidence that was presented and perhaps even the laws of this nation regulating the conduct of war.

These people have undoubtedly viewed Lieutenant Calley's conviction simply as the conviction of an American officer for killing the enemy.

I would prefer to believe that most of the public criticism has come from people who are not aware of the evidence, either because they have not followed the evidence as it was presented, or having followed it they have chosen not to believe it.

Certainly, no one wanted to believe what occurred at My Lai, including the officers who sat in judgment of Lieutenant Calley.

To believe, however, that any large percentage of the population could believe the evidence which was presented and approve of the conduct of Lieutenant Calley would be as shocking to my conscience as the conduct itself, since I believe that we are still a civilized nation.

If such be the case, then the war in Vietnam has brutalized us more than I care to believe, and it must cease. How shocking it is if so many people across this nation have failed to see the moral issue which was involved in the trial of Lieutenant Calley — that it is unlawful for an American soldier to summarily execute unarmed and unresisting men, women, children, and babies.

But how much more appalling it is to see so many of the political leaders of the nation who have failed to see the moral issue or, having seen it, have compromised it for political motive in the face of apparent public displeasure with the verdict.

I would have hoped that all leaders of this nation would have either accepted and supported the enforcement of the laws of this country as reflected by the verdict of the court or not made any statement concerning the verdict until they had had the same opportunity to evaluate the evidence that the members of the jury had.

In view of your previous statements concerning this matter, I have been particularly shocked and dismayed at your decision to intervene in these proceedings in the midst of the public clamor. Your decision can only have been prompted by the response of a vocal segment of our population who, while no doubt acting in good faith, cannot be aware of the evidence which resulted in Lieutenant Calley's conviction.

Your intervention has, in my opinion, damaged the military judicial system and lessened any respect it may have gained as a result of the proceedings.

You have subjected a judicial system of this country to the criticism that it is subject to political influence, when it is a fundamental precept of our judicial system that the legal processes of this country must be kept free from any outside influences. What will be the impact of your decision upon the future trials, particularly those within the military?

Not only have respect for the legal process been weakened and the critics of the military judicial system been given support for their claims of command influence, the image of Lieutenant Calley, a man convicted of the premeditated murder of at least twenty-one unarmed and unresisting people, as a national hero has been enhanced.

The jurors since rendering their verdict have found themselves and their families the subject of vicious attacks upon their honor, integrity, and loyalty to this nation.

It would seem to me to be more appropriate for you as the President to have said something in their behalf and to remind the nation of the purpose of our legal system and the respect it should command.

I would expect that the President of the United States, a man who I believed should and would provide the moral leadership for this nation, would stand fully behind the law of this land on a moral issue which is so clear and about which there can be no compromise.

For this nation to condone the acts of Lieutenant Calley is to make us no better than our enemies and make any pleas by the nation for the humane treatment of our own prisoners meaningless.

I truly regret having to have written this letter and wish that no innocent person had died at My Lai on March 16, 1968. But innocent people were killed under circumstances that will always remain abhorrent to my conscience.

Comment on Calley

Herbert Marcuse, the philosopher, wrote this commentary on the Calley case in May 1971.

THE OBSCENE HASTE with which a large part of the American people rushed to the support of a man convicted of multiple premeditated murder of men, women and children, the obscene pride with which they even identified themselves with him is one of those rare historical events which reveal a hidden truth.

Behind the television faces of the leaders, behind the tolerant politeness of the debates, behind the radiant happiness of the commercials appear the real people: men and women madly in love with death, violence and destruction.

For this massive rush was not the result of organization, management, machine politics — it was entirely spontaneous: an outburst of the unconscious, the soul. The silent majority has its hero: a convicted war criminal — convicted of killing at close range, smashing the head of a two-year-old child; a killer in whose defense it was said that he did not feel that he was killing "humans," a killer who did not express regret for his deeds; he only obeyed orders and killed only "dinks" or "gooks" or "V.C." This majority has its hero — it has found its martyr, its Horst Wessel whose name was sung by hundreds of thousands of marching Nazis before they marched into war. "Lieutenant Calley's Battle Hymn Marches On," the record, sold three hundred thousand copies in three days.

How do Calley's worshipers justify their hero?

The act which Calley is accused of was committed in warfare and is thus subject to special consideration. Now Calley was tried and convicted, after long deliberation, by a military tribunal of his peers, of whom it may be assumed that they knew that he acted in war. In fact, he was tried and convicted under the international rules of warfare. The rules of his own army stipulate the duty of disobedience to illegal orders (a disobedience which, as the hearings showed, was actually practiced by other American soldiers at My Lai).

What Calley did was widespread practice. Scores of men have come forth denouncing themselves as having done the same thing Calley did. Now the fact that one murderer was caught and brought to trial while others were not does not absolve the one who was brought to trial. On the contrary, the others, having voluntarily confessed, should also be tried. The man who wrote on the windshield of his automobile: "I killed in V.N. Hang me too!!" may well have meant it. People madly in love with death, including their own.

Everyone knows there are few genuine civilians in Vietnam today. A most revealing statement, which admits that the war is waged against a whole people: genocide.

Society is to blame. This is perhaps the only weighty argument. It moves on several levels:

(a) If society alone is to blame, nobody is to blame. For "society" is an abstract which cannot be brought to trial. It is true that this society is (and must be) training its young citizens to kill. But this same society operates under the rule of law, and recognizes rights and duties of the individual. Thus it presupposes individual responsibility, that is to say the ability of the "normal" individual to distinguish between criminal and noncriminal behavior (Calley was declared "normal").

(b) If the argument implies that all individual members of society are to blame, it is blatantly false and only serves to protect those who are responsible.

The reason for the "paroxysm in the nation's conscience" is "simply that Calley is all of us. He is every single citizen in our graceless land," said the Very Reverend Francis B. Sayre, Jr. Blatantly false, and a great injustice to the Berrigans, to all those who have, at the risk of their liberty and even their life, openly and actively fought the genocidal war.

To be sure, in a "metaphysical" sense, everyone who partakes of this society is indeed guilty — but the Calley case is not a case study in metaphysics. Within the general framework (restrictive enough) of individual responsibility there are definite gradations which allow attribution of specific responsibility. If it is true that Calley's action was not isolated, but an all but daily occurrence in Vietnam (which would corroborate the findings of the Russell War Crime Tribunal and call for the prosecution of all cases recorded there), then responsibility would rest with the field commanders, and, in the last analysis, with the supreme commander of the United States armed forces. However, this would not eliminate the responsibility of the individual agents.

(c) Technical progress in developing the capacity to kill has led to "death in the abstract": killing that does not dirty your hands and clothes, that does not burden you with the agony of the victims — invisible death, dealt by remote controls. But technical perfection does not redeem the guilt of those who violate the rules of civilized warfare.

What does this all add up to? Perhaps Governor Maddox gave it away when he exclaimed at a rally in support of Calley: "Thank God for Lieutenant Calley and thank God for people like you." Blasphemy or religious madness? The convicted war criminal an avatar of Jesus, the Christ? "He has been crucified," shouted a woman, berating the court-martial in a German accent (one wonders?!). "Calley killed one hundred Communists single-handed. He should get a medal. He should be promoted to general." And a Reverend Lord (!) told a rally: "There was a crucifixion two thousand years ago of a man named Jesus Christ. I don't think we need another crucifixion of a man named Rusty Calley."

Has the lieutenant taken our sins upon himself; will he redeem our sins? What sins? Could it be the wish to kill, kill without being punished? Has the lieutenant become the national model for a new superego, less exacting than the traditional one, which still preserved a trace of thou shalt not kill?

The old superego still stuck to the memory of this prohibition even in war. The new superego is up-to-date. It says: you can kill. No — you can waste and destroy. Calley never used the word "kill." He told a psychiatrist that the military avoided the word "kill" because it "caused a very negative emotional reaction among the men who had been taught the commandment "Thou shalt not kill." Instead, Lieutenant Calley employed the word "destroy" or the phrase "waste 'em." A pardon for Calley, who did not kill but only destroyed and wasted 'em would, according to some, be a "constructive step to restore the morale of our armed forces and the public at large."

The mad rush away from individual responsibility, the easygoing effort to vest guilt in anonymity is the desperate reaction against a guilt which threatens to become unbearable. Infantile regression: Billy cannot be punished because Maxie and Charlie and many others did the same thing: they do it daily, and they are not punished. People incapable of the simplest adult logic: if Maxie and Charlie did the same thing, they are equally guilty and Billy is not innocent.

Has the sense of guilt, the guilt of a society in which massacres and killing and body counts have become part of the normal mental equipment, become so strong that it can no longer be contained by the traditional, civilized defense mechanisms (individual defense mechanisms)? Does the sense of guilt turn into its opposite: into the proud, sadomasochistic identification with the crime and the criminal?

Has the hysteria also gripped the Left, the peace movement

which finds in the indictment of Calley an indictment of the war? A strange indictment indeed which regards the war criminal as a scapegoat — scapegoat for anonymous, for other scapegoats? Even Telford Taylor, who spoke so eloquently at the Nuremberg trials, thinks that the sentence may have been too harsh. And Dr. Benjamin Spock thinks that it is unjust to punish one man for the brutality of war.

Compassion. But has it ever occurred to all those understanding and compassionate liberals that clemency for Calley might indeed "strengthen the morale of the army" in killing with a good conscience? Has it ever occurred to them that compassion may be due the men, women and children who are the victims of this "morale"? Once again, we are confronted with that principle of diseased justice which was pronounced at Kent State and which expresses so neatly the perversion of the sense of guilt: "not the murderer but the murdered one is guilty."

Testimony of a Veteran

Navy Lieutenant John Kerry testified for the Vietnam Veterans Against the War before the Senate Foreign Relations Committee on April 22, 1971.

I WOULD LIKE TO SAY for the record, and also for the men behind me who are also wearing the uniform and their medals, that my sitting here is really symbolic. I am not here as John Kerry. I am here as one member of the group of one thousand, which is a small representation of a very much larger group of veterans in this country, and were it possible for all of them to sit at this table they would be here and have the same kind of testimony.

I would simply like to speak in very general terms. I apologize if my statement is general because I received notification yesterday you would hear me and I am afraid because of the injunction I was up most of the night and haven't had a great deal of chance to prepare.

I would like to talk, representing all those veterans, and say that several months ago in Detroit, we had an investigation at which over 150 honorably discharged and many very highly decorated veterans testified to war crimes committed in Southeast Asia, not isolated incidents but crimes committed on a day-to-day basis with the full awareness of officers at all levels of command.

It is impossible to describe to you exactly what did happen in Detroit, the emotions in the room, the feelings of the men who were reliving their experiences in Vietnam, but they did, they relived the absolute horror of what this country, in a sense, made them do.

They told the stories. At times they had personally raped, cut off ears, cut off heads, taped wires from portable telephones to human genitals and turned up the power, cut off limbs, blown up bodies, randomly shot at civilians, razed villages in fashion reminiscent of Genghis Khan, shot cattle and dogs for fun, poisoned food stocks, and generally ravaged the countryside of South Vietnam in addition to the normal ravage of war, and the normal and very particular ravaging which is done by the applied bombing power of this country.

We call this investigation the Winter Soldier Investigation. The term "winter soldier" is a play on words of Thomas Paine's in 1776 when he spoke of the "sunshine patriot" and "summertime soldiers" who deserted at Valley Forge because the going was rough.

We who have come here to Washington have come here because we feel we have to be winter soldiers now. We could come back to this country, we could be quiet, we could hold our silence, we could not tell what went on in Vietnam but we feel because of what threatens this country, the fact that the crimes threaten it, not Reds, and not redcoats, but the crimes which we are committing that threaten it, that we have to speak out.

I would like to talk to you a little bit about what the result is of the feelings these men carry with them after coming back from Vietnam. The country doesn't know it yet but it has created a monster, a monster in the form of millions of men who have been taught to deal and to trade in violence, and who are given the chance to die for the biggest nothing in history — men who have returned with a sense of anger, and a sense of betrayal which no one has yet grasped.

As a veteran and one who feels this anger, I would like to talk about it. We are angry because we feel we have been used in the worst fashion by the administration of this country.

In 1970 at West Point Vice President Agnew said, "Some glamorize the criminal misfits of society while our best men die in Asian rice paddies to preserve the freedom which most of those misfits abuse," and this was used as a rallying point for our effort in Vietnam.

But for us, as boys in Asia whom the country was supposed to support, his statement is a terrible distortion from which we can only draw a very deep sense of revulsion; and hence the anger of some of the men who are here in Washington today. It is a distortion because we in no way consider ourselves the best men of this country, because those he calls misfits were standing up for us in a way that nobody else in this country dared to, because so many who have died would have returned to this country to join the misfits in their efforts to ask for an immediate withdrawal from South Vietnam, because so many of those best men have returned as quadriplegics and amputees, and they lie forgotten in Veterans Administration hospitals in this country which fly the flag that so many have chosen as their own personal symbol — and we cannot consider ourselves America's best men when we are ashamed of and hated what we were called on to do in Southeast Asia.

In our opinion, and from our experience, there is nothing in South Vietnam, nothing which could happen that realistically threatens the United States of America. And to attempt to justify the loss of one American life in Vietnam, Cambodia or Laos by linking such loss to the preservation of freedom, which those misfits supposedly abuse, is to us the height of criminal hypocrisy, and it is that kind of hypocrisy which we feel has torn this country apart.

We are probably much more angry than that, and I don't want to go into the foreign policy aspects because I am outclassed here. I know that all of you talk about every possible alternative for getting out of Vietnam. We understand that. We know you have considered the seriousness of the aspects to the utmost level, and I am not going to try to dwell on that. But I want to relate to you the feeling that many of the men who have returned to this country express because we are probably angriest about all that we were told about Vietnam and about the mystical war against Communism.

We found that not only was it a civil war, an effort by a people who had for years been seeking their liberation from any colonial influence whatsoever, but also we found that the Vietnamese, whom we had enthusiastically molded after our own image, were hard put to take up the fight against the threat we were supposedly saving them from.

We found most people didn't even know the difference between Communism and democracy. They only wanted to work in rice paddies without helicopters strafing them and bombs with napalm burning their villages and tearing their country apart. They wanted everything to do with the war, particularly with this foreign presence of the United States of America, to leave them alone in peace, and they practiced the art of survival by siding with whichever military force was present at a particular time, be it Viet Cong, North Vietnamese or American.

We found also that all too often American men were dying in those rice paddies for want of support from their allies. We saw firsthand how monies from American taxes were used for a corrupt dictatorial regime. We saw that many people in this country had a one-sided idea of who was kept free by our flag, as blacks provided the highest percentage of casualties. We saw Vietnam ravaged equally by American bombs as well as by search-and-destroy missions, as well as by Viet Cong terrorism, and yet we listened while this country tried to blame all of the havoc on the Viet Cong.

We rationalized destroying villages in order to save them. We saw America lose her sense of morality as she accepted very coolly a My Lai and refused to give up the image of American soldiers who hand out chocolate bars.

We learned the meaning of free-fire zones, shooting anything that moves, and we watched while America placed a cheapness on the lives of Orientals.

We watched the United States's falsification of body counts, in fact the glorification of body counts. We listened while month after month we were told the back of the enemy was about to break. We fought using weapons against oriental "human beings," with quotation marks around that, we fought using weapons against those people which I do not believe this country would dream of using were we fighting in the European Theater or let us say a non-Third World people theater, and so we watched while men charged up hills because a general said that hill has to be taken, and after losing one platoon or two platoons they marched away to leave the hill for the reoccupation by the North Vietnamese because we watched pride allow the most unimportant of battles to be blown into extravaganzas, because we couldn't lose, and we couldn't retreat, and because it didn't matter how many American bodies were lost to prove that point, and so there were Hamburger Hills and Khe Sanhs and Hill 881s and Fire Base 6s and so many others.

Now we are told that the men who fought there must watch quietly while American lives are lost so that we can exercise the incredible arrogance of Vietnamizing the Vietnamese.

Each day, to facilitate the process by which the United States washes her hands of Vietnam, someone has to give up his life so that the United States doesn't have to admit something that the entire world already knows, so that we can't say that we have made a mistake. Someone has to die so that President Nixon won't be, and these are his words, "the first President to lose a war."

We are asking Americans to think about that because how do you ask a man to be the last man to die for a mistake? But we are trying to do that, and we are doing it with thousands of rationalizations, and if you read carefully the President's last speech to the people of this country, you can see that he says and says clearly: "But the issue, gentlemen, the issue, is Communism, and the question is whether or not we will leave that country to the Communists or whether or not we will try to give it hope to be a free people." But the point is they are not a free people now under us, they are not a free people and we cannot fight Communism all over the world, and I think we should have learned that lesson by now.

But the problem of veterans goes beyond this personal problem, because you think about a poster in this country with a picture of Uncle Sam and the picture says: I WANT YOU. And a young man comes out of high school and says: "That is fine, I am going to serve my country," and he goes to Vietnam and he shoots and he kills and he does his job or maybe he doesn't kill, maybe he just goes and he comes back, and when he gets back to this country he finds that he isn't really wanted because the largest unemployment figure in the country — it varies depending on who you get it from, the V.A. 15 per cent, various other sources 22 per cent — but the largest corps of unemployed in this country are veterans of this war, and of those veterans 33 per cent of the unemployed are black. That means one out of every ten of the nation's unemployed is a veteran of Vietnam.

The hospitals across the country won't or can't meet their demands. It is not a question of not trying; they haven't got the appropriations. A man recently died after he had a tracheotomy in California, not because of the operation but because there weren't enough personnel to clean the mucus out of his tube and he suffocated to death.

Another young man just died in a New York V.A. hospital the other day. A friend of mine was lying in a bed two beds away and tried to help him but he couldn't. He rang a bell and there was nobody there to service that man and so he died of convulsions.

Fifty-seven per cent, I understand 57 per cent of all those entering the V.A. hospitals talk about suicide. Some 27 per cent have tried, and they try because they come back to this country and they have to face what they did in Vietnam, and then they come back and find the indifference of a country that doesn't really care.

Suddenly we are faced with a very sickening situation in this country, because there is no moral indignation and, if there is, it comes from people who are almost exhausted by their past indignations, and I know that many of them are sitting in front of me. The country seems to have lain down and shrugged off something as serious as Laos, just as we calmly shrugged off the loss of seven hundred thousand lives in Pakistan, the so-called greatest disaster of all times.

But we are here as veterans to say we think we are in the midst of the greatest disaster of all times now because they are still dying over there, and not just Americans, Vietnamese, and we are rationalizing leaving that country so that those people can go on killing each other for years to come.

Americans seem to have accepted the idea that the war is winding down, at least for Americans, and they have also allowed the bodies which were once used by a President for statistics to prove that we were winning that war to be used as evidence against a man who followed orders and who interpreted those orders no differently than hundreds of other men in Vietnam.

We veterans can only look with amazement on the fact that this country has been unable to see there is absolutely no difference between ground troops and a helicopter crew, and yet people have accepted a differentiation fed them by the administration.

No ground troops are in Laos so it is all right to kill Laotians by remote control. But, believe me, the helicopter crews fill the same body bags and they wreak the same kind of damage on the Vietnamese and Laotian countryside as anybody else, and the President is talking about allowing that to go on for many years to come. One can only ask if we will really be satisfied only when the troops march into Hanoi.

We are asking here in Washington for some action, action from the Congress of the United States of America, which has the power to raise and maintain armies, and which by the Constitution also has the power to declare war.

We have come here, not to the President, because we believe that this body can be responsive to the will of the people, and we believe that the will of the people says that we should be out of Vietnam now.

We are here in Washington also to say that the problem of this war is not just a question of war and diplomacy. It is part and parcel of everything that we are trying as human beings to communicate to people in this country: the question of racism, which is rampant in the military, and so many other questions; also, the use of weapons, the hypocrisy in our taking umbrage in the Geneva Conventions and using that as justification for a continuation of this war, when we are more guilty than any other body of violations of those Geneva Conventions, in the use of free-fire zones, harassment, interdiction fire, search-and-destroy missions, the bombings, the torture of prisoners, the killing of prisoners — accepted policy by many units in South Vietnam. That is what we are trying to say. It is part and parcel of everything.

An American Indian friend of mine who lives in the Indian nation of Alcatraz put it to me very succinctly. He told me how as a boy on an Indian reservation he had watched television and he used to cheer the cowboys when they came in and shot the Indians, and then suddenly one day he stopped in Vietnam and he said: "My God, I am doing to these people the very same thing that was done to my people," and he stopped. And that is what we are trying to say, that we think this thing has to end.

We are also here to ask, we are here to ask, and we are here to ask vehemently: Where are the leaders of our country, where is the leadership? We are here to ask where McNamara, Rostow, Bundy, Gilpatric and so many others, where are they now that we, the men whom they sent off to war, have returned? These are commanders who have deserted their troops, and there is no more serious crime in the law of war.

The Army says they never leave their wounded. The Marines say they never leave even their dead. These men have left all the casualties and retreated behind a pious shield of public rectitude. They have left the real stuff of their reputations bleaching behind them in the sun in this country.

Finally, this administration has done us the ultimate dishonor. They have attempted to disown us and the sacrifices we made for

this country. In their blindness and fear they have tried to deny
that we are veterans or that we served in Nam. We do not need
their testimony. Our own scars and stumps of limbs are witness
enough for others and for ourselves.

We wish that a merciful God could wipe away our own memories of that service as easily as this administration has wiped their
memories of us. But all that they have done and all that they can
do by this denial is to make more clear than ever our own determination to undertake one last mission, to search out and destroy the
last vestige of this barbaric war, to pacify our own hearts, to con-
quer the hate and the fear that have driven this country these last
ten years and more, and so when in thirty years from now our
brothers go down the street without a leg, without an arm, or a
face, and small boys ask why, we will be able to say "Vietnam"
and not mean a desert, not a filthy obscene memory, but mean
instead the place where America finally turned and where soldiers
like us helped it in the turning.

Mankilling Is the King's Game

Halldor Laxness, Iceland's Nobel Prize novelist, wrote this commentary on war in the spring of 1971.

WHEN AS A YOUNGSTER I went to a Jesuit school (Osterley, London, 1923–24) I learned this: "Mankilling is the King's game."

I forgot to ask who wrote it; it sounds Shakespearean. To me it had a homely strain. From my Old Norse textbook back in Iceland I had become familiar with battle poetry rooted in sea-robber experience and the warlike spirit of petty Scandinavian kings, the so-called scaldic poetry. This heroic literature from the turn of the first millennium, two hundred fifty years plus or minus, is not to be confused with the Edda poetry, which never describes a battle and is exclusively legendary and mythological and probably of a younger date.

Although this scaldic poetry is high-class poetry in its own right, it has never been as popular as the Eddas. It is relatively voluminous; the Copenhagen-Christiania edition from the Icelandic vellum is more than twelve hundred double-columned pages in quarto. If you fastened the poems together end to end this poetry would be almost a mile long. Most of it is composed by Icelandic scalds (poets or bards) either itinerant or engaged as house poets of kings and pirates.

This is a poetry of grim beauty composed by happy warriors in the most intricate of meters. It is considered by encyclopedists to contain some of the most beautiful verses inspired by fighting in any age and any nation. Modern battle descriptions, including death rolls (anemic impersonal body counts; Hill No. this or that) make pale reading to Icelanders compared to the scaldic accounts of the famous battles of yore in which a great hero is dying a formidable death in almost every verse and battle is praised as the acme of human existence, war as the consummate glory of man.

This poetry is very particular about light and color in a battle, and about the right hour of day to fight one. The hour before daybreak is all right because it lends to the crimson of liquid blood a nice admixture of an azure sky and the silvery grey of a fading moon. Most good battles take place at dawn when you may behold the blue of your naked steel reddened by your worthy enemy's blood in perfect juxtaposition with the golden radiance of the rising sun. You delight in the frolics of blue colliding edges, accompanied by that seething din which this poetry holds to be characteristic of lethal wounds. Spears are singing and skulls crack with a thundering sound. The "flower of the wound" is one of the beautiful names given to a sword.

A battle is the "divine service," or mass, of swords; it also is the fun of swords, a happy bout of carnage, a kill spree. In all the poems the names of places where famous battles were fought are given; so are the names of chieftains and prominent heroes. A single poem might record a few dozen battles; one mentions fifty. Battles and heroes may or may not have their origin in reality. But you are left in the dark why all these battles were fought. The question seems never to have arisen. For all you know they might have been fought for fun, maybe not for fun of those who were actually slain, but for the many others who were supposed to hear the story and learn the poem. It is significant that a scaldic poem never misses one elaborate passage of big joy, that is the joy of the hungry raven and the eagle and the swift-moving wolves amidst the fresh-reeking carrion of the battlefield. At times you might think the only idea of all the wars was to produce plenty of "warm prey" for empty-stomached scavengers.

In the Norse war poetry you will note that a battle story never stands as a substitute, symbol or *exemplum* for anything outside itself; it never tries to put over on you any moral or give you tips about how to change the world for the better or save it. Evidently these poets were living in a perfect world.

To them war is the real thing; moreover, it is the thing of which it is always real fun to hear the news, the game of games, the Super Olympics of which other Olympics are a substitute or a symbol.

The situation has not changed much since scaldic times; anything to do with war still makes good copy. As our ancestors, we have the feeling that war is always with us, a *casus belli* is always round the corner. There are always plenty of facile "becauses." You open a war with someone because you think he is weaker than you or because he is your equal or you fear that he is stronger than you — all equally natural and legitimate arguments in favor of declaring war: let us go ahead and kill them! If you are afraid of being killed yourself, you are a scoundrel and a coward.

Matching the "Shakespearean" phrase about war as the game of kings, "war as a man's glory" is the unadulterated moral of our good old Icelandic classics. In modern times there are notions about wars being caused by people having different ideas, diverging *Weltanschauungen,* colliding philosophical, economic or theological theories, or not agreeing on the interpretation of Bible phrases and suchlike.

This conception does not get much support from serious scrutiny of human history or natural history in general, of which wars are part and parcel. Ask Dr. Konrad Lorenz or, say, the American ethnologist Robert Ardrey. To me these notions have the flavor of modern cant, a sham moralism ascribing sublime motives to war-making in order to excuse war. In the pre-Christian and even the medieval North we never seem to have had such dear moralizing aunts who did not know that war is supreme fun for everybody except the man who is being shot at, and maybe his mother. There is a widely held opinion among scholars, supported by established fact, that our old war poetry was memorized by old women and recited by them in the process of putting children to sleep.

In our Western cultures male adulthood means being ripe for a kill spree. This is called conscription age. Nice people say war is all right as long as only young men are sent off to die honorably on the battlefield, but think it is immoral to kill girls, old men and kids. Why?

In this case, as so often in ethnology, we do not have the rationale. Some enlightening stories about this thing may be read in fairy tales, mythology and poetry, even in the Bible: Saul killed one thousand, David killed ten thousand. Prophets and scientists, students of this syndrome, have several explanations about why only young men should be shot, but not girls, etc., but each one of their conclusions is disputed by the next bunch of experts.

Looking at the matter from the outside, for instance from the Moon, which might be as good a place for wisdom as any (or Iceland, for that matter), war looks like the fulfillment of a pact between two partners of mutually executing each other's young men. In recent years there have been symptoms, even forebodings, of a conceivable reverse in the situation. If wonderful young men with the future in their lustering eyes should take over one of these days as they threaten to do, let us pray they are not going to march us old devils off to die honorably in some faraway hell of which you don't even know the name, still less the number of the hill on the top of which you are going to be killed.

A famous scaldic poem ends on this bit of moral: "Why should a boy be nearer to death than other boys although he be placed in the front rank in a battle?" (Fate decides the issue.) "Many a man has led a long life of grumbling although he never was eaten by an eagle at a spree of swords. It is said to be hard work to raise the spirits of a coward: the heart of a coward is a useless thing to him." But this bit does not take us far either; these might just as well be the maxims of a desperado.

There is nothing that seems to stop a dedicated mankiller.

Hitler and Stalin had their sprees all right and it is for the next generation of suckers to understand and forgive. The question remains open from one generation to the next what was the reason for this and that war, or did war come first and reason as the runner-up or vice versa: the old dispute about hen and egg.

Then there is the question who was the better man, Hitler or Stalin: who represented the just cause; whose was the more sympathetic side? It is almost safe to say now that they were both very good buffoons. Many would say that Hitler was the greater buffoon though. But Stalin was a very good buffoon too. If their greatness be measured in body count as that of other mankiller kings on record, they are both great. Doubtless, both are passable stuff for that rather inane fiction called World History. Even a moralist would be hard put to decide who was representing the good side and who the bad side. A computer would have a hard time solving it. It depends on your own bias. And there you are. The Soviet Socialism of one and National Socialism of the other, yes, but who stood for Revolution and the revolution of what; and who was on the side of Reaction — to what?

When you travel in the East you sometimes see lepers sitting crosswise on the sidewalks sticking out at you their rottening limbs proudly, hatefully, defyingly, as if saying: "We are holy. We alone belong to God." To leprosy there is only one side, the side of leprosy. There you have a circumscription of war as good as any: War is the leprosy of the human soul. As in leprosy, there is only one side in war, the side of war.

THE EDITOR

Harrison E. Salisbury is Associate Editor and Editor of the Op-Ed page of the *New York Times* and a well-known foreign correspondent. He is the author of many distinguished books, including *American in Russia, The Shook-Up Generation, The Nine Hundred Days: The Siege of Leningrad,* and *The Many Americas Shall Be One.* He has received many distinguished awards for his reporting, among them the Pulitzer Prize and the George Polk Memorial Award, and several honorary degrees.